JAMES I.

JAMES I.

Artist Unknown—German School?

JAMES I.

BY

CHARLES WILLIAMS

ROY PUBLISHERS
NEW YORK

JAMES I

MADE IN GREAT BRITAIN
PRINTED BY MORRISON AND GIBB LIMITED, LONDON AND EDINBURGH

PREFACE

THE following pages are concerned with James Stuart, and not with the history of England except as it affected James Stuart. It is why the Gunpowder Plot appears only briefly, and the Gowrie Conspiracy at length, for the first was part of his indirect experience, the second of his direct. The Overbury affair, for the same reason, is presented, not chronologically, but as he became increasingly aware of it. The European situation at the end of his life was, no doubt, more important than his knowledge of it, but it is his knowledge which is here the subject. A lucid survey of the whole political situation in England will be found in Mr. Evan John's *King Charles I*.

Among the many tales which the gossips have recorded of James one can but exercise an intelligent discretion. I have not omitted anything probable merely because it threw light on a horrid streak in his character, but I have not put in anything improbable merely for that reason. Nor have I included every one even of those which are credible. I should like to think that this book was more than a string of haphazard anecdotes, and that it had a relation to the whole personality of the most grotesque of our Kings. On a score of things it is impossible to feel certain ; it is only possible to feel reasonably persuaded. To explain the reasons in more detail than the book itself provides would be to write a different kind of book. This is a book of one kind and not of another.

My gratitude is especially due to Mr. J. D. Meikle for the books he has lent me, and to Mr. R. D. Binfield for his continual vivid assistance.

C. W.

CONTENTS

INTRODUCTION

By the death of Charles Williams in 1945 the world sustained
the loss of a genuinely original mind. Like many others in
this rare kind, he developed slowly, his early work being
somewhat uneven, tentative and derivative ; but from the
moment that he achieved his characteristic style and outlook
he set his own stamp upon everything that he touched.
There is scarcely a paragraph in his mature work that could
conceivably have been written by anybody else, and it is
already not hard to recognise, among the younger generation
of writers and candidates for the priesthood, those who
passed through his hands as students in London and Oxford.

Williams was original—not only in the sense that he
was a source, from which others received the waters of truth,
but also in the sense that his truth, however strange its
savour might seem to the unaccustomed palate, was
grounded immutably in its Christian origins. The doctrine
was traditional and perennial ; his apprehension and
presentation of it so individual as at a first encounter to
disconcert, perplex, or even antagonise those on whom it
did not, on the contrary, break as a sudden light to them
that had sat in darkness. He was called from his work at
the very moment when it was beginning to reach and
influence a wider public. It is now arousing a stir of interest
in America and on the Continent of Europe ; and in this
country his books—many of which have been for some time
out of print—are happily again being made available to the
increasing band of readers who have been plaintively
clamouring for them.

All the works of his maturity—novels, plays, poems,
and essays in theology or literary criticism—form a closely
connected unity, throwing light upon one another,
si ch'ogni parte ad ogni parte splende.

They illumine one another, and illumine also those other
writers of the central tradition from whom their author
himself derived illumination.   If Williams is a pregnant
interpreter of Dante, Dante is equally a pregnant interpreter
of Williams.   So too, with Shakespeare, Milton, Wordsworth :
they and he are " set on the marble of exchange." Similarly,
that which in one of the novels or plays may seem merely
entertaining, romantic, or fantastical is seen to be but the
exposition in action of some profound and challenging
verity, which, in the theological or critical books, is
submitted to the analysis of the intellect ; and conversely.

It is therefore most desirable that the complete works of
Williams should be obtainable by those who want to study
him.   Since his death, many volumes which had been
squeezed out of print by the exigencies of war have appeared
in new editions.   The whole series of novels is now again
complete, and 1950 saw the reissue in one volume of the
two essays *He Came Down from Heaven* and *The Forgiveness
of Sins*.   The former of these, the earliest of the theological
works, is in many respects a key-book.   Almost all the
great themes which Williams made peculiarly his own are
here outlined with remarkable lucidity, and in direct
relation to the dogmas of the Incarnation and Atonement
from which they derive.   The book is perhaps chiefly
memorable as making comprehensible and actual the nature
of that " knowledge of good and evil " which so mysteriously
and painfully distinguishes man's awareness from the
innocence of God on the one hand and of the beasts on the
other.   But it contains also the first exposition of the
theology of Romantic Love—later developed in *The Figure
of Beatrice* ;   the first guidance on the approach to God by
the Way of the Affirmation of Images, as also on the Practice
of Substituted Love, shown as its most triumphant in the
novel *Descent into Hell* and at its most moving in the poem
called *The Death of Virgil* ;   the doctrine of the Coinherence
of all men, which later received a fuller exposition in *The*

Descent of the Dove ; the doctrine of the City. This essay, important in itself, and rich in those epigrams which seem to condense centuries of Christian experience into a single saying, is thus important also as constituting a kind of handbook to Charles Williams. The second, though less satisfactory in its workmanship, remains nevertheless searching and disquieting in its examination of the ever-present and ever-insoluble problem of reconciling the Law with the Gospel, and expands and completes that chapter in the earlier essay which is concerned with " The Mystery of Pardon."

Of all Charles Williams's works, the Arthurian cycle known generally as " The Taliessin Poems " is, admittedly, the most " difficult " ; it is, indeed, the only part of the Williams country in which the experienced and properly-equipped explorer need ever find himself at a loss. Dr. C. S. Lewis, however, in *Arthurian Torso*, has cleared away much entanglement and erected many useful signposts— not only by providing help with the symbolism, but also, and chiefly, by the simple process of putting the Taliessin poems into a logical and chronological order. The appearance of this book, together with the recent republication of both parts of the cycle (*Taliessin through Logres* and *The Region of the Summer Stars*) has opened up this country to adventurous spirits, who are thus enabled to go forward, map in hand, to the discovery of its noble landscapes and its rich mines of religious and psychological imagery. The interpretation of the poems can be greatly aided by a study of the critical volumes, *The English Poetic Mind* and *Reason and Beauty in the Poetic Mind*. These, stimulating and original in the handling of their own subject-matter, are important also for the light they throw on the writer's own attitude to poetry and its function, and on the sources of his own poetic inspiration.

By issuing this new edition of *James I*, Messrs. Barker have reintroduced us to what is, on the whole, the least known and the least considered part of Williams's output :

the purely historical works. It may be left to speak for
itself to those who are interested in a crucial transition in
the history of Britain, and in an enigmatic personality whom
there have been, generally speaking " none to praise, and
very few to love." (It is characteristic of Williams that he
should have been able to find both love and praise for his
subject.) One thing may strike us in reading this book, as
it strikes us also, and most forcibly, in reading that masterpiece of sympathetic interpretation, *The Figure of Beatrice*.
That Charles Williams had an acute sense of the living
movement of history is made abundantly plain by his
brilliant handling of the development of the Christian church
in *The Descent of the Dove*. But he was singularly free from
that hypertrophied " sense of period " on which our generation tends to pride itself rather too much, and which tends
to inhibit judgement by turning all action in the past into
a kind of " costume-piece." To make " period " the sole
criterion to which human thoughts and deeds can be
referred involves the total subjection of actuality to
relativity, and opens between ourselves and our forefathers
a gulf over which understanding cannot stride. For Charles
Williams, that gulf did not exist. He saw a historical
situation and human beings in that situation, but he never
saw them as the mere creatures of a situation. He would
have been quite incapable of that somewhat too-famous
passage in which Lytton Strachey sought to build up a
romantic mystique of incomprehensibility between us and
the men of Elizabeth's time. " By what art are we to
worm our way into those strange spirits, those even stranger
bodies ? "[1] It would have needed more than the passage
of a few centuries, or the disguise of ruff and bombast, to
make either body or spirit strange to him. He observes
that Dante " was so touched by the habits of the Middle
Ages . . . that he believed it to be less important that men
should think for themselves than that they should think

[1] Lytton Strachey : *Elizabeth and Essex.*

rightly " ; the row of dots indicates the slipping-in of the sly parenthesis " which he, of course, did not think were the Middle Ages ; he thought he was a modern." Williams never forgot that every age is modern to itself, and that this fact, or illusion, links it with our own. Thus to all men in all ages he has the same direct approach ; the same readiness to accept their behaviour as human (and not " strange " or " quaint ") ; the same charity, to which irony gives a certain wholesome and astringent edge.

This freedom of judgment is not to be obtained except from the viewpoint of a theology which postulates an absolute truth, and which, moreover, sees in the material facts of history the symbol and expression of that truth. When Charles Williams died, the lament went up from the Church : " Who will now show us the Way of Affirmation ? " That Way—less thoroughly charted by the theologian than the Way of Negation, though more frequented by the artist and poet—possesses few regular doctors : Dante and Charles Williams—it would not be easy to add many more names. The whole of Williams's work may be seen, from one aspect, as a reconciliation of the two Ways ; " This also is Thou ; neither is this Thou " ; we must still believe that after the rejections the greater affirmations are to return " ;

> " between city and convent, the two great vocations,
> the Rejection of all images before the unimaged,
> the Affirmation of all images before the all-imaged,
> the Rejection affirming, the Affirmation rejecting, the
>   king's poet
> riding through a cloud with a vowed novice,
> and either no less than the other the doctrine of largesse."

That final phrase is possibly the best summary of the doctrine of Charles Williams, now presented to a world which, with greater ease of communications, is rapidly losing its coinherence, and which, while insistently making larger demands upon life, appears at times most singularly lacking in largesse.

                                        DOROTHY L. SAYERS.

CHAPTER ONE

The Three Birthdays

ABOUT two in the afternoon the father of the child, the Lord Henry Stuart, Earl of Darnley, sometimes called the King, came into the chamber where his wife lay. He had been brought with her to the Castle of Edinburgh only for this moment, and had been lodged in the Castle to await it, along with other great persons—the Lord John Erskine, Earl of Mar, Captain of the Castle ; the Lord James Stuart, Earl of Murray, the Queen's half-brother ; two or three territorial chieftains, such as the Earls of Argyle and Atholl ; the Queen's ladies. The Captain of the Queen's Guard, the Lord James Hepburn, Earl of Bothwell, was discreetly lodged a little farther away from his mistress, in the town at the foot of the Castle. It was Wednesday, the 19th of June 1566, when the Queen's pains began ; betwixt ten and eleven that morning, after some danger, she had been delivered of a male child. Now she sent for the father to do his part : publicly to acknowledge his paternity and the legitimacy of the child. He was to do it before the company in the chamber, and through them before the kings and queens of Europe, before the Pope, before John Knox and the other ministers of the Reformed Kirk of Scotland, before the Scottish families related to the royal line, branches of the Stuarts and the Hamiltons, even before his own father, Matthew Stuart, Earl of Lennox, and himself. In the future neither he nor any one else should be able to deny the child's rights.

The Queen had no other desire or need of her husband. The passion in which she had married him a year before,

and had then under his power conceived, perished soon
after the marriage. Since then she had but once been
captive to him, and then but for a few minutes, and at
that but a physical, not a spiritual, prisoner ; in the
February now four months gone. He had held her by his
arm around her while his confederates had, from her very
supper-table, dragged her Italian secretary, David Rizzio,
to his death ; one of them, Andrew of Feardonside, had
even pointed a pistol at her own person. She had been
compelled to make use of Darnley afterwards in order to
escape from the band of them, and now she was determined
to make use of him once more in order to counter the
slander that the child was David's. Legitimate, it was the
strong support of her claim to the Crown of England ;
with it, she offered her Catholic supporters in that country
not a single person but a dynasty. It was for the sake of
the young dynasty that she sent for her husband. She was
twenty-four and he twenty-one.

He came in ; Mary of Scots lay in her bed and waited
for him. When he was by : " My lord," she said,
" God has given you and me a son, begotten by none but
you."

He reddened ; he bent and kissed the child. The
Queen took it in her arms, discovering its face to all present,
and said again : " My lord, here I protest to God, and as
I shall answer at the great day of judgment, this is your
son and no other man's son. And I desire all here, both
ladies and others, bear witness." She could not stop ; she
added across the child : " For he is so much your son that
I fear it will be the worse for him hereafter." Before he
could say anything she looked away again to one of her
gentlemen, Sir William Stanley. " This is the son," she
said, " who, I hope, shall first unite the two kingdoms of
Scotland and England."

Sir William knew, as they all knew, the tales of the
perilous health of the Queen of England and the prospects

of her perilous throne. He answered : " Why, madam, shall he succeed before your Majesty and his father ? "

The Queen said : " Because his father has broken to me."

Darnley, harassed as she meant him to be, broke out : " Sweet madam, is this the promise you made to forgive and forget all ? "

" I have forgiven all," the Queen said ; " I will never forget. What if Feardonside's pistol had shot ? What would have become of him and me both ? Or what estate would you have been in ? God only knows, but we may suspect."

" Madam, these things are all past," Darnley said.

The Queen answered : " Then let them go," and with that for dismissal she let him also go. But she did not forget ; she had not forgotten when, eight months later, she in turn went out from his bedside on that last evening of his life, and paused as she went to say : " It was just this time last year when David was slain." Nor, for all her precautions, did the world forget, either kings or crowds, for though " these things " never hampered the child in his claim to either of the kingdoms his mother desired for him—he was to have them both, and to have them, by Fate and his own choice, at her cost—yet years afterwards they served for laughter and abuse, as when Henry IV. of France jested at " Solomon, the son of David," or the populace of Perth cried out : " Thou son of Seigneur Davie, come down ! "

It was, as she feared, the worse for him that he seemed to have in him much of his father's weak, wandering, and egotistical spirit. But it was the worse for her that he had also, under it, much of her resolution and capacity. He inherited from both of them, and there was in him something else, some twist and check of nature that seems to receive and continue the spectacle of that February night.

B

It is an often-repeated, and rather doubtful, tale that the
flashing of steel before the eyes of his mother as the conspirators seized Rizzio gave him a lifelong aversion from
naked swords. His fear of steel has been exaggerated.
But there was another fear which had in it a fascination
for him—the fear of unseen powers and supernatural hosts
of darkness, such a thrill of horror and defiance as went
through the Queen's body when she looked up from the
lit supper-table to see in the darkness of the doorway the
grotesque figure of the Lord Ruthven who led the band of
murderers, tall, old, emaciated by sickness, with a gown
cast over his armour, looking down terribly on her friend.
There was also in him a physical longing for a personal love
and a fascination by it, which (natural as it is) possesses a
nervous excitement, a clutch of possession, as if from some
communicated knowledge of the friend whose fingers had
had to be torn from the Queen's skirts while she yearned
for his salvation in vain. His secrecy, his cunning, his
vigilant caution, seem to prolong, after a vaguer manner,
the hostility with which his mother strained against his
father's arm, the cunning she exercised through the hours
of the night and the day till she had lured her husband to
abandon his companions and be her escort to his own murder.

Whether from that night or from other causes, the child
of whom the foreign ambassadors wrote admiringly to their
sovereigns was a twisted growth in the Stuart line. He
was the gibe of life at their house, its beauty and tragedy.
He was to take himself seriously and be everlastingly comic ;
to think himself touched with " sparkles of Divinity "—
thus finally ousting any suspicion of Rizzio in his blood—
and to be everlastingly taken as an example of the lack of
divinity ; to be indifferently honest and suspected of the
foulest crimes ; to be indifferently continent and become a
byword for the most sentimental incontinence. He was
the forfeit that his house paid to existence for their

romantic glory, being the one member of it to whom the word could, in no sense whatever, be applied.

The child was born. The General Assembly of the Reformed Kirk of Scotland, in high session upon the dangers which threatened the pure Presbyterian religion, heard of it. They sent one of their number, John Spottiswoode, Superintendent of Lothian, to congratulate the Queen, and to desire that the Prince should be baptized according to the Reformed rite. Of this the Queen said nothing, but she caused the child to be brought ; the Superintendent briefly prayed over him, and with a good humour rare in the ecclesiastics of the day, told the baby to say Amen. The joke lasted, for the Queen called the Superintendent her " Amen," and when the Prince was grown he took it over—he called him " my Amen."

The child was born. Letters went to foreign Courts announcing it. A politician of Scotland, Sir James Melville, mature, intelligent, and pragmatic, was chosen to carry the news south to the Court which it affected most of all. Both France and Spain, in their growing rivalry, took an acute interest in him. But England was bound to have more than an interest ; her Government was bound to find him a continual preoccupation. It was historic ; English Governments had always been preoccupied with Scottish heirs. But this boy was something more than the heir of Scotland : he was the heir to England. There was a story that Mary of Scots had once, with her train, been in an Edinburgh house where was a picture of Elizabeth. The courtiers had disputed whether it were like the Queen of England till Mary interrupted them : " No ; it is not like her, for I am the Queen of England." It was not, however, in such terms that Sir James carried the news, but discreetly as became queen and sister communicating such joyful tidings to queen and sister. Four days later Cecil, hearing it privately from him, went into the hall at

Greenwich where the Court was dancing. Elizabeth—then thirty-three—was also dancing. He went up to her and whispered in her ear. She stopped abruptly and sat down, her cheek on her hand. In the immediate silence of the Court she broke out with the news to her people and to herself : " The Queen of Scots is leichter [lighter] of a fair son, and I am but a barren stock." It was a moment of which she never quite lost the sharpness ; she could never quite forgive James for being there, and never with equanimity contemplate his being where she so long had been. In the hours during which she suffered a divided heart over Mary's fate, there was always the knowledge that Mary's son must defeat her at last. Yet, could she have foreseen the comparisons of the histories between him and her when he too was dead, she might have felt that she was the victor over both her rivals in the end.

The next day, when Sir James made his official visit, she had recovered. She assured him, meeting him in her finest clothes, smiling and delighted, that she had recovered, upon the news, from a sickness that had held her a fortnight. Sir James enlarged upon the difficult delivery, telling her how Mary had wished she had never been married. " This I said," he explains, " to give her a little skar to marry, by the way." Elizabeth listened sympathetically ; she would not have been scared from marrying by such simple efforts. Sir James invited her, in his sovereign's name, to stand as godmother, and to come in person ; it would give her the opportunity to see Mary which she had often desired. Elizabeth promised to act, but doubted if her affairs would permit her presence ; she promised a noble embassy. Presently Sir James came to the underlying matter of his audience. He proposed the immediate official declaration of Mary Stuart as " second person," heir presumptive to the English throne, saying that he was sure the Queen of England had only delayed it until the birth of a child of Mary's body ratified the succession. The birth of a child of Mary's body ! He went on to argue that the declaration would settle the minds of many in both countries who desired to see the matter put out of doubt ; he undertook that Mary would never seek any right or place in England but by Elizabeth's forwarding. Twenty-one years later, in a more agitated moment, Elizabeth found her true answer to that enticement. on behalf of the son then as on behalf of the mother now : " By God's passion, that were to cut my own throat ! " Mary indeed need do nothing ; there were plenty to seek and give her right and place in England by Elizabeth's foundering, in deposition or death. The Queen answered mildly and sweetly now ; she was sure the birth of the Prince would be a great spur to the most skilful lawyers to use greater diligence in trying out the matter. She herself was of opinion that Mary's claim was just, and hoped that so the lawyers would decide. Sir James pointed out that when last he was in England Elizabeth had been saying the same thing ; would it not be delightful if he, who had brought one kind of joyful news south, could bear those other joyful news north ? Elizabeth, wanting no more of the conversation, told him she hoped to satisfy the Queen of Scots when the embassy went to the baptism. Sir James was dismissed ; the next day two grooms-in-waiting brought him the gift of " a fair chain." With that for himself, and another message for his Queen, he set out again. Francis Walsingham was soon to take charge of the affairs of Scotland.

The other message Sir James bore was a letter from his brother, Sir Robert, then ambassador in London. If the anxiety of the loyal English had been heightened by the birth of the child, the anxiety of the loyal Scots was not much lessened. The more sedate diplomats knew that their own Queen was an uncertain quantity. Sir Robert permitted himself an appeal, at the end of a paper of advice, that her Majesty, seeing the great mark she shot at, should be more careful and circumspect, that since her desires were now so nearly obtained, they should not be over-thrown " for lack of secresie, gud handling and prencely behaviour." The letter was delivered, but now, though the Melvilles did not know it, the uncertain quantity had endured the intrusion of two more certain elements—the spectral memory of Rizzio's death, the living presence of the Lord Bothwell. Mary went unhappily in a Court and a land overnetted with violence, and by the end of the year she was sick with anger and love. The child had been sent to Stirling Castle, which was to be his home for twelve years. As if to leave the whole stage free for him, his mother and his father played out their parts swiftly, before he could walk or speak or know them. He was left to him-self, except for the necessary guardians, and even there his mocking fortune found him. It is said that the woman who suckled him was a drunkard ; alternately, it is said that he endured " some ill treatment " in his infancy, by which his legs were left weak afterwards, and he was always inclined to shamble through his palaces. Meanwhile his mother and father were concerned with loves and crowns and quarrels and creeds.

They found little joy. Darnley, despised and neglected, drifted about from place to place. He thought of leaving the country ; his wife forbade it. She herself caused scandal by riding thirty miles and thirty miles back in one day to visit the Lord Bothwell, who had been wounded in a fight on the borders of which he was Warden. Sir Robert Melville's advice was divided against itself : it was a princely deed, but it was not good handling. She fell into illness and despair ; from the fever she recovered, not from the despair. She remained " in a deep grief and sorrow," wrote the French ambassador, " nor does it seem possible to make her forget the same. Still she repeats these words, ' I could wish to be dead.' We know very well that the injury she received is exceeding great, and her Majesty will never forget it." " There were," said Sir James Melville, " overfew to comfort her."

Preparations had to be made for the baptism of the child. His physical health, between them, might be injured, but his spiritual state was a matter of high political, as well as private, necessity. In December he was to be born again into the Church of Christ : with Catholic rites, the arrangements for which were put in the hands of the Protestant Bothwell. The magnificent sponsors — the Protestant Queen of England, the Catholic King of France, the Catholic Duke of Savoy—were preparing their presents and dispatching their proxies. This union of the Churches was sardonically reflected in a still wider union which occurred in December at Craigmillar, near Edinburgh, when Mary found some few to promise her a dangerous comfort. Bothwell was there, and her brother Murray, the defender of the Kirk, and Huntly, the Catholic lord of the north, and Maitland of Lethington, the Secretary and sceptic. They conferred together ; they laid before the Queen proposals for dealing with her husband—divorce or nullity, on the grounds of consanguinity, since there had been some irregularity in the Papal Bull of dispensation for the marriage of cousins, or of treason, or of adultery. The Queen insisted that whatever was done must carry no peril to her child's legitimacy ; sooner than risk that she said she would endure all torments and abide all perils. The succession must be secure, and the further succession over which the agitated Commons in England were daring to trouble their Queen, desiring once more her own marriage. Bothwell, in answer, said his own father and mother had been divorced, yet he had come to his inheritance ; why should not the Prince

2

do the same ? Maitland went farther ; he promised that
those present, " the principal of your Grace's nobility and
Council," should find a means to rid her of *him*, without
prejudice to her son. He added the immortal sentence
that though " my lord of Murray be little less scrupulous
for ane Protestant than your Grace for a Papist, I am assurit
he will look throw his fingers thereto." The Queen protested that she would have nothing done to hurt her
honour or her conscience ; better leave things as they were
till the goodness of God provided a remedy ; perhaps what
they thought would do her service would turn to her hurt
and displeasure. Maitland left God to mind His own business and keep out of theirs : " Madam, let us guide the
matter amongst us, and ye shall see nothing but good,
and approved by Parliament." The cool voice came from
an intellectual world beyond the turmoil of her love, her
hate, and her belief. To that reposeful and alien intelligence, and to Bothwell's ardent strength, she left all. Half-
acquiescing and half-rejecting, she left them, the conference broke up, and on the appointed day the mother and
father were both with their child in Stirling.

But while the child and the mother were the centres of
magnificence, the father moved on the outskirts, between
it and the dark. Presents were offered to the mother from
the great gossips : from the Queen of England, by the
Earl of Bedford, a golden font, weighing 333 ounces, decked
with precious stones ; from the King of France a necklace
of pearls and rubies, with two most beautiful ear-rings ;
from the Duke of Savoy a large fan with jewelled feathers,
worth four thousand crowns. The father tried in vain to
get speech with the French ambassador, M. du Croc. He
sent three times, but Du Croc had instructions from his
king, and at last Darnley received the answer that the
ambassador said his apartment had two doors, and if the
King entered it by the one, he himself would be compelled

to go out by the other.   Meanwhile the special proxy of
France, the Comte de Brienne, himself carried the Prince
from his room to the chapel between two rows of gentlemen, holding every one a pricket of wax.   After him went
Atholl, carrying the great sierge of wax; the Earl of Eglin-
ton carried the salt, the Lord Sempill the rood, and the
Lord Ross the basin and laver.   The Earl of Bedford, a
strict Puritan, refused to enter; he, with the other Reformed lords, including Bothwell, stood at the door.   He
gave the Queen's illegitimate sister, the Countess of Argyle,
a ruby worth five hundred crowns to act in his stead.
She did (and was afterwards forced by the Assembly of
the Kirk to do penance in time of preaching for this sub-
servience to Papistry).   There was one other notable
absentee: Darnley was not within.   The Archbishop
Hamilton, with three bishops and other ecclesiastics,
officiated in pontifical habits " such as had not been seen
in Scotland these seven years."   By the sacramental water
and the sacramental formula of fifteen centuries the child
was regenerated.   He was restored to his spiritual integrity
and the kingdom of God militant upon earth; the tragic
harlequinade of religion that had already begun to surround
him could not alter the act of Christendom.   He was
received into salvation.

The Christian names given him were Charles James—
Charles being the name of the King of France, and James
that of " the good kings of Scotland, his predecessors,"
who had been closely allied to France.   They were the
choice of the Queen, who had herself by her first marriage
been for so short a time Queen of France.   He was proclaimed Prince and Steward of Scotland, Duke of Rothesay,
Earl of Carrick, Lord of the Isles, Baron of Renfrew.   Latin
elegiacs by George Buchanan, humanist and Kirk convert,
before now the tutor and afterwards to be the accuser of
the Queen, were sung.   A letter from the Pope, saying

that he had conceived great joy over the birth of the child, brought his prayers for increase of joy to the mother, and preservation of grace and bestowal of divine gifts to the child. Long afterwards one person—Charles James himself—believed the second part of those apostolic prayers to have been granted. The first, every one knew, was wholly denièd.

In the evening there were masques and triumphs, again with a note of prophecy. They were designed by the Queen's servant Bastian, already concerned with his own approaching marriage in February. It cannot yet have been settled that the festival of his marriage was to be the reason for his mother to leave Kirk o' Field and return to Holyrood before the slaying of the father. Bastian displayed his skill, and the associates in the new plot watched it. There came in, running before the meat when it was brought, satyrs, with long tails and whips. The English gentlemen in attendance on Bedford were sitting in the hall. The Scottish satyrs, observing them, put their hands backward and wagged their tails derisively. The English, in high dudgeon and with a good deal of noise, rose from the table and, as a protest, sat down on the floor behind it. One was heard to threaten that, saving the Queen's presence, he would put a dagger into Bastian's heart. Mary and Bedford, hearing the disturbance, interfered and appeased the angry Southerners. The Prince (it is to be hoped) was in bed, but some such satirical tail-wagging was to go on for years under his rule before his Highness succeeded in appeasing the two nations, and in other days the wagging of copes before the angry North was to help to bring his son to his death.

The second birthday ended. Charles James had entered into natural and supernatural life. There was to be a third which should peculiarly combine both ; so he was to believe, and so some others. But for that he had to wait another seven months—fourteen in all between the first and the third. The grand company of splendour dissociated. His mother, attended by Bothwell, rode off to spend Christmas with the Lord Drummond at Drummond Castle. His uncle, the Earl of Murray, beginning the process of preparing his fingers, went off with the religious Earl of Bedford to St. Andrews. His father wandered away, still solitary, to his own father's house at Glasgow; there he fell ill of the smallpox. In January Mary was writing of his reported intention to seize the person of the Prince and rule in his name. She did not, she said, altogether believe the reports, though she knew that he, his father, and their folk were willing to give trouble. " But God moderates their forces well enough."

Man moderated them further. Another of those strange "bonds" or agreements was in preparation of which the whole period is so full. There had been one against Rizzio; there would be others for and against Bothwell. It would not do to say that there was then no political cause and effect. But our knowledge is still so limited, and their subtlety was so great, that we are left with a sense, greater than intelligence admits, of gazing at a number of violently discrete moments rather than at a series of logically consecutive moments. We can trace logical connections, but we can never be sure we are right. Bonds, associations, movements, are unrelated except by the dim and passionate destiny that rules all. Moment after moment expands with its stillness of sinister preparation or its violence of action, and disappears, and when the next rises in its turn everything is changed. These great persons exist discontinuously; to us, as to themselves (we seem to think), they live in their immediate knowledge of passion, and the flood of their passion withdraws into darkness and then hurls itself again towards us in another manner under a different sun. In the next century the darkness lifts;

we can understand the movements of the tides.   The execution of Charles I. is comprehensible ; in the execution of Mary there remains a mystery, in the explosion of Kirk o' Field a deeper mystery.   The curious figure of James stands at the change of the centuries.   The splendour of the Renascence *homo* is becoming the clarity of the seventeenth-century gentleman.   In those earlier lives we are conquered by shocks of vision.   Their drama is ostentatious and spectacular ; so are their lives, but each with its core of night.   Cecil, Walsingham, Maitland—these, and a few others, exist continuously, by their steady prolongation of purpose ; the rest in moments, many perhaps, but always moments.   It is from apparent discontinuity to apparent continuity that James is the transition.   After him, the great moment disappears except by an accident of logic ending in a spectacle, as in the execution of his son.   But before him the spectacle leaves its real logic concealed, as in the execution of his mother.

The child was brought to Edinburgh.   The rush of his parents to destruction grew quicker.   They came, both of them together, to Edinburgh, Darnley still ill.   He was lodged in Kirk o' Field, the Queen went to Holyrood.   A year after David was slain, Kirk o' Field went up in fire. Mary, professing that neither she nor her son was safe, delivered him to the custody of the Earl of Mar, who held him safely at Stirling again.   There the Earl heard news after news—heard of the placards against Bothwell fastened by night on the Tolbooth, of the demands for justice by Lennox, father of the murdered man, of his wife's reasonable answers, of Bothwell holding Edinburgh with four thousand men and Lennox gathering three thousand, of Lennox forbidden to bring more than his personal household to Edinburgh when he came to the trial of the accused Bothwell, of Lennox refusing to come.   In April he heard of the trial, where no witnesses could be offered and no

verdict but of acquittal found ; of honours showered by the
Queen on Bothwell, of his triumph, of the meeting of the
Estates of Scotland. He heard of the great supper at
Ainslie's tavern where the high lords pledged themselves
to stand by Bothwell if, for his infinity of good qualities,
the Queen should be moved to choose him as a husband.
On the 21st of April the Queen, without the Lord Warden
and Lord Admiral Bothwell, appeared before the Castle,
come to visit her son. There was a reason for the visit
besides motherhood, though the Lord Mar did not know
of it till three days afterwards. But he was wary of his
charge ; he would allow only two women to follow their
mistress into the princely presence. Rumours went abroad
of the meeting between Mary and her child. She had gone
to kiss him ; he had pushed her away, and tried to scratch
her with all his little strength. It is likely enough that
the small Charles James tried to push away a strange
woman when he found her kissing him ; babies do. But
the English agent wrote to Cecil, apparently in complete
seriousness, of impossible things. The Queen had given
him (at ten months old) an apple, which he had refused to
take. It was thrown to a greyhound and her whelps, all
of which ate it and presently died. She had brought a
sugar-loaf also, which was "judged to be very ill com-
pounded." This it is to have agents who gather for their
letters news more startling and more incredible than is
found in any of the sober papers of our modern age. A
witch in the north had prophesied—Bothwell would die
within the year ; Mary would have two more husbands,
and in the time of the fifth would die by fire.

But before that necromantic fire was well heard of,
the Queen had left Stirling, to be met and seized by Bothwell, hastily divorced from his wife, and soon afterwards
married to his sovereign. They returned to Edinburgh,
and from there messages came to Stirling demanding the

delivery of the child. Mar, having his charge from the
Estates of Scotland, refused, but he grew anxious of the
strength that Bothwell could bring, and he heard more
rumours that Bothwell had sworn, could he once get the
Prince in his hands, he " would warrant him for avenging
his father's death."

Mar negotiated, encouraged by Sir James Melville. The
split in the House of Stuart was already begun. Bothwell
and Mar prefigured the schism between Mary and Charles
James. The serious honesty of the Earl to his charge
began the seclusion of the son from the mother which was
to end in her final seclusion from him at Fotheringay.
There, at any rate, was continuity. Mar argued that there
was no place, outside Stirling, sure enough to hold the
Prince if he were yielded up. He was reminded of Edinburgh Castle. He allowed of Edinburgh, but he had another
objection. Being (they said) a bad dissembler, he had to
make his objections out of such facts as he could find.
Fortunately in Scotland then there were always facts to
which objection could be taken. He said he could not
trust the governor of Edinburgh Castle. But already the
discussion was becoming irrelevant, and the great bond of
Ainslie's tavern already negligible. The lords were gathering against Bothwell. Mar knew it ; very soon Bothwell
and the Queen knew it. The idea of seizing the child was
abandoned ; the lovers fled to Dunbar.

Of all this anxiety on his behalf Charles James knew
nothing. The routine of his life went on—after he had
endured the single incursion of the strange woman who had
tried to kiss him. He never saw her again, though as he
grew older he heard of her often enough. He heard of
her for the last time, except as a memory, twenty years
after at Fotheringay ; when he did, he knew that part of
his royalty was at last quite finally his, and did not make
any grand outcry beyond bidding the preachers pray for

her. But at present she could not come, though she begged to, because she was shut up in the Castle of Lochleven, while Bothwell lurked in the Orkneys, and there she signed her renunciation of the Crown. Instead of her, there came, one day in July, many masculine visitors. The Castle was full of armed men. Charles James found himself carried about into another place—the church near by. The men-at-arms were at their posts ; the Castle guns were ready. In the church there was movement and voices ; a man with reddish hair, inclining his body and laying his hand on the Book of the Gospels, read in the child's name the long oath of the King of Scots. It was James Douglas, Earl of Morton, selected for that service because of his other great services to the royal house of Scotland—he had held Holyrood for the conspirators while they slew Rizzio and threatened the Queen, he had signed the bond to stand by Bothwell and had then besieged him, he had put himself on the Council of Regency named in the paper the Queen had signed. In the name of Almighty God he read : how he—James, Prince and Steward of Scotland —would serve " the Eternal, my God, to the uttermost of my power . . . maintain the true religion of Jesus Christ . . . abolish and gainstand all false religion . . . rule according to the will and command of God . . . and according to the lovable laws and constitutions received in this realm. . . . The rights and rents, with all just privileges, of the Crown of Scotland I shall preserve and keep inviolate. . . . I shall forbid and repress, in all estates and all degrees, reiff, oppression, and all kind of wrong. In all judgments I shall command and procure that justice and equity be kept to all creatures, without exception . . . and out of all my lands and empire I shall be careful to root out all heretics and enemies to the true worship of God that shall be convicted by the true Kirk of God of the foresaid crimes."

The Earl finished the oath. The ceremony again went on. They set over the small head the ancient Crown of Scotland ; they brought up the other royal hallows—the " honours of the realm ":—and laid the small hand on the sceptre and the sword. They gave way to Adam, Bishop of Orkney, who had three months before married Mary to Bothwell, and he anointed the child. They swore their oaths of allegiance. The ceremony drew to a close ; the instruments of royalty were borne back to the Castle, each by one of the great lords, and with them went the Lord John Erskine, Earl of Mar, bearing the chief instrument of royalty, the little body that had received the unction and the homage, incarnated Majesty, James the Sixth of Scotland. John Knox preached on the event that same day in the church of Stirling, from the text, " I was crowned young."

It was his third birthday ; now he was man, and Christian, and King. What those three things meant to him is his biography ; what they meant to others is history. He set out, from those immingling nativities, under the charge of the lords. Before him, in due course, lay Edinburgh and London. Shakespeare and Bacon were to be his servants ; Harvey his physician, Donne his chaplain. Ben Jonson was to write him masques, and Lancelot Andrewes arguments. He was to be the patron of the great English book that declared the coming of the Prince of Peace, and to see himself as a prince of peace, bringing rest to the afflicted churches and nations. But war in Europe and war in England were to open over his grave ; the gossips were to spice their scandalous talk with his name ; and afterwards everybody was always to laugh or shudder at him for ever.

CHAPTER TWO

The Education of the King

THE lords had received during these months of militancy signs of the care which other Governments had for the Prince. The Queen of England caused her agent to propose that he should be brought to England for safety; she sent word to Mary at the same time, pointing out " how much good may ensue to her son to be so nourished and acquainted with our realm "—so much (Elizabeth added) that Mary ought rather to be petitioning for the removal than she herself proposing it. The King of France offered Murray almost anything he wanted if he would procure the dispatch of the Prince to France; he was said to be determined to get the child into his hands, " either by hook or by crook." The Spanish ambassador in London, not seeing any chance of abducting the Prince for his own master, urged Cecil to secure him lest France should get him. Mary at the moment, what with Kirk o' Field and what with Bothwell, was not popular with the Catholic sovereigns. But to have possession of the undoubted heir to Scotland and possible heir to England would be to hold a figure of very high potential value. In the end, however, none of them got him. The lords, and Murray, now on his way back to accept the Regency, realized James's value; they kept him in Stirling under the sure vigilance of Mar; to whom presently came the final news of Mary's escape from Lochleven, of her stand at Langside, of her flight to England, and of the sinister hospitality extended by Elizabeth. James was doubly orphaned—of his father by death, of his mother by exile.

C

One last message she left him—in those short days of her freedom she dashed down a revocation of her surrender. The Throne was hers and not his ; she, and only she, was the sovereign ruler of Scotland. By the time he knew of it he had been taught, and profoundly believed, otherwise.

James underwent three educational experiences. They were not, indeed, so markedly separate as his three birthdays, for each of them to some extent reflected and overran the others. But their intensities were different. From 1569 to 1579 he was under serious tutors, officially appointed, and learned his proper lessons, especially Biblical. From 1579 to 1582, under the influence of his first passion, he learned amorous emotions, royal emotions, and some sense of the facts rather than the bogies of the Continent and Christendom. From 1582 to 1583, in a captivity to his own servants, he learned to meet circumstantial hostility with caution and guile. After his escape from that captivity, at the age of seventeen, his education ends ; his experience as a man begins. That experience itself divides naturally into two parts : formally, by his accession in 1603, at the age of thirty-six, to the Throne of England ; actually, by the change in his circumstances which opened to him the relaxation and in the end the defeat of his spirit.

The Earl of Murray was Regent, having reached that position by a series of inspired absences from any spot where a murder happened to be taking place. In the history of the world no one else can have been away at the right moment quite so often as the Earl of Murray. He had lately broken his rule so far as to be present at the launching of accusations against his sister the Queen in England. But in the matter of physical or spiritual absence he could not teach Elizabeth anything. She too was never there, in any real sense, when she was wanted unless she also wanted to be. She had not been there now, either physically or spiritually. She had said, almost in so many words, that it was all very sad, and with that the raging Mary and the reluctant Murray had to be content. He returned to Scotland.

His Chancellor was the Earl of Morton, who, unlike Murray, had generally been either present or near at hand during the murders. The alliance worked admirably. Both Murray and Morton were professors of the Reformed Kirk, though even the Kirk was sometimes a little uneasy about Morton. But that was rather because of his abruptness with the ministers than because of the murders. Of Murray, however, they had no complaint. It was his nephew James who called him afterwards " that bastard who unnaturally rebelled, and procured the ruin of his owne sovran and sister."

In August 1569 the Estates of Scotland considered their King's education. They appointed four preceptors, two more especially tutorial : Mr. David Erskine, Mr. Adam Erskine, Mr. Peter Young, Mr. George Buchanan. The first two were known respectively as the Abbots of Cambuskenneth and Dryburgh, being lay persons who had, by permission, impropriated the revenues of those foundations. They were described as " wise and modest " ; certainly for nine years they took no prominent part. Peter Young was a minister, twenty-five years old, recently returned from Geneva. He was liked when he was noticed, but he was not usually noticed. The accident which sent him to Stirling as the younger coadjutor of Buchanan determined that his life should thereafter fall in pleasant places. He was afterwards made master-almoner ; he was sent on a few minor diplomatic missions, especially in connection with the King's marriage ; he followed his master to England in 1603, and in 1604 was made tutor to Prince Charles ; in 1605 he was knighted ; in 1616— at the age of seventy-two—he became master of St. Cross

Hospital, and there he died three years after his master.
So steady a list of continual quiet occupations and pro-
motions suggests a real affection between Peter Young
and his pupil. He was something like James's first love,
that steady young Calvinist Master of Arts, and outlasted
many later and more splendid rivals. Alas, he wrote no
Memoirs !

But the chief preceptor was a very different person.
No one had heard of Peter Young, but every one had heard
of George Buchanan. He was a humanist with a European
reputation. He had taught at Paris and Bordeaux, where
young Montaigne had been one of his pupils ; he had been
imprisoned for heresy by the Inquisition in a Spanish
monastery and released ; he had been tutor to the sons of
James V., of the Earl of Cassilis, of the French Marshal de
Brissac. He had formally abandoned the Church for the
Kirk in 1563, and had been made by Murray Principal of
St. Andrews College. Once, on her first coming to Scotland,
he had been a friend of the Queen's ; he had written her and
her ladies little complimentary poems in Latin. They had
read Livy together. In him alone of all the strong Scottish
Protestants she enjoyed scholarship and poetry. But then
there had come the catastrophic change. He was a man,
says Melville, " of good religion for a poet, but he was
easily abused, and so facile that he was led with any company that he haunted for a time." Whether from company
or from judgment he had believed the worst, and recorded
still worse, of his sovereign and sometime friend. He also
had returned but lately from residence in England, where
he had assisted Murray's arguments against Mary, and
had stood up to swear to her handwriting in the Casket
Letters.

During the first two years of his preceptorship he had
another great work on hand besides the education of the
son. He was busy in the detection of the mother. As

the months went by he went, day by day, from proposing the Latin sentences by which he taught James to polishing the Latin sentences in which he denounced Mary. He poured into that work all the baser scandals and all the fouler fancies ; it was the occupation of his leisure hours, and it was infiltrated with anger and hatred and scorn. That labour of darkness alternated with his labour of light. In the year 1571 the book was published—*Detectio Mariae Reginae*. It was probably at some moment when his two labours had become confused in his mind that he once called his pupil (as was reported) " a true bird of that bloody nest."

With these four there was Lady Mar. She had a severity, but more than Buchanan she remembered the person of the King. Buchanan and she both " held the King in great awe." The King remembered Buchanan for the rest of his life. In 1619, when he was fifty-three, he dreamed of his old master " checking him severely, as he was wont to do, and his Majesty in his dream seemed desirous to pacify him," but he turned away " with a frowning countenance," and repeated verses that the King, on waking, " perfectly remembered." Buchanan did not stop at a severe countenance. There was certainly one occasion when James with other boys made too much noise, even after admonition, upon which Buchanan, who was disturbed in his reading, leapt from his chair, caught hold of the King, and thrashed him. Lady Mar, whom the cries of James brought on the scene, protested at this treatment of Majesty, and was promptly and coarsely snubbed. Against all such behaviour Peter Young, " who was loth to offend the King at any time," seemed doubly amiable.

James learnt, and he learnt well ; no doubt he had to, but the capacity and the inclination were both there. " They gar me speik Latin ar I could speik Scottis," he said afterwards, and he was always inclined to be conceited over his correct pronunciation, which he justly attributed to Buchanan. On the other hand, Ben Jonson found fault with his manner of speaking verse ; he was apt to fall into a common error—" his master, Mr. G. Buchanan, had corrupted his ear when young, and learned him to sing verses when he should have read them." They taught him the Bible and the great texts that proved this or the other according as the wisdom of warring saints and doctors bade. They taught him history, ancient and modern, even at last the most modern history of all—of the Queen who had once dwelt with the leopards of France, and then for a little driven the unicorns of Scotland, and now lay in the castles of the lion of England ; of the woman who (they said) had been art and part in the killing of his father, and had debauched herself with lovers, and had been rightly chained from her wickedness by the holy champions of God ; of his mother. They taught him theology—the nature of God and of the Gospel, and the many enemies who opposed the Gospel, as the Roman Pontiff with his idolatries and the covens of witches with their necromancies. They taught him geometry and physics, logic and rhetoric, dialectic and astronomy. At times they showed him off to distinguished visitors. The Reverend James Melville and the English agent Killigrew both saw him in 1574, when he was eight. He was walked up and down by Lady Mar and made to display his capacities. " The sweetest sight in Europe for strange and extraordinary gifts of ingine, judgment, memorie, and language," wrote Melville. Killigrew heard him translate " any chapter " of the Bible out of Latin into French, out of French into English—" a prince of great hope."

When he was five they took him to open Parliament. In the canopy above him there was a rent. He asked what all this was ; they told him the Parliament. " There is a

hole in the Parliament," he said solemnly. Parliaments
were to be a great trouble to him—Parliaments in which
he would find so few convenient holes. Buchanan had
theories of the relation of a king to his people, of his responsi-
bilities, duties, and subordination. He wrote another
book and put them in—*De Jure Regni Apud Scotos*—and he
dedicated it to James. It was a statement of constitutional
monarchy, unexceptional in the abstract. But a constitutional monarchy presupposes a general agreement,
not merely on the monarch but on the constitution. It
was precisely this that was lacking. The King must not,
all were agreed, be an absolute monarch on his own behalf.
But any one of the lords who would so soon be in his
train might at any moment want to use the monarch
against some one else ; in which case the more absolute
the monarch was the better. Potential necessities clashed
with absolute needs. And even Buchanan, teaching duties
and limitations, still could only teach them as duties and
limitations of the central fact which created them as its
own characteristics. The King had duties because he was
the King. His own mind grasped that fact, and grasped
also the fact that in all Scotland there was no one like him.
Whatever it meant to be supreme, that he was, and he
alone. If James had grown up in any sort of even occa-
sional propinquity to his mother, if Mary had still ruled
Scotland he would have met another and a greater person
of this strange kind that they call Majesty. He would have
endured—agreeably or disagreeably—relations with her.
He might have quarrelled ; he would not have been
solitarily royal. But he never did. They told him he was
a phœnix, and all they told him besides of the proprieties of
his phœnixhood could not compensate for the lack of the
physical shock of another phœnix.

Gradually there appeared another element—the wish
of the phœnix. The Lady Mar and George Buchanan had

held him in great awe. But, slowly, other people entered.
He was invited to have preferences, and to express them.
He was urged to have royal wishes. The great world of
Scotland had been proceeding briskly in its activities all
those ten years. The Regent Murray ruled three years,
suppressing the Hamiltons, the Gordons, and the Borderers,
and was assassinated. The Regent Lennox, Darnley's
father, ruled in his stead for six months, and was killed in
a skirmish with the Hamiltons. The Regent Mar succeeded,
leaving James at Stirling in the custody of his brother, the
Master of Mar, ruled for a year or so, and died of fever.
The Regent Morton succeeded, and was still governing the
country, not ineffectively, by a steady process of stamping
out what remained of rebels and reivers, when the shadow
of Stirling began to creep slowly over his world. " There
was not another Earl of Morton to stir up factions," remarked the observant Sir James Melville. But there was
something else, which the Lord James Douglas in an
extremely busy and bloody life had almost forgotten :
there was the other James for whom he had sworn so many
remarkable things.

One day a gentleman of his household ventured a
reminder. He pointed out that the Regent, in general, was
both envied and hated throughout the country, and even
in Stirling. Gentlemen of note were going there ; the Earl
of Argyle was said to have been given, " by the King's
wish," a room in the Castle. There was feud between
Argyle and Morton. Even George Buchanan was said to be
very apt to speak evil of the Regent, who had once by chance
bought a hackney that had been stolen from Buchanan,
and would not give it up. The Regent was not usually a
fearful man. But once he had a leman, who had been wise
in necromancy, and made prophecies, and told him how
in the end the King should be his destruction, and the
doubt of that doom disturbed him now. He sent gold to

Stirling, to be discreetly bestowed on any there who spoke evil of him : except, certainly, George Buchanan. The gold was taken, and the gentlemen changed their tune. Presently the King, with the inconvenient accuracy of intelligent children, noticed to his surprise that the tune had changed. He spoke of it aloud, somewhat to the scandal of his household. It was found that his memory would " check up "—the phrase is Melville's—" any that he perceivet had first spoken evell, and then began to speak gud again." He said something about turncoats. It was his first intricate glance into the less violent methods of governing the opinions of the King.

The Lord Regent—it would not be altogether out of tune with the tragi-comedy of Scotland at this time to call him the Chief Brigand—found that bribery had failed. He had converted the gentlemen ; he had not influenced the King. He began to contemplate that chief act of brigandage which was so common—at least, as an effort— in both Scotland and England, the seizure of the person of the King. He determined to get into his power the anointed symbolical source of government ; and he determined to do it before that source could, as it showed signs of doing, divert its waters down other channels. But even here he was hampered, for the Master of Mar, following the precedent set by his dead brother in dealing with the Queen, would not allow even the Regent to enter the Castle save as a private person and a guest. Followers were not allowed. The Regent yielded the point, and went as a private person.

He was introduced into the Presence. He saw before him a boy of twelve, well made, but already somewhat ungainly, incapable of standing easily, and inclined either to loll in a chair or to wander up and down the room ; with large and noticeably rolling eyes, and hands that were constantly fiddling with his clothes. Before those remarkable

eyes the Lord Morton began to spin an attractive web.
He bowed to them a head grown old, as it were, in the
service of the State—Rizzio murders, accusations against
Mary, and such-like. He indicated his wish to retire in
favour of personal government by James. As a preliminary
he invited the King to come to Edinburgh, into the Castle
there, the Regent's own particular pet parlour. He
described the parlour : the Castle was in a fine situation ;
there were pleasant fields, and the sea, and many ships.
James was a free King ; let him express his wish and he
would be obeyed. Let him leave Stirling and come.

The boy fidgeted and rolled his eyes and said nothing
much to the point, until after Morton had withdrawn,
when he let out to his guardians that the Earl was tired of
the Regency. The general discontent gathered itself into
a regular confederacy. It was noticed that in certain
places the arms of the House of Douglas had appeared
instead of the more correct emblazonment of the royal
arms. Before any further substitution could be made,
Erskine and Buchanan, Argyle and Atholl, determined to
strike. James lent his name. In the most solemn manner
the Regent was summoned to do what he had said he was
longing to do. Without the King in his own hands he did
not venture on battle. He assented ; at a high ceremony
at the market cross of Edinburgh, proclamation was made
of the resignation of the Regent, and the assumption of
the government by the person of the King's Majesty.
The Chief Bandit retired to Lochleven and gave himself
to gardening, making the walks even and such simple
employments. The King remained at Stirling under the
care of the other bandits. " All the devils in hell are
stirring and in great rage in this country," wrote the
English ambassador to his Queen, but added hopefully,
" yet are we in hope of some good quietness, by the great
wisdom of the Earl of Morton."

The resignation had taken place in March. Towards the end of April the nephew of the Master, the young Earl of Mar, came as he sometimes did to lodge in the Castle. He was the head of his house, and he was jealous of the authority the Master exercised by virtue of his office. The possession of the Castle and its royal inmate, the Earl felt, were his by right, and the great wisdom of the Earl of Morton had secretly agreed with him. So far the assent of the King had been attempted by persuasion or petition. It was now time for deeds. Early one morning James was awakened by an uproar in the hall. He came out of his room, and saw below him a tumult. The Master, clutching a halberd, among a few of his servants was being surrounded and pressed back by a greater crowd. The abbots who were the King's preceptors were shouting at him; the Earl of Mar himself was there, also ·exclaiming. Voices were crying " Treason ! "; some one went down in the mêlée, and was trampled and crushed. The brutality, the noise, the shining steel—the things his mind despised and his nerves hated—were raging and threatening. The boy clutched his head and shrieked for the Master. Argyle hurried from his room and ran down to pacify the tumult. The King was soothed, composed, and told his governor was safe. They were right; but the governor's son died the next day of his trampling. The raid had succeeded. Morton came riding hard to Stirling, and took possession. For long, James had nightmares; the steel and the cries troubled his sleep; he woke by night shrieking of the brawl and of the armed forms that terrified his unguarded hours, and when he woke at morning the visions of his sleep yielded to the vision of the day, the presence of Morton. The Master of Mar, at whose danger he had cried out, was driven from the Castle; Morton remained. Through the early May the young King was aware by night of the brawl, by day of the victor in the brawl.

Night and day presented him with two sides of a single
fact, doubly repugnant to him. He had lost the Master ;
he had, instead, a more dominating master. The confederates, even if for their own purposes, had been urging
and directing him to the assertion of himself. They had
required him to profess his royalty. But the restored
Regent, even though he did not formally revoke the King's
assumption of government, disallowed any further action.
James was checked at precisely the moment when he had
approached " the two great ends of liberty and power."
There was riding and gathering and negotiating ; Parliament was held at Stirling ; at last Morton and his enemies
came to an agreement. The Regent, in effect if not in
title, had triumphed. As if delighting in his renewed
power, he became even more confident, " supposing that
it lay in his power to form the Court at his pleasure ; be
his great substance to won as many as he thocht necessary ;
and be the multitude of his friends to bear out his business."
He abode " always starkest about the King." The oracular
fate which had been prophesied for him seemed to have
been met and defeated, and his fear began to pass, as if
Macbeth had seen Birnam Wood thronging in a mass of
climbing verdure about Dunsinane, and had by the force
of his own breath blown it far back from the walls.

It was the autumn of 1579. James was thirteen.
Such affection as he had hitherto felt, so far as it can be
traced in that remote castle, had been for Peter Young
and for the Master. But now the Master was distant
and Peter Young was ineffective, and only Morton abode
stark about the King. In the crowd of lesser gentlemen
James had taken note of one, a soldier, the son of Lord
Ochiltree, of his own clan, bearing indeed his own name,
James Stuart. He was a fine figure of a man, and he
belonged, as far as any of those militant adventurers could
belong to any, to the anti-Morton group. But his time

was not yet ; the secret bitterness of the boy, his sovereign, had first to be tempted by more delicate food. Some splendour, some ostentation of beauty, was needed ; some rich weather to nourish royalty into flower. The boy was the child of Mary as well as of Darnley, and he was yearning for something more wonderful and more passionate than Peter Young or the rest of his Douglas and anti-Douglas Court could furnish. He went on secretly pluming himself on what he was, but all that in truth he was remained useless amid all that he was beside. He was royal and learned, but he was young, awkward, nervous, and un-certain ; he needed belief. The possibility of belief arrived, that September, from France.

There disembarked in Scotland a gentleman almost of the Blood ; the grand-nephew of the late Earl of Lennox, nephew to the dead Darnley, cousin of James—Esmé Stuart. In the fifteenth century an ancestor of his had helped to defeat the English in France, and had been granted the seigneury of Aubigny for his services. The new arrival was the sixth seigneur—a simple French gentle-man, an accomplished French courtier. He descended upon that armed and Calvinistic court, an adorned wonder of a brilliant civilization. He came to the King of Scotland, and all the heraldic beasts of the royal coat of arms grew sleeker at his coming.

The thistle rather than the lion had hitherto been for James the emblem of his royal office, but now he began to enter into a more beautiful and more dangerous world. He himself was no lion ; a mule in a lion's skin would have been a truer description, were it not that all his uncouthness and awkwardness, his uncertain legs and large tongue, did not quite conceal a certain swiftness and ferocity of spirit. He was the son of Mary of the leopards of France, and now, called by its French mate, the leopard in him began to stir and emerge from its spiritual lair. The King was thirteen

when the stranger arrived ; he was sixteen when they were
parted for the last time. In the short three years he had
been given something more than flattery—more even than
friendship ; he had been given himself. As he wandered
with and talked with the stranger, he beheld in a mirror
the image not of the clumsy youth but of the cultured,
unscrupulous, and exquisite Majesty of France or Scotland.
His own nature was Stuart ; he became as much open
Stuart as it was possible for him to become. He clasped
his friend " in the embraces of his great love " ; to the
free passion of that released love a later observer attributed
all ". the sweetness of his nature." But that sweetness
possessed now a new and dangerous spirit, felt in him by
others ; within a year the English agent in Scotland wrote
that the lords found it wiser and safer to keep the King's
favour by yielding to the course of his affection rather than
to risk the peril of plainly dissuading him from his pleasures
and openly withstanding the counsels and devices of his
favourites and minions.

The conquest was immediate and lasting. The stranger
was a man of over thirty, sure of himself, of his culture,
and of all his shining French background. He was a
Catholic ; physically, intellectually, spiritually, the Continent entered into the harsh castles of uttermost Thule,
and the half-barbarian prince of Thule avidly welcomed it.
D'Aubigny was given a suite of rooms next the King's.
By the end of the month, when the King paid his first
visit to Edinburgh, the Frenchman, acknowledged Favourite, rode with him. Away in Greenwich or Nonesuch the
Queen of England had her Favourites, as the King of
France in Paris or Orleans had his. But no other Favourite
of them all could give what this one was giving, for those
sovereigns knew very well what they were, and James was
only now discovering it. His eyes followed the stranger
everywhere ; he leaned on him and played with his clothes.

Had he not been the King he would have hung about
D'Aubigny's house and haunted him with a continual
presence. But he was the King; in an exquisite and thrilling union his submission and his supremacy were combined
and flattered. The very man at whose feet he was ready
to fall, fell humbly at his own. His master attended on
him, and the self-conceit of the delighted boy received
homage from his hero.

D'Aubigny found he had much to teach—among other
things a certain amplitude of giving. His pupil was ready
enough, for now he realized that he could give. Being the
King, he had things to give—lands and titles—and being
the King, he was free to give as he chose. Peter Young
had of himself at least been a Calvinist and a minister,
but this new friend was nothing in Scotland except by royal
favour. He gave James much; he took much in return,
and even in taking he gave, for he took from the King's
hand what no hand but the King's could give.

Within the first six months the Earldom of Lennox was
revived and bestowed; it had been promised to another,
but that other had to be content with the Earldom of
March. He was furnished with revenues and estates.
He was made—at first indirectly; afterwards directly—
Governor of the Castle of Dumbarton, the great key fortress
of Scotland, which gave access to and from France. Before
the first year of his advent was over he had become a duke:
there had been, outside the royal family, but one other
duke in Scotland, when, for a little while, Mary had made
Bothwell Duke of Orkney. This new creation was either
an acknowledgment of the Blood or an advancement to
the glory of the Blood, and either way an extraordinary
favour. More significant still—for himself—than all such
benevolence and beneficence was the kingly display in
which James indulged. He went, in 1580, on a royal
progress, and the Earl of Lennox went with him. Every-

where the shows and pageants, the gifts and offerings, proclaimed the presence of the King and his elect. And all the while the earl's tongue murmured of kingship as it was in France, and courts and learning and splendour and beauty—all as they were in France.

There was, between James and his beloved, but one rift, but one thing they did not order better in France; and that was religion. The Earl of Lennox may have regarded himself as a Catholic; James certainly so regarded him; and so, with even more horror and alarm, did the ministers and true men of the Gospel. Among the many agitations which the coming of the " parahelius " [1] had produced in both the northern and southern kingdoms the religious was of extreme importance. The ministers of Edinburgh kept a close watch; it was said that Lennox could not open his pack in any corner but it would be " seen and published in pulpit." It was known he had come from the Catholic House of Guise; it was asserted that he had come entirely to overthrow religion, to recover for the Roman household the Steward of Scotland, and with him the lands of his stewardship. The preachers inveighed against him and his friends—" Papistes with great ruffs and side bellies " were suffered in the King's chambers. The King himself argued with his friend. It seems likely that Lennox would have been entirely out of his depth in theology, whereas James was fully at ease. There were few things James liked better than arguing theology; certainly he liked to win, and he disliked an obstinate heretic who would not be converted. But he liked to think the heretic had been converted by reason and not by royalty; it was more glory and more delight for the victor. By a graceful compensatory act of devotion

[1] " That is, when the sun finds a cloud so fit to be illustrated by his beams that it looks almost like another sun " : so, of Lennox, a late contemporary.

the earl allowed himself to be converted. He indulged the
King and himself with the only unity that was lacking ;
spiritually, as corporeally, they embraced. The Protestant
mouth of the young ruler, earnestly setting forth the true
meaning of a hundred texts, opened a golden pathway—
of theology—to his cousin's view. Light broke on the
idolater. He allowed it to become known to the ministerial
champions of the Kirk that he had seen his errors. He
told them that a preacher—a French preacher—of the
Reformed Religion should be procured from London to
instruct him. At first some of the ministers were much
impressed by this notable conversion ; later, they complained to the King that nothing had been done. The King
promised to excite the earl to action. But both the King
and the earl found it more delightful to confine religious exposition to their own duet than that Lennox should sit away
from his friend under a strange Huguenot importation.

Meanwhile the stark Morton began to be troubled by
the influence of the new moon of royalty. " The flexible
nature of the King in these tender years " was becoming
daily more antagonized, both personally and politically.
The King was never quite as flexible as his baronial psycholo-
gists thought. But at present he did not want scenes
and quarrels in his presence, and the surest way of avoiding
them was to be as charming as he could to every one.
His conversation, his manners, were precociously flexible,
but not his spirit. Even with the beloved Lennox he was
firm on two things ; he never thought of abandoning his
Protestantism, and he never showed any inclination to
take refuge in France. Lennox may not have suggested
or proposed such a removal, but the fear of it agitated
Morton and Morton's friends the English. Sir Robert
Bowes, the Treasurer of Berwick, was sent as a special
agent into Scotland to undermine Lennox ; he wrote long
letters home to Burleigh and Walsingham. Morton, in a

D

secret interview by night, complained to him that the
King began " to commend and be contented to hear the
praises of France, beyond his accustomed manner," that
he kept D'Aubigny's secrets and revealed Morton's. Bowes
urged on his government the need of a judicious expenditure on pensions and bribes. He could, had he the money,
purchase almost any one in Scotland, save only Peter
Young and—an ominous exception—the ministers of the
Kirk. The surrender of Dumbarton Castle to Lennox
raised wilder fears. Through the year 1580 the English
statesmen grew more despairing. Morton kept on asking
for money ; Elizabeth kept on refusing to give any to him
or any one else. Cecil foresaw every kind of disaster ;
he continually prophesied catastrophe. Walsingham, out
of his fervid Puritanism, beheld the Mass coming back ·
everywhere in Scotland. Paris, or Madrid, or both Paris
and Madrid, were preparing armies to land there, restore
old things, and march through the postern gate on England.
Elizabeth wrote letters, varying from kindly friendship to
shocked maternity. She reminded him of all that she had
done for him ; she even allowed Bowes, in two interviews, to
touch on that thing, unmentionable, yet now becoming
as clear to James's eyes as it had so long and so painfully
been clear to hers—the succession. The crown that he hardly
yet wore in Scotland was but a reflection of the greater
crown that floated before his eyes away over the Border.
There, sooner or later, was to be his future, and as his nature
throve in the propinquity of Lennox it fixed itself the more
obstinately on its destiny. He began to know the obstacles
— the nightmares of raid and rebellion in Scotland, and
the hindrances—two women, his godmother on her throne,
his mother in her prison. As he grew and throve, in a
double adolescence of manhood and royalty, he saw always
before him the two shadowy women who claimed the crowns
that were his own.

Elizabeth was to attempt to touch that nerve in him many times in the next twenty years. In the warnings against Lennox which came to him she used a phrase strangely reminiscent of her own past and her fortune. She bade him " rather to fear (for) his ambition than to comfort and delight his affection." Ambition was too strong a word ; he did not purpose all the activity it implies. She did at one time encourage Morton to " lay violent hands" on Lennox, but after the letter had gone she considered that violence, once begun, might lead anywhere—to the abduction of the King into France or the induction of the French into Scotland ; she wrote the next day forbidding it. And she persistently refused to send money.

There were good reasons for this. She never wanted to spend ; she had far too many necessary affairs to spend on, and far too little money to spend on all ; she was never clear how far the expenditure of money in the Scottish waste of nobles might be profitable, how far the money might bind any of them to her or how far, having taken the money, they would neglect her. She had (or so Walsingham at one time thought) " a strange disposition " not to enter into any formal agreement with the Scottish government while Queen Mary was alive. " Such scruples," he remarked, " are rather superstitious than religious." But Walsingham was not a crowned prince and could not possess the sensitiveness of princes concerning the other members of their guild. It was not only Mary but James of whom it is tempting to think that Elizabeth had a more intuitive knowledge than any of her advisers. Perhaps, remembering her own girlhood, the imagination may be justified. She too had been a child alone among bullying or luring lords and princes ; she had had affections and subdued them to her interests ; she had watched the slow approach of a Crown ; she had displayed everything but herself until she and the Crown were one. When all was said,

there was something which the two distant cousins, in
their distant palaces—the boy of fourteen and the woman
of forty-seven—had in common which none of the others
possessed—not Lennox nor Cecil nor Morton nor Walsingham nor Bowes : the habit of royalty in their blood. For
all her letters of promises or threats, Elizabeth did not
really think that James would surrender that habit to
any masculine or feminine domination. She was entirely
right ; she was, in another sense than the religious, the
spiritual godmother of James, and she knew if that spiritual
kinship held that he must inevitably win, and she must
inevitably lose, the Crown that was still hers. He was
fourteen and she was forty-seven. Time had given him a
sufficient and certain bribe ; she need do no more, and
they both knew it. It was not to France or Spain, Lennox
or Morton, baronage or clergy, love or anger, that he would
surrender his own future. Nor to that other solitary figure,
his unknown mother, Mary, held in an English prison. In
the end certainly a yearly pension of four thousand pounds
was forced out of Elizabeth for him. But it was unnecessary, and she knew it ; it was, in its way, a defeat. The
battle, however, had been between her and Cecil and Walsingham ; not between her and James. It was their fears
which defeated her ; they did not understand the spirit
or tenacity of kings, or of the leopard that prowled patiently
round the Northern gate.

As for Morton, she could not believe that Morton really
mattered now. Bowes wrote that Morton was anxious for
the King to have a personal guard. The King also wished
for one. There seemed to be no money in Scotland to
provide such security. Morton hinted that if Elizabeth
supplied the money and he the men, the King's person
would be more adequately secured. Elizabeth did nothing.
Presently, however, a guard—or the equivalent of a guard
—appeared. The Earl of Lennox became Lord High

Chamberlain ; under him there were four-and-twenty ordinary and five extraordinary Gentlemen of the Chamber, sons of nobles. The captain of this company was James Stuart, son of Ochiltree. He also had become a close friend of the Favourite. They were at the King's disposal ; he was at theirs. It was time to deal with Morton.

The late Lord Regent, despairing of England, was beginning to open negotiations with Lennox. Bowes, after a last interview in which he solemnly warned James of his rashness in preferring an Earl of Lennox to the Queen of England, had been recalled. The Favourite, having become a Protestant, was making efforts to become a popular Protestant. He had begun " to creep into credit even with the ministers at Edinburgh." Morton was warned publicly by a mad seaman, when he was with the King and Lennox, that his destruction was drawing near. Without Elizabeth's aid and with the dubious support of the godly he saw no chance of laying violent hands on Lennox. But the original intention of seizing the King and murdering the Favourite became known to the intended victims. Christmas came ; on the next day James took Morton out with him for a day's hunting, and showed him a favourable kindness. It was on the last day of the year (1580) that the blow came.

The King was at Council. He lolled, attentive and expectant, in his chair ; his lords were round him—Lennox, Morton, Argyle, Angus (also a Douglas), Lindsay, Cathcart, and others. The Captain of the Guard, James Stuart of Ochiltree, came into the room and fell upon his knees before the Presence. He was asked what brought him there. Still kneeling, he made answer that he had come to charge James Douglas, Earl of Morton, with high treason in that he was privy to the horrible murder of the late King Henry, his present sovereign's dearest father. The King saw Morton come to his feet, saw him turn his eyes,

after one glance at the Captain, upon himself ; heard him
speaking of the low degree of his accuser, of his right to
despise the accusation, heard him saying something of his
innocence.   But he and every one there knew that the
Captain of the King's Guard would not bring such an accusation without the assent, willing or unwilling, of the King,
and knew also that the King would have willingly consented
to anything that promised the Earl's overthrow.   Still
kneeling, the Captain asked, if the Earl of Morton were
innocent, " why did he prefer his cousin Archibald Douglas
to be a Senator of the College of Justice, who was known
to have been an actor in that murder ? "   He sprang up,
seizing his sword.   Morton caught at his own ; as they
moved, the Lords Lindsay and Cathcart came between
them.   Morton was thrust away, out of the council-
chamber, and into the chapel.   Stuart retired into another
room.   There was a discussion ; the law-officers were
consulted.   Morton was brought back ; Stuart pushed his
way back.   The King received the advice of his councillors, though Lennox refused to vote against his enemy,
and Angus in favour of his kinsman.   At last the Earl was
removed to ward in the Castle.

Elizabeth at first moved to save him.   Her agents laid
plots in Edinburgh ; an army of two thousand men approached the Border under Lord Hunsdon ; the English
ambassador Randolph denounced Lennox. before the
Estates of Scotland.   None of these methods saved the
Earl.   The plots fell through ; the Estates were hostile ;
a shot was fired through Randolph's window.   None of
the Scottish lords rose in arms, and Elizabeth, unprepared
for an invasion in full strength, withdrew her force.
On June 1 Morton was brought to trial ; on June 2
he was beheaded, in full expectation (according to his
own words) of entering into the felicity of Almighty
God.   On the steps of the scaffold was the Earl of Arran,

a title just bestowed on James Stuart, Captain of the King's Guard.

The execution of Morton was the greatest achievement of this second period of the King's education, which lasted for little more than a year longer. During that year he enjoyed the company of Lennox and, in a lesser degree, of Arran, to his high content. The King "can hardly suffer him out of his presence," they said of the pre-eminent Favourite. The removal of Morton had left the world freer to those other plotters who, on the whole, were more sympathetic to James, to the Catholics. Mary, in England, was attempting to operate through Spain ; Lennox wished to operate through France. On both sides Catholicism was made as attractive as possible, and it was understood James was by no means in-different. Mary had greatly offended her son by giving permission to the French envoy to address him as King. She now put forward a scheme of Association, by which he and she should reign conjointly. Jesuit priests were introduced into Holyrood. Lennox wrote to Mary, talking of an army with himself at its head. The Scottish Catholic earls would rise. The King would be converted, by grace, reason, or force. But it would make a good deal of difference whether the accent of his new creed were French or Spanish, and the con-version of Scotland by either France or Spain (could it be secured) might throw the other government on to the English side. The Scottish Catholic earls were, in a general way, willing to co-operate with whichever would foot the bill for expenses.

News of the plots in operation began to leak out. One of the Edinburgh ministers, John Durie, prophesied in his sermons against the courtiers who persuaded the King to write to France and Guise. Other ministers forced an interview with him and exhorted him to his face at great

length.   They offered to name godly men who could guide
him, and they had the names ready.   James, quite frankly,
fled.   He could face swords, though he never cared to use
one ; he could not face sermons, though as he grew older
he came to like delivering them.   Other troubles were the
Bishop of Glasgow and the horses of the Duke of Guise.
Bishops in the Reformed Kirk had been abolished ; a few .
lingered.   The King had given the bishopric of Glasgow
to Lennox, who appointed a certain Robert Montgomery
to be a tulchan Archbishop, the channel by which the
revenue should flow in to the patron's hands.   It is said
that he was scornful of Greek and Hebrew ; that he condemned " the particular application " of Scripture, that he
disparaged the ministerial commission to direct kings, and
had even called the ministers "men of curious brains."
Durie threatened him with excommunication.   The Duke
of Guise sent the King a present of horses ; they had hardly
arrived before James found Durie on his threshold, bidding
him refuse the papistical steeds ; it was the will of God.
James promised to obey the will of God, but he went to
see the horses first, after which they disappear from
history.   .

Some time between June 1581 and June 1582, he began
indulgence in another delight.   He experimented in verse.
A " Song " exists which is said to be " the first verses that
ever the King made," and also " the King's verses when
he was fifteen years old."   If they are both (which seems
unlikely), then Lennox was the godfather of his poetry.
The " Song " runs :

> Since thought is free, thinke what thou will,
>   O troubled hart, to ease thy paine.
> Thought unrevealed can do no evill,
>   Bot wordes past out cummes not againe.
>   Be cairfull aye for to invent
>   The waye to gett thy owen intent.

To pleas thy selfe with thy concaite
 And lett none knowe what thou does meane,
Houp aye at last, though it be late, .
 To thy intent for to attaine.
  Thoght whiles it brake forth in effect,
  Yet aye lett witt thy will correct.

Since foole haste comes not greatest speede
 I wolde thou shoulde learne for to knoaw
How to make vertue of a neede,
 Since that necessitie hath no law.
  With patience then see thou attend
  And houpe to vanquise in the end.

A little less discreetly than this suggests, the King in
May 1582 took action against Durie ; he compelled him to
leave Edinburgh. In June the Kirk replied by excom-
municating Montgomery in Glasgow Cathedral. In July,
after great preaching against Lennox and Arran, a series
of articles was presented to the King, protesting against
his negligence of the Kirk and his friendship with " bloody
murtherers and persecutors." Arran in a rage demanded
who dared subscribe such articles. Andrew Melville,
Rector of St. Andrews University, one of the great Kirk
leaders, cried : " We dare and will subscribe them, and
render our lives in the cause." He seized a pen, wrote
down his name, passed it to another minister, and so one
by one they all signed. While Edinburgh was thus in
open rage, a more secret plot was arranged by the Protestant
lords. Angus had interviewed Elizabeth, who had either
given him money or come convincingly near it.[1] The other
lords were warned that Lennox was about to take action
against them. James, for once divided from his beloved
and from Arran, had gone to Ruthven Castle, belonging
to the Earl of Gowrie, for the hunting. He rose on the
morning of August 22, 1582, to find throngs of armed men

[1] He asked for " four thousand crowns to every earl and two thousand
crowns to every baron " who armed against Lennox.

outside the Castle. Gowrie, Mar, the Master of Glamis, Lindsay, and other lords entered his room. He was told he must remain where he was for a while. He went towards the door, meaning to leave the room ; Gowrie (or, as some say, Glamis) insolently thrust his leg across it in front of him. The boy, surprised and shaken, gave way to tears of anger. The Master said callously : " Better bairns greet than bearded men." Some one called out for a rocking-horse to be brought to the King. James uttered incoherent words of vengeance ; it is by that we know his tears to have been of rage and not of fear.

He was in their hands. He was told that Arran also had been taken in an ambush. Lennox fled to Edinburgh, but without the King's person he could do nothing. From his window, plucking at his beard, he was compelled to watch the return of John Durie, who came back in lowly pomp, received by ministers and townsfolk singing the 124th Psalm (" If the Lord had not been on our side "), and singing it with especial ardour outside the house of the Papistical stranger. The Raid of Ruthven was accomplished ; the third period of the King's education had begun.

It did not take James long to grasp the situation. He was a prisoner ; he was not too secure of his life. His lovers were helpless ; he was uncertain of theirs. The net was about him. Within it the leopard faded into an inner darkness ; a lamb began softly to emerge. Once before he had been seized, by Mar and Morton, but then he had been very young ; since then he had been the captive of passion, not of fear. Now he was captive, yet he must act. Mary and Elizabeth, France and Spain, Morton and Lennox, had all his life been plotting and dissimulating. He entered fully into that world. He spent, of necessity, almost a year in it ; it was his University. By a symbolical geography he left it at St. Andrews.

It was a University in which the dour dons, unconscious of their academic office but soon to be conscious of the result, had great difficulties. Sir Robert Bowes arrived again from Berwick to hearten them. He found them mutually suspicious ; agreed only on the necessity of getting Lennox out of the country ; more and more reluctant to bear the expense of continually attending the royal person and maintaining the necessary force about him. They received Bowes with demands for money. Bowes, having little, gave less and husbanded the remainder for a crisis. He wrote urgently to Walsingham : let the Queen only send money, and all would be well. He had interviews with the King who, for all his young dissimulation, could not yet conceal " the great affection " that he bore towards the duke ; in October, indeed, Bowes heard that he had been brought again to those angry tears by something in the behaviour of the lords—it seems, by their intended Declaration of the causes for their action : " he entered into a great passion and sorrow to behold himself and his honour, · as he thought, so greatly wounded thereby." Bowes continually urged him to put his love and trust in Elizabeth. Certainly, hereditary passion was in him, but passion which is thrillingly beautiful in a beautiful Queen becomes laughable in a provincial and awkward precocity. It had been allowed free play, and now in an unhappy freedom it was weeping for its beloved and for its own ill-luck. He was compelled, for his love's safety and his own, to drive the beloved out of his land. He had to dry his own tears, to find his own consolation. He had to deny his passion the freedom it had so recently found. The persons of the lords were about him ; the voices of the ministers in his ears ; the admonitions of the English ambassador were substituted for the sweet devotion of his own duke. He was invited to love, to trust, to admire an old woman at a distance instead of a splendid masculine beauty at his side. He inhibited his display of love and sorrow. Awkwardly he sat, no longer tearful, listening with rolling eyes to the exposition of Sir Robert Bowes, who begged him to accept Elizabeth's sympathy and support. He did so—gratefully he showed a proper disposition to turn from France and rely on England. He said that he had heard that the Queen had heard " he was by nature inconstant and dissembling " ; he was anxious to remove " all such distrust " and " approve his thankful and constant mind."

He was indeed constant to actuality. He had been brought back to Edinburgh ; and there also one evening came a secret messenger from Lennox. He got into touch with John Gibbe, a page of the chamber. Gibbe whispered news of the interview in the King's ear. The King, pretending " to go to the stool," called Gibbe to go with him, and in that place of intimate channels listened to the duke's messages. But for answer he only said hastily that if the duke were wise he would not thus send to him to their hurt and his danger, and as hastily went away. He had realized that Lennox could raise no party, and that, even could he, his own perilous position would not be improved. He allowed himself to become more and more placable to the lords and Bowes ; as the months went by he issued orders to Lennox to yield Dumbarton and to leave the kingdom. What might happen after that was another matter. If James was ever to enjoy again the company of the Favourite, it was above all things necessary that James and his Favourite should be alive and free : he went on directing Lennox to go. At the end of December, reluctantly, Lennox went, after a little counter-conspiracy at the end of the preceding month to recover the Person, by bringing a company through the chapel up a dark stair to the gallery over the chapel while James was at supper, and introducing them into his presence when the lords in attendance had gone to their own supper. It failed, and James again accepted actuality.

The opening of the year 1583 found him still surrounded by the lords of the Raid, with Bowes's expositions and admonitions for diversion. The departure of the Duke of Lennox had coincided with the arrival of a new ambassador from France—indeed of two new ambassadors, charged to offer James the sympathy and aid of the French king who had heard that his Scottish Majesty was held prisoner. James exhibited to them an ostensible freedom ; he listened to their proposals, promises, and prophecies of the future. The English agents could not tell what to make of him. He appeared to be wholly disposed to Elizabeth, yet sometimes " the King's own disposition and liking of this present company with him have been called in doubt upon sundry circumstances noted lately in him." It became more and more obvious that everything depended on James's own deliberate choice, and to fix that choice the French and English agents continually laboured. The Ruthven lords " had the wolf. by the ears," but what was to happen when they let go ?   Could the wolf be trusted to do what the bleat of the lamb had promised ?   And how long could they hold on to the growing and sometimes growling beast ?

Had Mary of Scots been already dead, it is just possible that James might have accepted the French alliance. But she was not, and (what had again offended him very deeply) the French ambassador spoke to him as Majesty by permission previously obtained from Mary. The more he gave himself to the French the more likely it was that he would be subordinated to the closer of those two watching women across the frontier. Yet his only alternative was to lean towards the other. The second ambassador, defeated by the measureless swamp of the appetite of the nobles for gold and by the stone wall (which could never be

eventually disguised) of James's own Protestantism, at
last departed. James went on bleating affection and
devotion to Elizabeth ; Bowes, worried and hampered,
half-believed, half-distrusted. Lennox had gone ; the
lords of the Raid were at a loose end in policy. They
disputed, quarrelled, left and returned. Gowrie himself
was—not without cause—distrusted by his companions.
They did not know in the least what to do next.

There was to be a vague " convention " of the nobility ;
the King was to be allowed to go on a progress and enjoy
himself with hunting. Some small effort was made to
remove Arran and restore the true earl (who was mad), but
James demurred and deferred action. In May, Bowes had
a long interview over the Association project, which James,
without any need for dissimulation, thoroughly disliked :
" it was," he said, " a matter dangerous to his estate and
tickle to this crown." He let it be known that during the
summer he would leave all affairs of State to " old councillors " ; he would give himself up to hunting. Meanwhile he was holding other interviews with the old Sir
James Melville, whom he had recalled from his retirement,
and to whom he let something of his underlying spleen
appear. " Other princes," he complained, thought him
but a beast to suffer so many indignities ; the French
ambassadors perhaps had not altogether concealed their
incredulity. Melville rather discouraged change, and
delivered a lecture on the state of countries during the
minority of princes. But the King was fixed : " he took
up a princely courage either to put himself to face liberty
or to die by the way." He did not propose, however, to
die by the way. He had written to divers lords of the
opposed party or of none, to come to the convention. He
rode to St. Andrews, arriving there a day or two before the
new lords. Certain of the Ruthven lords followed him
up hastily. While the King was at supper it was suggested

to him that he should walk in the Abbey yard until the castle was ready for him. But men in armour had been seen in the yard ; news of them was brought ; the King got himself by another way to the castle. Even in the castle on the next day it was a touch-and-go business ; at the stair-heads and galleries there were other armed men of the Ruthven faction. Melville acted swiftly ; many young men were introduced, belonging to the Earl of March, and as many of the townsfolk as the provost believed loyal. Gowrie wholly swayed on to the King's side ; no one quite liked to take the risk of beginning a definite rebellion in blood. The day slipped dangerously by ; by night the King was safe.

The next day he made a speech. He was to be " a universal king " ; that is, indifferent and equal to all his subjects. He acknowledged the good intentions of the managers of the Raid ; he would overlook everything, if they would seek remission and oblivion. As a spectacular exhibition of peace, he dined with Gowrie at Huntingtower ; who, after dinner, kneeling down, lamented that the King should have been detained " at that unhappy house," on the last occasion of his being there. He himself, he said, had supposed nothing more but that a supplication was to be presented ; the ensuing detention had been " a purely accidental fault." The King forgave him ; so amazing a statement could at least hardly be called dissimulation. The future was the Earl of Gowrie's business ; if the earl should slip into another accident, it might also be James's. Meanwhile the King enjoyed his sensations, and awaited the first favourable opportunity to recall Arran to the Court.

Sir Robert Bowes was told by " discreet persons " that the King had undergone a great change. They reported that he was purposed to try what he could get from Elizabeth by fair words, while yet he would proceed in his own

ways—" wherein he is thought to be so earnest of late as
hardly can be withdrawn from the thing that he desireth."
The Ruthven Raid had had its lasting effect : " surely
many note great alteration both in his mind and also in his
face and countenance." There was one sign of this that
troubled Bowes. The King had now a trick, " far beyond
his own wont," of himself keeping the key of the coffer
wherein his papers lay, " so as hitherto," Bowes added,
" I cannot get any certainty of the contents." It was a
permanent alteration ; he locked his coffer ; he locked the
more secret coffer of his mind—the more James he. It
was the picturesque conclusion of his education.

CHAPTER THREE

THE LEOPARD AMONG THE THISTLES

THE youth was just seventeen. He sat at St. Andrews among his own lords, or those who were temporarily his own, and saw on all sides of him a world of enemies. He saw too a world of friends, for he liked men and women, and liked to be at his ease with them. He knew he was different from them, for in his body he was mysteriously impregnated with a kind of Divinity, and therefore his judgment, when that was stirred, was wiser and better than ordinary men's. Wise men recognized that. But he had not any personal pride ; he was not in the least an aristocrat, and his tastes were not aristocratic. He was the King. He did not in the least want always to be on his guard. But he knew he had to be ; habitually now he was on secret guard. There were so many dangers.

He was James VI., King of Scotland and heir of England. There were some who wanted to destroy him and some who wanted to possess him. In Scotland there were the lords, any of whom were likely to try and hold this sacred person of his. Some of them were Catholic, some were Calvinist, most were neither in particular, a few were both by turns. There was, especially, Gowrie, to whom he was now reconciled ; like his mother, he would forgive but never forget. There was Arran, whom, as soon as might be, he would call back to his Court, especially since his dearest Lennox could never return, for he was by now dead in Paris. This was what Gowrie and his friends had done. But the dead—even though the dead were Lennox—must not interfere with the actuality of living. Arran was alive.

There were the Catholics, mostly away in the Highlands of
the North. He had a good deal of feeling for the Catholics ;
they were mistaken, of course, but if it had not been for the
woman in England who wanted, and whom they wanted,
to take or share his throne, he could have been quite
friendly with them. And a large part of England was
Catholic, and he would not antagonize his future people, if
it could be helped—it could not always be helped. There
were the Catholic kings beyond the seas, who had never
yet recognized him as the King because of that woman who
was his mother. If she was his mother she was—but his
mind stopped there. It was literally impossible for James
to imagine that she might be Queen. He had had it driven
into him far too profoundly that he was the King, that
the body of which he was so intensely aware was the
body of the King, for that was why so many dangers
surrounded his body. He accepted actuality ; he was
the King, and so Mary could not be the Queen. No one
could make her so ; the Catholics might want to, or his
brothers of France and Spain might play with the idea, but
that could only be done by a great invading army which
could hold the whole country down. He did not want a
great invading army, not even if they had been willing to
keep him on the throne, for then he would be expected to
become a Catholic himself, and that was impossible. The
texts and the Fathers were against it ; even Lennox had
seen that when the King had explained. But the texts and
the Fathers did not justify all the preachers of the Kirk
in wanting to direct and control him in everything. They
held their pulpits as sacred and inspired places. Once in
them the Spirit might move them to any madness. They
were mad and tiresome, and they were very difficult.
Andrew Melville in this very town, for example. Over in
England things were much better ; his godmother Elizabeth
had her Puritan fanatics much more in hand. But she

had no General Assembly of the Reformed Kirk to manage, and she had bishops. Bishops were consecrated beings, meet for a King, justified by Scripture and tradition, a hierarchy of sacred officers under the sacred throne. Elizabeth did not want his throne, but she wanted to govern him while he sat on it, through the solemn exhortation of Sir Robert Bowes. But when all was said, he could wear Elizabeth down. Yet the two strange women fretted him sometimes ; they were incarnate rejection and procrastination. One claimed his present throne ; the other occupied his future. But still God had meant him for King of Scotland and England. God even had His enemies ; he knew that, scattered through the land, there were witches and covens of witches—in high places sometimes. His uncle, Murray, had burnt Lyon King at Arms for sorcery ; the house of Ruthven was said to be tainted with it ; even Lady Arran, whom he liked, was looked at askance by the Kirk. There was yet a kind of fascination as well as horror in the dream. But he was an anointed King ; he must destroy this wickedness. He hated it, but perhaps he was unaware that he did not altogether hate destroying it.

A world of enemies. He could see it from St. Andrews, as he sat there, his education done, precocious and ignorant, awkward and royal, nervous and confident. He was free, and he had had his way—by a symbolic action he had shown the world that he was free. His career lay before him, and he would be faithful to it.

It was not easy. Again and again, in the next twenty years, he went down thistly or stony ways. Again and again the lithe swift spirit of the leopard in him twisted itself out of the prickly circle of hunters or took advantage of some enemy's solitude to destroy him. Again and again the beast shoots in and out, and it is hard to determine whether the resulting ravage is but an incident of the hunt after him or the destructiveness of his own nature. There are the bleeding bodies—but who caused them ? Could we attribute to the beast such ingenuity of savage craft, it would be one of the most marvellous in the whole darkening jungle of the sixteenth-century day : the more marvellous that when we trace it to its lair we find, as by an exhibition of animal necromancy greater than any among the spell-winding women of contemporary legend, no dazzling and lovely creature such as, eighteen years before, sat in a glory of colour on the Throne, but (again according to legend) an awkward stammering booby, dribbling with nasty fondness and shaking with nervous fear.

It is hard to believe. Clumsiness and craft never so wholly existed in unison. The two legends, destroying their incompatibilities, leave, at least and at last, the form of a man. " He is, for his age," wrote a careful observer about this time, " one of the most remarkable princes that ever lived." His qualities, during the first half of his life, were in quicker and more effective action than during the second. He loved ease and peace, but if he was stirred he was capable of carrying himself with dignity, at the head of his troops or alone. He loved loose freedoms and gross pleasures, yet he never lost himself in them. He loved arguments and theological hair-splitting, yet he had at any moment that sense of actuality which is rare in such theoretical minds. He loved idleness and pleasure ; but when he was rebuked for it he answered by saying that he did more work in an hour than others in a day, but his body was too weak to work without interruption. He added that he was like a Spanish jennet which could run one course well but could not hold out. In every single spasm of labour he " could listen to one man, talk to another, and observe a third. Sometimes he could do five things at once." And as in labour so in temper. He was good-humoured and kindly, and loved it in others, but if his spiritual nerves were touched, especially the nerve of his kingship, by conspiracies of swords or spells, he was capable of spasms of vengeful cruelty, and of disguising them from himself.

He gave himself in the next few months certain private pleasures. He sent over to Paris for Ludowick, the young son of the late Duke of Lennox, had him brought to Scotland, a boy of ten, invested with his father's duchy, educated, attached to the Household. It was perhaps not merely affection, for he was of the Blood, and might indeed be reckoned as heir-presumptive. At least he was so near it that he was a pawn of value in the game. But the mere doing it was a sign, an obstinacy of free choice, a rebuke and a retort to those who had expelled the father. The King might be baffled for a while ; he was not beaten. There came with Ludowick one who was afterwards to become important—Patrick, Master of Gray. While the convoy was making ready to depart for France, James expanded his royalty at home. He had promised to pardon the Ruthven raiders ; so he would, but they must ask for it, as Gowrie had done. Perhaps Gowrie's action had put the idea into his mind. Each of them who desired pardon must come and kneel and entreat. The King found himself loving those moments—the feel of power, the paw of the good-tempered leopard touching the prey. There were perils in it he did not understand : that the enjoyment of power might become an enjoyment of suffering, the protraction of suspense and subordination end in actual cruelty ; and another, that so long as a pretended power was there, he would not trouble about the actuality of power. Of the two, the second was the more remote danger ; his natural common sense was too strong for him not to know when he was taking part in a mere show of sovereignty. But before he died, when away in England his favourite and his son drove him, with less and less deference, along a road he did not want to go, he did know it.

He recalled Arran. Arran was never one of the greater loves of his life ; he was of too violent and haughty a spirit. But he had been a friend of Lennox ; he was a friend of the King's ; he was a foe of the Ruthvens and of the ministers ; and he saved the King a great deal of trouble. Besides, James liked Lady Arran—who was " generally accused of sorcery," but that was by the thwarted ministers of the Kirk. He let the earl have the custody of Stirling and Edinburgh castles ; he made him chancellor and left him to preside at the council board while he himself went hunting. The continual intrigues with and against England went on. As a special peal of thunder after and against the overthrow of the Ruthven lords, the great Secretary Walsingham himself came north. From all that he heard and all that he saw he grew confident that the new state of things could not last ; from Newcastle he even wrote that " this dissembling king, both with God and man, will not long stand." Walsingham was quite often wrong, but hardly ever more entirely wrong than in that letter.

He — and Bowes — were received on September 9. Bowes had on earlier occasions been hinting pretty broadly that if James drove Elizabeth to extreme courses, anything might happen. He had pointed out that James could not possibly resist " her puissance " without " the succour of strangers," and his own people would be more likely to rebel than to endure such an invasion. The new interview was unsatisfactory. Walsingham began by telling James how wrong he had been in everything. James became restive ; he had not restored himself in Scotland to be orated over by Walsingham. He said with an angry insolence that he would be glad if Elizabeth would leave him to take his own order with his own subjects ; she need not be " more curious to examine the affection of his councillors than he was of hers." Walsingham was coldly angry in return.

He rebuked, rated, and almost threatened the King. But —a thing of which Walsingham hardly understood the importance to James—he was, of course, bareheaded in the Presence. He probably enjoyed the interview more than James. But it meant much more to him than to James. He was unused to scolding royalty. In London, he might be rated like an errand-boy by the Queen. James was used to being scolded by Andrew Melville, John Durie, and others, at much greater length. He scarcely needed even to harden his heart ; he merely waited for the verbose lecture to stop, and got rid of his lecturer as soon as possible. When the Secretary retired he was in turn scolded, this time by a woman called Kate the witch, whom Arran had hired " at the price of a new plaid and six pounds in money," to shriek abuse after the solemn great man. But Walsingham knew nothing of the trick, nor of the other trick by which Arran's avarice substituted a crystal for a diamond in James's farewell gift of a ring. He went off and wrote a letter to Elizabeth in which he attributed this shocking behaviour to Mary of Scots, Spain, and the Pope. He was of opinion that " his mother, who is the layer of the plot, will work his confusion, and though she cannot live many years shall before her end see his overthrow." There was another interview, not much more satisfactory, after which the Secretary returned to England to do his best to shorten the mother's years, delaying only on his way to " endeavour to lay some such plot as he (the King) may be bridled," peaceably if possible, violently if not. He sent an urgent messenger south with a sketch of the scheme. But Elizabeth put a stop to it, and it had to be dropped.

Irritated a little by the intrusion, and also with some general idea of circumventing his mother, James began to play with the Catholics, at the same time that his minister was offering himself on terms to England. James did not altogether understand—perhaps he did not at all understand—the nature of the Roman See. But at least, having a clearer sense of historical theology than almost any one else in Scotland, he knew it was a See, and the Patriarchate of the West. He knew that if he wanted anything like actual peace with Catholicism he must deal with the Pope. He wrote, secretly, to the Pope ; also to the Duke of Guise, intimating that without Papal aid—which meant money— the extreme Protestants would have it all their own way. The Papal aid was not, at the moment, forthcoming, and a sudden shock threw him violently back on Arran.

Certain of the Ruthven lords—Angus, Mar, Lindsay, and others—had retreated to England. Walsingham went to work to unite them and all other discontented elements against Arran : assassination or banishment for him, Ruthven domination for James, dependence of Scotland on England for the rest. Gowrie was again drawn in ; he hesitated, but he agreed. Elizabeth did not interfere, though she encouraged at the same time a secret negotiation with Arran through Lord Hunsdon. Her servants were scornful of and angry with each other. The Queen watched and disapproved and approved and found fault whenever any scheme went wrong. The Walsingham scheme went wholly wrong. The exiled lords crossed the Border, but Arran was master of their fate. He had Gowrie arrested. He put the King at the head of an army, and marched against the revolt. The lords fled back to England, pursued with ostentation, and with ostentatious lack of success, by a freebooter baron, Francis Hepburn, the new Earl of Bothwell. James and Arran, after hanging a few minor captains, returned in triumph to Edinburgh. A number of ministers also fled south, to join Andrew Melville.

Melville, who was called *exactor episcoporum*, the flinger out of bishops, had got himself into trouble with the Council for asserting that whatever was said in the pulpit, even though it were treasonable, ought first to be tried in the presbytery, nor might the King or Council meddle with it till later. He had gone on to declare that James was perverting the laws both of God and man, and had then thought it wise to take refuge in Berwick. The pulpits lamented him continually. They had also to lament the Earl of Gowrie, who, by a detestable trick of Arran's, was convicted and executed. Nothing connects James with the trick, except that Gowrie died. The leopard leapt over the first of the bodies and wandered off to play. The King found himself, for the first time for months, briefly at peace from his foes—without danger and without dread.

Arran, now in supreme control, encouraged him to go hunting again, a pastime which he had not happily enjoyed since the fatal day of the Raid ten months before. It was an occupation to which he was always devoted ; it gave him a maximum of the excitement which he loved with a minimum of responsibility and fear. In the hunt he could be " bloody, bold, and resolute " without any distress supervening if he failed. He could pursue, he could enjoy the suspense he inflicted ; he could act ; and he could rely on his hounds. It was a little later that he took in his hand a paw of one of them, named Tell True, and said : " Tell True, I drink to thee above all my hounds, and would sooner trust thy tongue than either Craig or the bishop "—Craig was one of the ministers ; the bishop was Montgomery.

Hunting was not his only pleasure. In the year 1585 there appeared, " imprinted at Edinburgh, by Thomas Vautroullier," a little book, entitled *The Essayes of a Prentise, in the Divine Art of Poesie*. There was no name on the title-page ; there was no Preface. But the author-ship was given away in the prefatory sonnets by other poets—the Prentise was the Prince himself. It contained a number of poems and translations, and also a small treatise on *The Reulis and Cautchis to be observit and eschewit in Scottis Poesie.* The monarchs who have written on prosody have been few; uttermost Thule furnished this instance. It does not go very far into its subject, and it lays down some very debatable rules. On the other hand, it talks in a very agreeable way of *Flowing*, rather as Gerard Hopkins talked of Sprung Rhythm; and it has a few peculiarly just counsels. Care is to be taken, wrote the august author, that " in quhatsumever ye put in verse, ye put in na wordis, ather *metri causa*, or zit [yet] for filling furth the nomber of the fete, bot that they be all neccesoure, as ye sould be constrainit to use thame, in cace ye were speiking the same purpose in prose. And thairfore that your wordis appeare to have cum out willingly, and by nature, and not to have bene thrawin out constrainedly, be compulsioun." He went on to advise various kinds of diction: for love — common language, with some passionate words; for tragical matters—lamentable words, with some high, as ravished in admiration; of " landwart " affairs—" corruptit and uplandis wordis." He had a strong feeling for alliteration—let all your verse be Literal, so far as may be. " Be Literall I meane, that the maist pairt of your lyne, sall runne upon a letter . . . :

" Fetching fude for to feide it fast furth of the Farie."

But before his readers came to read these rules, he hoped they would have found in themselves such a beginning of Nature that they would have practised the rules without realizing them to be rules. " Gif Nature be nocht the cheif worker in this airt, Reulis wilbe bot a bond to Nature . . . quhair as, gif Nature be cheif and bent to it, reulis wilbe ane help and staff to Nature."

The practice of the young poet did not always rise to his own rules, as he ingenuously explained in the preface to a translation of Du Bartas' *Uranie* which appeared in

the book. He gave several good reasons for breaking
them, but perhaps the most touching sentences are in the
opening explanation :

" Having oft revolved, and red over (favorable Reader)
the booke and Poems of the devine and Illuster Poëte,
Salust du Bartas, I was moved by the oft reading and
perusing of them, with a restless and lofty desire, to preas
to attaine to the like vertue. But sen (alas) God, by
nature hathe refused me the like lofty and quick ingyne,
and that my dull *Muse*, age, and Fortune, had refused me
the lyke skill and learning, I was constrained to have refuge
to the secound, which was, to doe what lay in me, to set
forth his praise, sen I could not merite the lyke my self."

Indeed he was right in his judgment of himself. It is
not merely that the poems fail of perfection ; they tend
to wander along the roads that diverge from perfection.
They explain what the poet wishes to do rather than
attempt to do it. But he was young ; he was sincere ;
and he was devout in his poetic piety. His version of the
perpetual spring sonnet may be given.

And first, ô *Phœbus*, when I do descrive
The *Springtyme* sproutar of the herbes and flowris,
Whome with in rank none of the foure do strive,
But nearest thee do stande all tymes and howris :
Graunt Readers may esteme, they sie thy showris,
Whose balmie dropps so softlie dois distell,
Which watrie cloudds in mesure suche downe powris,
As makis the herbis and verie earth to smell
With savours sweit, fra tyme that onis thysell
The vapouris softlie sowkis with smyling cheare,
Whilks syne in cloudds are kepped closs and well,
Whill vehement *Winter* come in tyme of yeare.
Graunt, when I lyke the *Springtyme* to displaye,
That Readers think they sie the Spring alwaye.

Poetry and hunting were his two chief interests—these
and his loves. " It was very notorious that he dedicated

rainy weather to his Standish, and faire to his Hounds, or
anything else that owned the voice of pleasure," wrote a
hostile critic later.   In all of them he could enjoy the
world and himself, which meant that he could escape partly
from the difficulties of kingship, partly from the dangers
of the other world of devilish hauntings.   He knew he was
not a great poet—as Du Bartas seemed to him a great
poet ; so much his natural intelligence taught him.   He
was right, and he was therefore not disturbed by the world
of other dimensions which must continually distract those
imaginations.   He was free to move in this world, with
the definitions of this world.   He was the King taking his
pleasure.   At this point he was perhaps more free than
he had ever been—free even from the golden bondage of
his first love, from the adored Lennox ; free, certainly,
from the Ruthven lords, from the ministers, from the
solemn English envoys.   He rode out, among his courtiers
and huntsmen, and was genially at ease.   Sorcery fell
away.   The strong and splendid Arran ruled—by his permission and in his name.   Arran, for all his high spirit and
sumptuous circumstance, could never be Lennox.   But
the King had a great affection for him—both in himself
and as a kind of viceroy.   People complained of him ;
Sir James Melville complained.   James listened and was
shocked or complacent as need demanded.   But Arran
was far more important than Melville.   The King smiled
on the Chancellor still, and on the Chancellor's people,
among whom was that wonderfully beautiful young man,
also newly come out of France—Patrick, Master of Gray.

The great Lord Acton once complained that Bishop
Creighton treated morals far too lightly in his historical
works.   No doubt, fundamentally, Lord Acton was right.
But it is a question of energy : to exhaust oneself in disapproval wastes so much, and—since all those strange
figures are dead—does no good.   No living person is likely

to be improved by denunciations of phantoms, and as for the phantoms themselves, what purpose does condemnation serve ? " Shrilling on the wind," they go by ; there is something a little comic in trying to rebuke them. Besides, it encourages us to think that we are better than they. Private assassination has—in England—gone out of fashion ; private treachery perhaps—it is naturally more difficult to tell. It seems unfashionable now, as it was fashionable then. Certainly the Master of Gray lived at the very height of that fashion. He is an almost incredibly romantic figure—beautiful, cultured, ambitious, false. And the ridiculous thing is that he was precisely beautiful, cultured, ambitious, and false. The Master of Gray kneeling for the first time to James VI. is a figure worthy of the wildest melodramatic novel. But it is a mere fact of serious history. And to add to the whole romantic show, the Master nearly repented once—because of the coming of love, because of the person of Sidney.

At present, however, the Master was in Arran's train, his own patron, the new Duke of Lennox, having been placed, to finish his education, in the custody of the Earl of Montrose. Gray had brought with him to Scotland something to recommend him to Arran, and through Arran to the King. In France he had been a Catholic, a friend and client of the Guises, an intimate of Catholic conspiracy. He knew the intrigues that had Mary for their centre. He was prepared to lay them at the disposal of any one who would reward him. Until Arran was clearly the dominant power in Scotland, no useful use could be made of them, but now he felt the time had come.

In fact, two times had come. The Master, contemplating his surroundings and prospects, found Arran superfluous and rather tiresome. It seems likely, from the way he went to work, that he suspected the King also, on rare occasions, found Arran a little tiresome. The Earl, magnifi-

cent, haughty, and gallant, had not. always been able to
strike quite the right note to please James, who—as he
grew older—liked a whole orchestra of emotions in his
Favourites, although all must perform one symphony. He
was not, in the ordinary way, jealous ; he raised no difficulties when his Favourites, for example, had passionate
love-affairs of their own, of the more ordinary type. He
liked Lady Arran ; he assisted Somerset to marry Frances
Howard ; he took the Duchess of Buckingham into his
personal interest and affection—he had her children in the
palace and took a semi-paternal delight in them. But he
enjoyed feeling that his Favourites owed all they had to
him, including their married happiness. He liked being
God, and he liked being treated as God ; on that unspoken
understanding he was always willing to be a benevolent
and beneficial God. He was still young in his Deity.
Arran did not always sufficiently recognize the youthful
Deity. So far, however, there was no split. No one but
the observant Master had any hope of removing Arran—
except, of course, by assassination, but that was a universal
principle of the age. The Master approached Arran with
suggestions.

Since the collapse of the second Ruthven effort, the
English government had fallen back on the " by-course " ;
and since they could not remove the devil, were preparing
to sup with him. The long spoon in this case was Lord
Hunsdon. Burghley supported him ; in a draft of a letter
Walsingham wrote : " B. hath always liked to entertain
by-courses, which groweth from lack of resolution in him,
which, I pray God, may not prove the destruction of
England." Walsingham himself was still in favour of
provoking rebellion. The Queen, doubtful of the success
of any course, allowed all to be tried. Lord Hunsdon
himself had an idea of marrying James to one of the ladies
of his house. Arran—while his wife began secretly to get

into touch with Mary Stuart, in case anything could be done there—let it be known that he was prepared to come to a full understanding with England. The King was agreeable, on the understanding that the understanding involved an acknowledgment of the succession. Arran had an understanding with the Master of Gray. The Master of Gray, riding south with Arran and his five thousand followers, kept his further understanding of himself to himself.

Hunsdon and Arran had a private meeting at Foulden Kirk, not far from Berwick. The five thousand were at a distance ; five Privy Councillors accompanied the Chancellor to the church, and waited in the churchyard. The two representatives of majesty withdrew into the church alone. They came out very cheerfully, Arran making jokes about the peacefulness of men " accounted so violent and furious as we two are." He called forward the Master and presented him to Hunsdon : the rather feminine beauty of the young man in contrast to Arran's masculine grandeur, of whom Sir Edward Hoby, Burghley's nephew, wrote to his uncle that he was " goodly of personage, representing a brave countenance of a captain of middle age, very resolute, very wise and learned, and one of the best spoken men that ever I heard." Alone in all his great company he and the Master wore no secret mail, though he laughed over the numbers of men in his array who would be willing to cut his throat. The Master presented to Hunsdon, under those masculine eyes, a letter of commendation from James, and Arran and he proceeded to explain that the King was willing soon to send him ambassador to England, in order that he, who had been so deeply engaged, might explain all the plots of the captive Queen. " He is very young, and wise and secret, as Arran doth assure me. He is, no doubt, very inward with the Scottish Queen, and all her affairs, both in England and France ; yea, and with the

Pope, for he is accounted a Papist ; but for his religion,
your lordship will judge when you see him ; but her Majesty
must use him as Arran will prescribe to her." So Hunsdon
to Burghley. Burghley was to judge of his religion, and
Elizabeth to use him, in quite another way.

The conference broke up. Arran had made a
tremendous impression on the English. He returned, to
be welcomed at the Castle of Edinburgh by a salute of
cannon, generally reserved for kings and regents. " They
do not stick to say," Hunsdon had written, "that the King
beareth the name, but Arran beareth the sway." So much
they all knew ; so much, more and more, the King. There
was a Parliament at which there were heavy forfeitures that
went to the Earl and Countess. In the open street Lady
Gowrie attempted to present a petition to James, and
was pushed down by Arran, whose hand on the King's
arm brought him swiftly past. It was a significant incident. Arran was thrusting all the rebellious faction down
with one hand while he hurried the King on with the other,
He was a soldier, and a tried and effective soldier ; the King
felt in him a military temper, recognized it, and, himself
not wholly unmilitary, consorted with it. But he felt,
still, the hand on his arm, and the divinity in him was not
altogether pleased. By accident or design, he showed
something of his feelings to the English envoy Davison.
who wrote that : " he groweth full of their fashions and
behaviours, which he will sometimes discourse of in broad
language " ; and again, " they assure me the King himself
is growing weary of the insolence and rapine both of him
and his wife." A captured border ruffian swore he had
been hired by Arran and the King to shoot Angus. It was
unlike James ; it is more likely, if he were there at all, that
it was with Arran's hand upon his arm.

Yet, on the other hand, he had no liking for the exiled
preachers and lords. They also, at a distance, touched

royal rights even more intimate than those which Arran overbore. Slanders, he heard, were still spread by them of the nature of his blood ; they said he was not the King's son but Davie's. While Davison wrote of his restiveness under Arran, Lord Hunsdon wrote of the other misery. A friendly agent of Hunsdon's, one Cuthbert Armourer, had been with James at a moment of depression. They two alone, the King became sorry for himself ; with tears of grief or anger he spoke of the rumour—" not the King's son but Davie's." He was lonely, unhappy, and uncertain.

He was aware of Gray ; he was aware of two other lords of his train, both antagonistic to Arran. One was George, Earl of Huntly. Huntly was recommended to the King, not only by a personal friendship, but by the enmities they had had in common, for Huntly belonged to the great house of the Gordons which James's uncle, the Regent Murray, had for a while overthrown. It had risen again when its enemy was down, as the Scottish noble houses tended always to rise ; and the young Earl had supported Lennox against Morton. He was Highland and Catholic, one of those peers of Scotland who were not so much peers as sovereign princes, viceroys only occasionally acknowledging their King, and in both characteristics he was opposed to Arran. The other younger Favourite was Francis Stuart Hepburn, Earl of Bothwell. By a ridiculous trick of Fate he was kindred both to the lovers and the foes of Mary, the King's mother. He was twice her nephew, for his father had been a natural son of James V., and he was therefore a half-nephew to her and to Murray the Regent ; and his mother had been sister to the other Earl of Bothwell, so that there also he was nephew-in-law to the Queen. There had been a time when the elder Bothwell had been allied with Huntly's father in defence and support of the mother of James ; both their signatures had gone to the bond of Craigmillar which had promised her relief

F

from the father of James. But Murray and Morton had
defeated them, and mother and father had both perished
from Scotland. Bothwell had fled north to the isles, taken
for a brief while to piracy, landed in Norway, and found
himself at last held captive in Denmark, as Mary was in
England. During their imprisonment, in 1570, their
marriage had been declared null by the Pope on the assertion that it had only followed an outrage committed by the
man on the person of his sovereign. The castles of Denmark received Bothwell into closer and deeper captivity.
His mind broke ; his body yielded. In 1576 (the year that
the elder Huntly died) they declared he was dead—at least
he was never seen again, nor spoken of but as a thing that
had been. His nephew Francis received his titles. The
Border followed him as the North followed Huntly.

It appeared to the young Earl that there was room for
an effective champion of the Kirk ; he offered himself
unofficially for the post. At the same time he looked.
forward to gaining influence over the mind of the King.
He could not look forward to becoming King by marriage
as his uncle had almost done. But there were other
methods : . there was intimacy and there was overthrow.
The Lord Francis Stuart Hepburn, a great admirer of his
own good parts and a great believer in his own good
fortune, began to practise at both, and found himself by
both methods in hostility to Arran.

James listened to them all. " Owing to the terrorism
in which he has been brought up," wrote a French agent,
" he is timid with the great lords and seldom ventures to
contradict them." But he added, " Yet his especial anxiety
is to be thought hardy and a man of courage," and " he is
wonderfully clever, full of honourable ambition, and has
a great opinion of himself." He listened ; he meditated.
Presently he let the Master of Gray ride south, with a vague
commission " to treat, confer, deliberate, and conclude in

all matters." All matters were, in effect, three : the exiles, the succession, money. The Master occupied himself with charming Elizabeth, with openly pursuing the negotiations with which he was charged, and secretly pursuing others. He rehearsed to the Government all that he knew about Mary ; which was not much more than they did. The great game of bluff in which James and Elizabeth were engaged was approaching its temporary climax. He had threatened her, implicitly, with a Catholic invasion, and even with the support of Mary. She had threatened him with the loss of the succession and with an English invasion : Mary was but a dim threat, yet she was there. And both James and Elizabeth believed that Mary would abandon almost anything but her religion in order to achieve freedom and her throne. Sooner or later, and now sooner, one of them would be compelled to act unless one of them first died. Neither did. Elizabeth, by pressure from her own people, was beaten. She acted, and Mary died.

Out of the commercial flirtations of Elizabeth with the Master, out of the commercial interviews between Walsingham and the Master, out of the English Queen's public orders to Angus and his friends that they should withdraw from near the Border to Oxford, and the Master's private hints that at a suitable moment they might be " let slip " over the Border, there rose the clearer possibility of the league between the two countries. Through all that cloud of swirling and suspicious mist there broke one gleam of sun in clear air. The Master met Sir Philip Sidney ; they loved. They admitted pleasure in each other's beauty and chivalry. The Master, with Arran, had worn no secret shirt of mail. There was in him a high touch of debonair courage, and Sidney found it. They parted, and never met again. The Master rode north, with Sidney hidden in his heart, but his eyes on the lordly Arran by the throne. He hid Sidney more securely and set himself to his secret

work. Presently, Sir Edward Wotton came north to help
him, not so much an envoy as a partner of the King's
amusements. He brought presents—horses and buck-
hounds ; he delighted in hunting ; he talked of four
thousand pounds. He was a great success.

It would have been a longer business than it was if
chance had not helped him. The King was still reluctant
to consent to the return of the preachers and lords. Plots
for Arran's " removal " were begun and dropped. Arran
and the Master became hostile. The King listened to
them all, and went on hunting. But within him a certain
pressure of discontent grew greater, and he went on showing
favour to the Master of Gray.

There came, suddenly, a Border affray in which, by
pure ill-luck, the English Lord Russell was killed. The
Scottish warden, who had been present, was a friend of
Arran. Wotton hurried before the King demanding justice,
while Walsingham was demanding from the English warden
as black a report as possible on Scottish responsibility.
The King received Wotton, listened, and sent Arran to
ward. But he was still disinclined to abandon him in
favour of the less powerful, if less insolent, person of the
Master. He was indeed in as near a state of irresolution
as he ever was. He allowed Arran to retire to his own
house ; this by the advice of the Master (whom Arran had
either threatened or bribed—authorities disagree). Walsingham was shocked by the Master's apparent treachery
to his originally treacherous plan. No one, in fact, knew
where any one was.

It was a difficult moment for James, and he was only
nineteen. On the one hand was the mature strength of
Arran, fascinating but overwhelming ; on the other, the
younger and more obsequious favourite Gray, but behind
him were the lords of a new reckless faction and their
ministers. He did not want Arran to go, nor Andrew

Melville to come. But he wanted a check on Arran, such
as the Master could supply. He wanted a check on Elizabeth, such as Arran could supply. He, and he alone,
would have been content to maintain those swaying
counterbalances. He made efforts to get the Master to
meet Arran. But it was clear to all others, and probably
to himself, that it was now too late. The seizure of the royal
person was the only solution. Arran pressed forward his
own plot for this ; the Master wrote desperately to England :
everything was ready, if only the Queen of England would
" let slip " the lords. He himself went off to raise his men.

Elizabeth agreed. Wotton, to escape assassination, fled
back to England. The banished nobles, after a great
exercise of prayers, humiliations, and tears, at Westminster, came pouring over the frontier ; by the end of
October they were at Falkirk with eight thousand men
and marching on Stirling. Arran heard that they had
reached the Border, broke his ward, rushed to Stirling,
and clamoured for the arrest and execution of Gray. The
King consented, at least, to order his presence.

When the command reached the Master he knew he
was in the gravest danger. Arran was with the King, and
Arran might even now thwart the conspiracy if he could
sufficiently dominate James's mind and person. Only
the presence of the Master could check him, but if already
he had achieved his purpose and the Master was too late,
the end for Gray would be death. Yet he " had worn no
mail " ; he was the friend of Sidney ; he took the deadly
chance. He rode full speed to Stirling and James. In the
royal presence he defended himself—he does not tell us
how. Both of the hostile Favourites, and the King himself, knew that it was no longer a question of proof or
purgation. What would James say and do ? at that last
point of freedom, while still neither of them had men
enough to overthrow the household and seize the Castle,

which would he choose ?   He listened to the Master ; he
smiled and spoke friendlily.   Arran knew that his chance
was lost, unless—— There were hasty proposals to seize
the Master and stab him, in the King's very presence if
need be, but at any rate somewhere in the Castle.   While
still the wild talk went on, and still the King spoke with
the Master, there came more news.   The lords were
already within a mile of Stirling.   Arran rushed from the
Castle to the walls of the town.   All night he watched on
them in person ; away in the Castle the King and the
Master lay.   There were about the lordly rivals friends of
both.   But again no one, not even Arran, could trust any
one, not even his friends.   He " suspected falsehood in
fellowship "—terrible phrase !   With the morning the spears
of the army drew near the town, and some entered by back
ways.   Arran, on the wall, heard the cry that the town was
taken.   He did not dare defiance ; with one servant he
mounted and spurred over the bridge for safety.   His friends,
not being in such danger, did but retire into the Castle ;
through the rest of that day, the second of November, the
returning Lords of the Faction, with Bothwell who had
joined them, occupied the town, their men seizing, according to Border custom, all the horses they could find in it.

The Castle was untaken ; it had, however, one final
weakness—there was no store of food, and it was full of
people.   But it was not the King's purpose to stand a
siege ; had he meant that, the head of the Master would
have been thrown from the walls to greet the lords.   As
it was, Gray went out himself to conduct the negotiations.
He bore, on James's behalf, three demands—safety for his
person ; no innovation in the State ; security for such
lords as he should name.   The first two were purely formal.
Safety and innovation were ensured by the mere presence
of the lords ; the King was safe, for he was their purpose ;
and they needed no innovation, for they were themselves

sufficient innovation. As to the third, James insisted on
an assurance that no vengeance of private feuds should
be taken under cover of public necessity, which being
promised he consented to receive them.

They entered and fell on their knees. James made
a speech, graciously pardoning and accepting them. He
told them their exile had been their own fault, and warned
them to behave dutifully in the future. Only to one who
was with them, to Bothwell, he addressed a special word :
" What should have moved thee, Francis, to come in arms
against me ? . . . I wish thee a more quiet spirit." He
was free from the violence of Arran, which was to the good,
and he might yet avoid the violence of the ministers. He
accepted actuality, but as a King should—or at least as .
this King could. Actuality itself, having got its way,
was lectured and warned, and retired half-abashed. Like
the Stuart that he was, he was always adequate—after his
own grotesque manner—to the dramatic occasion.

As in the hall of St. Andrews his education was finished,
so in the hall of Stirling his own peculiar life begins. His
few people are behind him ; the gay diplomatic traitor, the
Master of Gray, " beautiful exceedingly," is by him ; before
him are the armed lords kneeling in a homage they only
partly mean, which is as much a threat as a service. The
awkward and solemn youth of nineteen—" ung vieulx
jeune homme," " an old young man "—looks down on them,
always restless, his eyes rolling from one to the other,
rolling sometimes towards the exquisite flattering courtesy
of the Master, his hands picking at his dress, and one
sometimes resting on the Master's shoulder or flung round
his neck, for affection, for support, for the indulgence of an
æsthetic delight in beauty, for the enjoyment of cerebralized
sensual emotion. His knowledge of himself and his kingship, his amorous attachments, his dissimulation (as it is
called, but a better word would be his privacy), all twined

together, have mingled in him, and the solemnity of his
being plays the others down. They are not quite certain
what is happening ; he is. He is pardoning the lords—
part by choice, part by compulsion. But he has accepted
the compulsion ; he has made it also his choice, so that, in
a sense even the very intelligent Master hardly understood,
he has regained his spiritual freedom. He has chosen
necessity ; therefore now again he is free to act as he will.
As he achieved one kind of freedom at St. Andrews, so now
he achieves another. It was well that Arran had fled over
the bridge, and his hand passed from the King's arm, well
for the King, and perhaps well for Arran ; he might have
met a more surprising, if not a more disastrous overthrow,
for certainly the King's freedom would, in a little longer
time, have been served. The King, in his loud voice, said
to the kneeling lords something to this effect : " To all
you who, as I truly think, have not meant any harm to any
person, I am pleased to give both my hand and my heart."
" So they arose one by one, and kissed his Majesty's hands "
—even Bothwell, who perhaps most despised him, and was
to be most utterly defeated by the thing he despised.

There are two postscripts. The first is the disappoint-
ment of the ministers who, back in their pulpits, found that
the lords displayed no noticeable zeal for the advancement
of Christ's Kirk and the establishment of holy discipline
over themselves, Scotland, and the King. Indignant
sermons had no effect, except to render more acute the
continual wrangle between the clergy and the Crown. The
second is the signing of a League with England. There was
a general vague understanding about the succession ; there
were guarantees of mutual aid in case of danger ; there was
to be a pension. Neither James nor Elizabeth got all they
wanted, and as the succession was not promised nor the
pension paid, the Treaty itself ensured no more than
necessity anyhow ensured. But it pleased Walsingham.

CHAPTER FOUR

" MORTUI NON MORDENT "

THERE are, close behind the realistic figure of James, during most of his life, two groups of followers—one comic and one horrible. Whatever he is about, sooner or later, there is heard the music of a harlequinade. The King seems often to have a touch of the buffoon in him, but even more than in himself it is discernible in others, and mostly in religion. Moments that should be solemn (and, at least once, dreadful) are invaded and transmuted by the grotesque. They are funny, but funny with something distasteful ; they are serious, but serious with something horrible. These are actual moments and actual facts. Against them, uncertain and dark, are the shadows of interpretations of facts. On one side in the actual day the realistic figure of the King seems to become a clown among clowns ; on the other, in the fabulous night, a conspirator among conspirators. The folly of men noisily attends him ; the wickedness of men softly. The King, and the comic King, and the sinister King, intermingle in those legends and tales and records which are all we have to make history, and only by a half-arbitrary decision can we determine which is he. Nor is there any more effective apparition of that riddle of con-joined realism, buffoonery, and death than in the autumn and winter of 1586.

On April 1 the Treaty was signed. Walsingham, having provided, subject to Elizabeth, a pension for the son, occupied the summer by providing—also, he feared, subject to Elizabeth—a more ghostly payment for the mother—her fee to Charon. He determined that Mary Stuart should, at last, die. Into the controversies of charge and counter-charge, factual and moral, which surround that action, there is no need to go. Walsingham was no innocent, and Mary was no fool. Murder, legal or illegal, was a habit of the age. If Mary was destroyed by injustice, it was an injustice with which she had provocatively flirted. To defend or attack her is as useless as to defend or attack Elizabeth. Thus, so far as we can understand—thus, in their hope and despair and anguish, those shining and sombre figures went through the world ; thus also they went out of it.

At the beginning of August, Mary's secretaries were seized, and she herself was taken into close confinement. Walsingham took care that adequate information was sent to James about it, and about the Babington conspiracy which had been the cause of and excuse for it. The King was not altogether displeased. He had been threatened, explicitly or implicitly, with and by Mary through all those years ; one of the drawbacks of any dealing on his part with the Catholics in the realm was the existence of Mary as the rightful Catholic sovereign. Her letters and appeals went out to the Catholic courts of France and Spain, who would send no properly accredited ambassadors to him because of her. He highly distrusted her activities, and it was not displeasing to him to have them hampered. Something of his satisfaction showed in his conversations with the now prevalent Master of Gray. He was content for her to be more strictly warded, for her correspondence to be stayed, for her " knavish servants " to be hanged, and to write letters of congratulation to Elizabeth on her escape from the plot. The French agent urged him to interfere on his mother's behalf. But he remembered that other French agents would not recognize him as the King because of his mother. He answered that she must drink the ale she had brewed. The Scottish lords, including Bothwell, spoke highly of arms and invasion. James reminded them that she had threatened him with the loss of all but the lordship of Darnley, " which was all my father had before me." He had judged what he thought likely to happen. He was wrong.

Meanwhile the Master of Gray, from the right hand of the Throne, was writing secretly to the Scottish ambassador in London—that same Mr. Archibald Douglas who had been privy to the murder of Darnley. In spite of the King's willingness to spare his mother, wrote the Master, "I pray you beware, for she were well out of the way." He was willing to advise what the English wanted; he was supposed to be pressing their policy on James. He had betrayed and insulted Mary, and if ever she could, she would have his head. If the Queen of England, he wrote, "could not preserve her own security without taking his Majesty's mother's life, *quia mortui non mordent*, yet it were no wise meet that the same were done openly but rather by some quieter means."

Before the end of the year he was in a strait. It became evident that Mary's life was indeed in danger. James realized his error. He conceived his honour concerned, but he knew actuality also. He thought nothing of the shouting romanticism of his nobles. Their ardour was not likely to burn for more than a few raids in force, unless he accepted the offers of Spain or France; and the Kirk and their friends would be themselves at once in arms against Spain or France, and he himself would be likely to disappear in the marching of Spain or France. The dilemma did not infuriate him as it would do some minds; it cooled and hardened him. He sent letters to Elizabeth, remonstrating and protesting, and demanded high activity for his mother's salvation on the part of Gray and Archibald Douglas. The King "apprehends the matter so vehemently," wrote Gray, and went on to discuss his own problem. The King had proposed to send him with Bothwell and Robert Melville on an embassy to intercede for Mary. Intercession, but not intervention, was his private formula. Mary was one of those two women. He had always known they were rivals ; he knew that the death of either was the other's gain. The death of his mother was his own greater gain, for the death of Elizabeth, if he waited, was sure. Yet—it was his royal and filial duty—he would intercede. He could do no more, effectively. With an almost awful accuracy he determined to do exactly what he could. He would send an embassy. He spoke of it to Gray, who saw himself either way in danger. If he refused to go and Mary died, James would suppose that he was in the secrets of the English Government, and therefore partly responsible, and would visit it on him. If he went and Mary died, men " shall think I have lent her a hand " ; whether he went or no, if Mary lived, she was bound to hate and hurt him because of his old treachery. Against his will he was compelled to accept. James provided him with long Instructions. He was to say this and that to Elizabeth— every kind of argument and remonstrance, but no kind of violent threat. In mere despair Gray determined to be honest. Sir Robert Melville was joined in the commission. There went with them another Stuart, a certain Sir Alexander, who is the most secret figure in the whole secret business. Riding south in December the ambassadors came to London. No paraphrase can equal the Master's own account of their audience :

" The 9th day we sent to court to crave audience, which we got the 10th day. At the first, she said, a thing long looked for should be welcome when it comes ; I would now see your Master's offers. I answered, no man makes offers but for some cause ; we would, and like your Majesty, first know the cause to be extant for which we offer, and likewise that it be extant till your Majesty has heard us. I think it be extant yet, but I will not promise for an hour, but you think to shift in that sort. I answered, we mind not to shift, but to offer from our Sovereign all things that with reason may be ; and in special, we offered as is set down in our general : all was refused and tho't nothing.

She called on the three that were in the house, the Earl of
Leicester, my Lord Admiral, and Chamberlain, and very
despitefully repeated all our offers in presence of them all.
I opened the last part, and said, Madam, for what respect
is it that men deal against your person or estate for her
cause ?　She answered, because they think she shall succeed
to me, and for that she is a Papist.　Appearingly, said I,
both the causes may be removed.　She said she would be
glad to understand it.　If, Madam, said I, all that she has
of right of succession were in the King our sovereign's
person, were not all hope of Papists removed ?　She
answered, I hope so.　Then, Madam, I think the Queen, his
mother, shall willingly demit all her rights in his person.
She answered, She hath no right, for she is declared unhabil.
Then, I said, if she have no right, appearingly the hope
ceases already, so that it is not to be feared that any man
attempt for her.　The Queen answered, But the Papists
allow not our declaration.　Then let it fall, says I, in the
King's person by her assignation.　The Earl of Leicester
answered, She is a prisoner, how can she demit ?　I
answered, The demission is to her son, by the advice of all
the friends she has in Europe ;　and in case, as God forbid,
that any attempt cuttis the Queen here away, who shall
party with her to prove the demission or assignation to be
ineffectual, her Son being opposite party and having all the
princes her friends for him, having bonded for the efficacy
of it with his Majesty of before.　The Queen made as she
could not comprehend my meaning, and Sir Robert opened
the matter again ;　she yet made as though she understood
not.　So the Earl of Leicester answered, that our meaning
was, that the King should be put in his Mother's place.　Is
it so, the Queen answered, then I put myself in a worse
case than of before :　By God's passion, that were to cut
my own throat ;　and, for a dutchy or an earldom to yourself, you or such as you would cause some of your desperate
knaves kill me :　No, by God, he shall never be in that place.

I answered, He craves nothing of your Majesty, but only of his Mother. The Earl of Leicester answered, that were to make him party to the Queen my mistress. I said, he will be far more party, if he be in her place through her death. She would stay no longer, but said she would not have a worse in his Mother's place; and said, Tell your King what good I have done for him in holding the Crown on his head since he was born, and that I mind to keep the league that now stands between us, and if he break it shall be a double fault: and with this minded to have bidden us a farewell; but we achevit. And I speak craving of her that her life may be spared for 15 days; she refused. Sir Robert craved for only eight days; she said not for an hour; and so geid her away."

The cunning of the Master was defeated by the superior cunning, or, more probably, by the sheer pedantic actuality of his own master. He was making out the best case for a respite that he could. But the King had written secretly and even earlier to the Earl of Leicester, announcing the ambassadors' departure, and proceeding:

" But to my first purpose, this far shortly may I say, I am honest, no changer of course, altogether in all things as I profess to be, and whomsoever will affirm that I had ever intelligence with my mother since the Master of Gray's being in England, or ever thought to prefer her to myself in the title or ever dealt in any other foreign course, they lie falsely and unhonestly of me. But specially how fond and inconstant I were if I should prefer my mother to the title let all men judge. My religion ever moved me to hate her course although my honour constrains me to insist for her life."

He wrote down exactly what he meant. He would never conspire with Mary against Elizabeth; he would never run any risk of preferring his mother to himself in the succession. His religion opposed itself to hers, and remembered the dangers which her religion put him in.

His honour constrained him to protest against her death. He thought it a shocking thing (as he wrote later) that "sovereign princes themselves should be the example givers of their own sacred diadems' profaning." It is possible that till the last he hardly thought Elizabeth would profane Mary so far. But he refused, as he always did, to see that his own royalty already profaned hers.

Meanwhile Alexander Stuart, behind the ambassadors' backs, was reassuring the English Court. He was said to have told them that if the King showed himself discontented at his mother's death "they might easily satisfy him in sending him dogs and deer." James, hearing of this, flew into a passion, and threatened to hang Stuart before he put off his boots. He wrote to Elizabeth to say that none but the ambassadors knew his mind ; " I pray you take me not to be a chameleon." To be fair to them, they did not ; they thought they knew his colour perfectly well, and that it would harmonize peaceably with the crimson of his mother's blood. They were so far right that Sir Alexander, on his return, was not hanged.

The ambassadors rode back, before the end of January. Then the harlequinade which attended on James broke out in full strength ; the fatuity of man once more embroidered the altar-cloth of religion. The King in Council commanded all the ministers to pray for his mother—that God would illumine her soul and preserve her body from danger. The ministers—at least, in Edinburgh—refused, upon which James, proposing to go himself to St. Giles', appointed the Bishop of St. Andrews to make intercession. News of this came to the ministers, and they sent up one of their youngest brethren, the Reverend Mr. John Cowper, into the pulpit before the King arrived. He came, in his state, entered, took his seat, and saw Cowper standing up to lead the congregation. The King called out to him that he could stop there if he would obey the charge " and remember my mother in your prayers." Cowper answered with the formula with which the ministers continually defended the freedom of the pulpit—that high place of inspired proclamation, the altar of the word ; he said he would do as the Spirit of God should direct him. The King bade him come down ; he moved to remain ; the captain of the royal guard went across to drag him out. He cried out : " This day shall be a witness against the King in the great day of the Lord ! " and then, prophesying woe to all them that dwelled in Edinburgh, descended.

Many rushed out of the church. The bishop hastened up and soothed and persuaded the rest of the congregation to prayers and tears, by expounding the duty of Christians to pray for all men ("he was a most powerful preacher"). Cowper was sent to ward ; Andrew Melville and the others were forbidden to preach. In a few days the other ministers and the King came to an agreement. It was decided that it was very desirable that Mary Stuart " should become a profitable member of Christ's Kirk."

By then she could at least belong to no other—neither of Rome nor Geneva, nor England, nor Scotland. While her son and her subjects wrangled over her soul, it had gone to its own place. She died. When, seven days after the execution, Roger Ashton, a Gentleman of the Bed-chamber, came in from England with the news, the King was in great displeasure and went to bed without eating ; the next day also he desired to be solitary, and rode alone to Dalkeith. But it was rumoured that, for all his displeasure, he could not conceal his inward joy, and that the Secretary Maitland had had to· put the courtiers out of the room. The tale is too gross ; it is more likely that displeasure and satisfaction contended. He had been insulted, but he was alone. The Queen of Scots was dead, against his will, but very much with his will the King of Scots was indeed the King.

He could hardly have prevented it, and for a wild dream of almost fabulous honour· he could hardly be expected to move—he who preferred reasonable ways and comfortable ways and profitable ways. He took them—all of them at once, and afterwards the irrational, uncomfortable, unprofitable thing avoided him for ever. He had no other chance of glory. The clumsy body imposed some image of itself on his spirit, and never again did he come so near healing. He had courageous moments and intelligent moments afterwards, but never again did the Spirit come so near saying to him, " Die ! " ; never again did he have the opportunity of losing his world. He could not be expected to do it ; it is only at such moments that man finds what may be expected of him, and usually (quite reasonably) does not do it.

So much for what the records suggest, and the realism of James's character. Yet here also there dances, in the magnified shadows which the fires of that winter cast on the walls of Holyrood and Greenwich, the sinister possibility. In those shadows the arm of James is round Sir Alexander's neck ; the mouth of the King near his ear. There seems to have been no opportunity for Gray to whisper in Elizabeth's, as was once said : the Scottish ambassador and the French bore witness to his honesty in London. Yet . . . an unrecorded whisper in Holyrood, a night visit to Walsingham in London, something—some lost hour— which history has had to miss, and only the grotesque shadows on the palace wall suggest, and the death of Mary becomes an even more sinful thing than it is. Beyond the problem of the forged postscript which slew her is the problem of the hidden utterances which allowed her death. At least, we know practically the last thing about Elizabeth in that moment ; the last thing is precisely what we do not know about James. We are certain—in the very end—only of that atrocious harlequinade in Edinburgh, preluding the hooves which through the February twilights bear the news of the slaying of the King's mother northward to the King.

G

CHAPTER FIVE

The Queen and the Witches

ONE of those two grey forms that floated over the Borders of England and within the borders of his mind had been dispelled into oblivion. Sixteen years were to pass before the other grey and haggard spectre faded also into the past, and the comfort and profit he desired were his. They were years of such continual difficulty that often it seemed impossible that he should win. But he did win. By luck, by cunning, by daring, by slipping here and striking there, by the continual imposition of his obstinacy, he brought Scotland to heel. When the day came that the King's train waited to start upon the month-long journey to London, and the King came out to join them, a steady peace lay round him. The dangers had rather been driven underground than abolished, as his son was to find. But they had at least been driven underground, and left the leopard to purr and stretch and expand and lie somnolently in his possessions, almost as if he had turned himself into a great fireside cat undisturbed.

It was largely luck—his Fortune, so to call the incalculable operation of things that partly determines a man's career—which carried him through to his peace. But there was something in his nature which secretly co-operated with his fortune. He was not one of those who strongly impose their will on a refractory world, but neither was he a mere negligible fragment of mortality pitched up at last on the dry footstool of the double Throne. He is at work; his nature is at work, all the time. He was indolent, capable of bursts of speed and business, incapable of pro-

longed industry and attention. But something deeper
than industry or intelligence runs through those sixteen
years.   It is the more difficult to define that there is through
them all no dominant Favourite—no D'Aubigny or Arran,
as before, no Somerset or Buckingham, as after. We
cannot, therefore, study the black shadow that is the
King in the surrounding light of the shining beauty that
falls on him. The nearest thing to a Favourite was, by
a trick of fate, usually hostile — Francis Stuart Hepburn,
fifth Earl of Bothwell, or George Gordon, Earl of Huntly.
There is the Chancellor, Sir John Maitland, younger brother
of Maitland of Lethington ; but he was forty-one years
old in 1587, and he does not come before us as one of that
shining and dangerous circle of loves. The curious Cupid
who presided over James's affairs did not shoot a dart on
his behalf. There is the Queen, but except by a fretful
and spasmodic opposition she did not greatly affect
the secret movements of her husband's mind and will.
There are the young men, such as Lennox ; they are there
certainly, and that is all they are. He is alone, and he
has—it would seem—no profound political intelligence.
What, besides his Fortune, brought him through ?

Chiefly, perhaps, his indefatigable belief in himself,
which sometimes looks like weakness and sometimes like
obstinacy, but is at bottom always James Stuart simply
and utterly convinced of James Stuart. He was so convinced of James as the King that he could afford to be
careless of James as James. His son, compared to him,
took his royal office solemnly, even to himself. But James
took it so simply that he did not need to be solemn. When
Mary was dead the last possible rival was gone, and the
last possible royal traitor. Even if that nightmare of his
youth, " the son of Davie," should recur, still—once his
mother was dead—there was no one who could substantiate
it. So far as it had substance, it drew that substance

from her substantial life ; when she passed to the spirits, it passed to fables. He had a complete belief, and he remained completely loyal to it.

In such a loyalty to a single fixed vision he was alone in Scotland. It is afterwards that the limitations of his vision become chiefly operative. Those limitations can be put in seven words—his vision could be and was achieved. It was possible. He could be King of England and Scotland, and he was. The kingdom was not quite all that he had hoped, but such as it was, there it was. One need but see him in relation to Francis Bacon to know the difference between the finite and infinite imagination. But the finite nature of his kingdom was only to be discovered afterwards, and in the infinite he never had much interest. It is we who remark the difference.

Its finity, its actuality, were his strength. The purposes of the lords might vary from day to day : they sought their own profit, and their profit was often changeable. His never was. The ministers of the Kirk themselves had to admit the reconciliation of some kind of show of temporal obedience with their fierce spiritual sovereignty. James needed no reconciliation in his mind. Andrew Melville came nearest to defeating him, because Andrew Melville came nearest to claiming and possessing a perfect sovereignty, and was least moved by James's own. Had the chance of history ever brought James face to face with any of the great Popes, he might well have gone down. But he hardly met, hardly even saw — save as a child of ten months—another sovereign. His amities and his hostilities with the other members of that unique guild of crowns were—save for a brief knowledge of the King of Denmark— always conducted by correspondence. They were therefore purely mental. He never received the shock of the physical presence of equal or superior royalty. That physical disturbance which is our only salvation from our own dreams and our own interpretations in this respect never touched him. He never beheld the mitred forehead of the Pope, or the vivid eyes of Elizabeth, or the callous smile of the French Valois. Only at long last there arose from near his Throne the obstinate gravity of his son, and pressed him from his seat. If Charles I. had been Charles II., things might have been different. The grandfather and the grandson had much in common; their son and father divided them, and lost the Crown in the division.

The corresponding exterior cause of the King's final success was the complete uncertainty which existed in all other minds on the strength of their position at any one moment. No one could tell, on any day, what enemies might denounce him in the Council or attack him in the country or the streets. Every one despised the King's power, but no one could safely guess at any moment on what other powers the King could call. Had the English government been stable in its intentions and credible in its promises, there might have been a firm weight in the other scale. But any one who supported England was likely to be betrayed by England, or at least thrown to James. By civil war, by assassination, by bribes, the various houses of rebellion and intrigue were continually weakened. In the midst of them went the person of the King, without a guard, without money, without a sure friend. But he was still the King to them as he was to himself, and still the mere name could summon men for the necessary month, and for the necessary moment the mere presence could cause hesitation and uncertainty. He was mocked; he was despised; he was supposed to be governed by favourites, to be dominated by the Chancellor. But one of Burghley's correspondents, a gentleman of the Court, wrote that the King himself " moved the Chancellor and all the rest as he turned, minions and all. . . . The

Chancellor is a great councillor . . . but he followeth directly
his Majesty's course in all."

So he shuffled forward, obstinate and alone. He had
a respect for Maitland and a fondness for Huntly and a
liking for Bothwell, but above all, through these years, he
respected his aim and liked himself.

After the slaying of Mary there was, for a brief while,
agitation. He let it rise ; he swept it over Scotland, a
vociferous and dangerous veil to trouble the South. The
Master of Gray was accused of treason, and exiled ; as
Davison in the South was imprisoned. Bothwell cried out
that mail was the only mourning wear ; the Hamiltons
offered to burn Newcastle ; the Catholic lords pressed on
their intrigues with Spain. The Borders became alive
with silence and spears. The Queen of England's messenger
was stopped on the frontier. Armed men interrupted all
correspondence, and Walsingham's secret service failed
him. There were wild forays all through the summer.
Walsingham sent a long letter pointing out how unwise
James would be to move by himself, how foolish to let
himself be converted to Spain. It was almost certain that
the King would not stir, yet Walsingham wished Elizabeth
would honourably console him with lands, titles, and
money. She would not. She had taken her risk ; the
succession would be her only bribe, and she knew it would
be sufficient.

The King called a Parliament. His majority was
officially declared ; he was twenty-one. He prepared for
himself, in that auspicious year, a feast of peace, not
without some hope that it might achieve over Elizabeth a
victory no less renowned than war's. The great houses of
Scotland were divided and ravaged by bitter feuds. The
King determined to end all that. He gathered all the
hostile lords at Holyrood, and by his own exertions he
brought them to a reluctant ostentation of peace. He

banqueted them there, and then he displayed his achieve-
ments before God and man.   He caused a procession to
be formed, two by two, each one of each pious or scornful
or bewildered pair handfasted to his worst enemy.   The
King came down and took his place at their head.   Out
from the palace the procession went, up the High Street
of Edinburgh, between the heads of gazing citizens, up to
the market cross.   There, by command of the magistrates,
a table had been spread, " even in the midst, among their
enemies."   Public proclamation of concord was made ;
foes drank to each other, and the King to all.   Amid general
applause from the pious and impious alike, the King led
the new-bathed lambs of peace back to Holyrood.[1]

In the Parliament, before it broke up, there was a great
scene.   All the white lambs, snowy with virtue, offered
themselves to follow their leopard against his sister, the
lioness in the South.   Maitland made a speech, the nobles
flung themselves before the King on their knees, and begged
to be allowed to offer their all to avenge the death of Mary,
if he would take up the quarrel.   James showed himself
deeply moved, and thanked them.   But for the moment he
postponed action.   Every one knew that Philip of Spain was
arming at last, and that sooner or later his fleet would come.
The King knew that he had no intention, unless driven to
it, of putting himself in the power of the Spaniards ; he
remarked that the only favour he expected from them
was that which Polyphemus granted to Ulysses—to be
devoured last.   But did Elizabeth know it ?   He exhibited
to her a united nation, a nation waiting only his word to
be hurled southward at her while the floating armies of
Spain barricaded and invaded her on other sides.   The
lords were all friends, and all burning for war.   If that did

---

[1] Only William, Lord Yester, refused to be reconciled with his enemy,
Traquair.   But a few months in Edinburgh Castle composed both him
and the quarrel.

not shake her, nothing would. She might guess more truly, but would she stand to her guess ?

She did—at least until the next year, when the Armada was circling England ; then she gave way. In July 1588, when the great foreign castles were already passing out of the Channel, a certain Mr. Ashby came riding in haste to Edinburgh, sent to promise James *something*. Exactly what, no one was very clear, not even Ashby, who like most of Elizabeth's servants was expected to act on his own initiative (" as from your own head "), in order that he might afterwards be disavowed if necessary. Elizabeth, quite honestly, expected no less of her servants, and she could never quite understand their reluctance or refusal. Her idea of loyalty was a man who risked his head on every action, and she did not expect him to complain, at the last moment, if it were convenient to her to take his head. It would be a meiosis to call this unjust. But something of that wild injustice became part of the irrational legend of Elizabeth. It is impossible to make a reasonable heroine of the great Queen, but then the effort need not be made. She demanded impossibilities, but she was herself an impossibility. She could not be, yet she was, and she went on being ; that was the indestructible centre of her renown. At least the chances she took were as great as any she asked of her servants.

The King received Ashby on July 24 and listened to his general exhortations and insinuations. The Armada came sailing northward, nearer to the Scottish coasts. The Kirk lamented and fasted and sought the Lord with petitions concerning the universal conspiracy " of the enemies of the truth against Christ's Kirk, to put in execution the bloody determination of the Council of Trent." If the Armada should unload its army on the Scottish coast, if there should join with it all the principalities of the North (the spiritual North of the devil and the geographical

North of the Earl of Huntly), if the unreliable and half-
papistical King should be wholly converted by force or
persuasion, then the professors of pure religion would be
lost indeed. The King remained, as it were, in secret.
Ashby wrote to Burghley on August 6 saying he had
thought it wise " to satisfy his Majesty." He had therefore
been driven to promise an English duchy, a pension of £5000,
a royal guard of fifty men, and a small force upon the
Borders. The King listened, accepted, proclaimed hostility
to Spain, called out the country against invasion. The
Armada disappeared into mists, except for the wrecks, the
bodies, and the survivors that were swept up on the shore.
On August 22, when he knew it, Walsingham wrote to Ashby,
finding fault with his promises, and Elizabeth refused to
ratify them.

In fact, having Elizabeth to deal with, James could
never win both ways. Her ministers would have bought
him with gold as well as with the all but inevitable Crown.
The Queen would not. If he must have the Crown he must
choose it and pay for it with his own goodwill, not with
hers. She continually defeated his continual efforts. But
this time he was very angry ; he said he had been " dandled
like a boy " ; he became friendly with Huntly.

The Lord who had thus redeemed the faithful poured
more gracious mercies on them by the end of the year.
Catherine de Medici died in France (" bloody Jezebel "),
and there followed in the same country " the maist remarkable work of God's justice . . . making first King
Henry to cause his guard stick the Duke of Guise under
trust, with the Cardinal of Lorrain ; and syne a Jacobin
friar . . . maist treasonably to stick the King : the Lord
working by maist wicked instruments maist wisely and
justly." The Kirk received an inrush of spiritual confidence ; the pulpits grew loud with denunciations. The
King was entreated—as by the prophets of the Lord—to

take strong measures against Papistry. But the Papists
were the King's only counterweight against the prophets.
He agreed, of course, but nothing immediately happened,
however much (as they told him) it was the Will of God.
That serene and indefectible power—of which, perhaps, the
only mortal praise is that of John Donne, King James's
later preacher : " Blessed be Thou, that Thou art only
Thyself "—that serene power was by three forces supernaturally invoked in Scotland and by one supernaturally
denied. The Catholic priests on secret missions, the Catholic
laity in more or less secret devotion, invoked it and reposed
upon it. The Presbyterian ministers—those who sought
to control all earthly activities from their pulpits, and those
who simply fulfilled day by day the ordinary duties of their
office—these with their lay-folk prayed to it and reposed
upon it. The King's Majesty, in the firm belief of an especial
relation to it, laboriously and sincerely accepted it and
reposed upon it. All these groups were apt to expound it,
and to explain all events by its immediate miraculous intervention. They saw it at work everywhere ; they seem even
to expect to see it in itself, in its own perfect beauty, round
the next corner. Contemplating so much sincerity of zeal,
one is shocked to realize that all those vehement controversialists turned the final corner of death before they could
experience its complete victory. Meanwhile the Divine
Will, in patience and irony, submitted its perfection to
their imperfections, and hid its judgments from their
angry eyes.

There remained the wizards and witches, or those who
imagined themselves to be so. Through the darkness, in
the screams of the tortured, it is all but impossible to
catch any note of sincerity. Credulity and cruelty lie all
about them. It is certainly better for man to disbelieve
that such communion of evil can be, for man is not to be
trusted with the belief. Perhaps it cannot. But it seems

likely that at least a few wretched men and women of the
time did believe that such blasphemous capacities were in
them, and sought to enjoy them. There was raid and
horror enough ; there was, perhaps, at best some self-
illusion too. Unless every one was lying under fear of
torture—which they may very well have done—there were
groups and covens of imbecile or sacrilegious folly. In
England, later on, the Countess of Somerset visited a reputed
magician for love-philtres : it is not impossible that wilder
minds might imagine themselves to be magically enlarged.
It is, at least—*ad hoc*—necessary to believe so much to be
true, it is necessary to feel the quiver of repulsion and
fear, or it is quite impossible to understand James. Great
men and great minds believed in it. It is no good to say
that they did unless we experience something of what
they believed—something of what, to James, rode in the
storms, or flickered sometimes on the swords of his enemies,
or touched the House of Ruthven with terror and shone for
a moment in Bothwell's eyes. It was the destruction of
the soul, the rejection of the Divine Will, the living effort
of rejection. " Thou shalt not suffer a witch to live."

The Armada had gone. This crisis, with the death of
the Guises and of Henry III. of France, left Philip of
Spain more inclined than he had been to suffer negotiations
hopefully with the Catholic Scottish lords. " Scotland,"
Maitland warned an English agent, " is his only card to
play against England, and that you will see ere long."
Huntly and Errol were in deep communication with Spain.
Burghley intercepted letters and sent them on to James,
who read them (so the story goes) in the presence of the
suspected lords. He was bored and unhappy. He liked
Huntly, who in the course of this year had married Henrietta
Stuart, daughter of the long-loved D'Aubigny and sister
of the present Duke of Lennox. James had given him
5000 marks to bring over the bride, presented him with

the Abbey—that is, with the revenues of the Abbey—of
Dunfermline, which had been taken from the Master of
Gray. He also wrote an *Epithalamion*, or verses for the
masque at the wedding, in which the gods were invoked,
by the King's past labours, to show beneficence to the
young couple, and consented.

> If ever I, O mighty gods, have done you service true,
> In setting forth, by painful pen, your glorious praises due . . .
> O Venus, make them broody als for to produce with speed,
> Wherein they may revive again, a blest and happy seed.

There was a good deal of it. James was anxious not to
please the Kirk by hurting his friends. But, marriage or
no marriage, Kirk or no Kirk, Huntly could not be allowed
to go on making plots which would, sooner or later, involve
the seizure of the royal person. He caused the earl to be
held in custody, but he took the Chancellor Maitland to
him there. They all dined together. The King patted
and caressed the earl in his usual self-indulgent way. He
indulged himself and annoyed the Kirk by letting him
out of ward. Huntly allowed his Catholicism to ally
itself with Bothwell's beliefs . . . whatever Bothwell's
beliefs were. He was officially a champion of the Kirk,
but the Kirk would have been in difficulties with him,
were it not that support of the Kirk in any nobleman
served almost as well as conversion. It had done so with
Morton. The two young men (Huntly was twenty-seven
and Bothwell was twenty-six) agreed to seize the third
young man, who was by now twenty-three, and to deal
with Maitland. The semi-favourites were shining in
opposition. With a sudden flirt of audacity the third
young man accepted the opposition. In a new and strange
movement of that everlasting dance of figures of fascination
about the King, the fascination breaks now into a show
of steel. As if flashing back those presumptuous rays of
battle, the King rode to Edinburgh, sent out a summons to

the conspirators to surrender their castles, and gathered forces. It had been intended that Bothwell should make business for him in the south, but the King disappointed their hopes. He left Bothwell till later, marched out, and pressed northward ; the rebels hovered in front of him. James came up with them, told his soldiers to stand no longer than they should see him stand, watched under the stars for one night with them, and in the morning found the hostile force dissolving. Huntly, with others, was taken ; the King brought them back to Edinburgh, where Bothwell, in Maitland's own garden, made submission. The King, in political satisfaction and personal glee, had them sent off to ward. He examined Huntly afterwards also in a garden—himself, the prisoner, a few of the Council. Huntly was brought to formal trial, imprisoned, and, in spite of the Kirk, released. Bothwell, in spite of the Kirk, was brought to formal trial, convicted after some difficulty, imprisoned, and released. But though released they were not pardoned. The sentence—" the doom," as it was called—was kept hanging over them for two years. It was a not unwise precaution, perhaps, but though the precaution was political the use of it was personal. James enjoyed having opportunities of keeping people in suspense. He dallied with cruelty ; there were to be later instances. At present his amusements were harmless, and neither Huntly nor Bothwell troubled about the suspended sentence.

It was the beginning of June. The King—both his companions being imprisoned and neither of his companions being (amorously) of the first importance—allowed his mind, as the summer passed on, to become occupied with another theme—that of his marriage. There had been all kinds of suggestions for the past ten years. Elizabeth, in an odd moment, had even spoken of herself. Leicester and Hunsdon had both thought of relatives of their own. Others had suggested the Lady Arabella Stuart (James's

English cousin), a princess of Spain, a princess of France, a princess of Denmark. Elizabeth was backing the sister of the King of Navarre, if James *must* marry. She did not see the necessity. She had, in old days, made Arran agree to keep him unmarried for three years ; she had intrigued through Wotton against the Danish proposal. The ambassadors who had come on political business regarded themselves as insulted, and only through Sir James Melville's interposition was the King made aware of their treatment. He sent them away soothed, borrowing (by an exquisite sense of kingcraft) a great gold chain from Arran, who had been partly responsible, for a parting gift. Arran, for fear of losing the King, lent it and lost it.

A little later, the King sent his old master, Peter Young, who was by now master-almoner, to Denmark to continue the rather vague negotiations. He was to bring back a report on the general appearance of the Danish princesses, the King probably feeling safer with such a Calvinistic Lancelot than with any of the younger courtiers. He went ; he returned, bringing accounts which persuaded James to send yet another embassy, more formal but still with only a cautious commission. It was just after their departure that M. Sylvestre Du Bartas arrived from France.

He had come in response to an urgent invitation from James, who had so great an admiration for his poetry. He is known to us chiefly as one of the poets who did not much influence Milton. But it is doubtful whether James could ever have cared for *Paradise Lost* as he cared for the *Creation* of the Frenchman ; he even translated some of it into the same long lines he used to bless Huntly :

> declare me what offense
> From Edens both, chas'd Adam's self and seed for his pretense. . . .

Milton, it is true, had not yet begun :

> Say first, for .heaven hides nothing from thy view
> Nor . . .

Du Bartas arrived, with a kind of underhand mission from the King of Navarre's secretary. The King was so taken with his verse that, had not the embassy departed, the northern marriage might have been stayed. Literary style curiously intermingled with James's business affairs. The Chancellor, who was against it, assured Du Bartas it would not take place. The King, agreeably anxious that the poet should enjoy himself, took him to St. Andrews, to hear Andrew Melville lecture, which he did—on the right government of Christ and the proper discipline of the Kirk, and against interference by the civil power. The sermon distracted the King from letters and made him " verie angrie all that night." But the next day they gave him a banquet and made him merry again.

Du Bartas prevailed so far that an embassy went to Navarre. He himself left in September, to translate into French the King's poem on *Lepanto*,[1] while James got to work on a return translation of the *Furies*. Presently his embassies returned, with pictures, upon contemplating which the King retired into devotion for a fortnight to seek the direction of the Lord. The Lord, it seems, counselled him to avoid the Princess of Navarre, who was said to be old and crooked. The English, however, the Chancellor, and the Council, neither intending to marry her nor having the advantage of fifteen days' prayer, still put difficulties in the way. The King (according to Melville) was driven to suggest, through some of his intimates, to the deacons of the Edinburgh crafts that they should cause a show of rioting against the Chancellor. At last, with general consent, the Earl Marshal was dispatched, on June 18, 1589.

The Princess Anne was married to the royal proxy on

---

[1] Otherwise, I think, unsung in English until Mr. G. K. Chesterton wrote on it. The curious will be profited by comparing the poems. The King's is the more statistical.

August 20, and prepared to cross the seas. Storms drove
her back. The young King was at Craigmillar, oblivious
(it is to be hoped) of the conference which twenty-three
years before had been held there to promise his mother
some kind of final release from the trouble of his father.
It was a sinister place to think of marriage. But what
with victorious war, what with absence of amorous delight,
what with a sense of his own chaste life, what with the
opposition to his own (and the Lord's) marriage decision,
what with devotion and poetry and love and conflict, James
was excited and fantastically exalted into the behaviour
of a royal lover. The first James of his house, centuries
before, had written poetry to his love. While the storms
raged over the North Sea, the King wrote sonnets. The
Court, which had been seriously disturbed at the King's
continence—" a prince without vice," an English agent
called him, and if an English agent called him that, his
vices must have been negligible enough—observed that
" he could neither sleep nor rest." When he could not
sleep he did sometimes " drop into verse " ; in the deep
midnight he once wrote a sonnet to Maitland. He now
wrote poems to his unseen princess, a girl of sixteen. But
he felt that something more was wanted, and by a happy
chance the instruments were provided.

Maitland had opposed the marriage. But the marriage
was now, by proxy, an accomplished fact. The Queen was
undoubtedly coming, and would some time reach Scotland,
unless the witches who, in Scotland and Denmark, had
raised the storm, stopped her. In Denmark they burnt
some of the witches ; in Scotland the Lord Chancellor
procured and fitted out a suitable vessel, and announced
that, by permission, he would himself go and bring home
the bride. The King was graciously pleased, but he saw
a better way—he would go himself and take the Chancellor
with him, since both of them agreed that, with the King

absent, it would be very unsafe for the Chancellor to remain
at home. The motives that drove James are dark, but
they can be guessed. The crudest is that he wanted a
complete holiday. The finest is that he was the King, and
the King should bring home his bride. Between those two
were others. He was young; he had persuaded himself
that he was in love; and there was, in that voyage over
the dangerous sea to Norway, where the Queen had taken
refuge, an adventure that lay between hunting and war.
It is not unlikely that he had some idea of annoying Elizabeth and some determination to defy the devilish powers
that thwarted him. The courage in him—and he had
courage—was still high. It would have been convenient
for us if the weakness or selfishness that had prevented him
from striking for his mother had also prevented him from
sailing to find his wife, or if the romantic adventure involved
in the voyage had had its counterpart in a war. But
James was not as simple as that. He knew the war would
not give him what he wanted; he thought the voyage
would. There was at least one other reason. He had heard
the gossip of the Court, the hints or the sneers at impotency.
He was determined to show that this was as much slander
as the false tales of his paternity. He had insisted on
making a public display of his freedom, and he would now
make as public a display as possible of his masculinity.
Whether he thought of it all for himself (certainly he
claimed to, "in the solitude of his own chamber") or
whether Maitland put it into his head first we do
not finally know. But he fell in love with the idea of a
hunting-party of so novel a kind, and he went—as secretly
as possible—to the ship, appointing a Council of Regency
and writing a letter to his people:

"In respect I know that the motion of my voyage will
be at this time diversely scanned, and misinterpreting may
be made as well to my dishonour as to the blame of innocents,

H

I have thought fit to leave this declaration, for resolving all good subjects, first, of the causes that moved me to undertake this voyage, then in the fashion in which I resolved to make the same. As to the causes, I have been generally blamed by all men for deferring my marriage so long, being alone, without father, mother, brother, or sister ; and yet a king not only of this realm, but heir apparent of another. This my nakedness made me weak, and mine enemies strong ; for one man is no man, as they speak, and where there is no hope of succession, it breeds contempt and disdain ; yea, the delay I have used hath begot in many a suspicion of impotency in me, as if I were a barren stock. These and other reasons moved me to hasten my marriage, from which I could yet have longer abstained, if the weal of my country could have permitted. I am not known to be rash in my weightiest affairs, neither am I so carried with passion as not to give place to reason ; but the treaty being perfected and the queen on her journey, when I was advertised of her stay by contrary winds, and that it was not like she should perfect her voyage this year, I resolved to make it on my part possible which was impossible on hers.

" The place where I first took this resolution was in Craigmillar, none of my council being present ; and as I took it by myself, so I bethought me of a way to follow the same. And first I advised to employ the earl of Bothwell in the voyage, in regard he is admiral ; but his preparations took so long a time, that I was forced to call the council, and send for the chancellor and justice-clerk, who were then in Lauder. When as they met, they found so many difficulties on sending forth a number of ships for the queen's convoy (for so I gave it out), and who should be the ambassadors, that I was compelled to avouch, if none should be found to go, I should go myself alone in a ship : adding, that if men had been as willing as became them, I would not have needed to be in these straits. This the chancellor taking to touch him (for he knew he had been slandered all that time of impeding my marriage) partly out of zeal to my service, and partly fearing that I should make good my word if no better way could be found, made offer to go himself in that service. This I embraced, keeping my intention from all men, because I thought it enough for me to put my foot in a ship when all things were ready, and from the chancellor himself (from whom I never kept any of my weightiest businesses), for two reasons. First, because if I had made him of my council in that purpose, he had been blamed for putting the same in my head (which had not been his duty), for it becomes no subject to give his prince advice in such matters ; withal considering what hatred and envy he sustained injustly for leading me by the nose as it were to all his appetites, as though I were an unreasonable creature, or a child that could do nothing of myself, I thought pity to heap more unjust slanders on his head. The other reason was, that I perceived it was for staying my journey that he made offer to go ; so was I assured, if he had known my purpose, he would either have stayed himself at home, or, thinking it too heavy a burden for him to undertake my convoy, he would have lingered so long as there should not have been a possibility for making the voyage. This I thought meet to declare (and upon my honour it is the truth), lest I should be esteemed an imprudent ass, that can do nothing of myself, and to save the innocency of that man from unjust reproaches. For my part, besides that which I have said, the shortness of the way, the surety of the passage, being clear of all sands, forelands, and such other perils, safe harbours in those parts, and no foreign fleets resorting in those seas, it is my pleasure that no man grudge at this my proceeding, but that all conform themselves to the directions I have given to be followed unto my return, which shall be within twenty days, wind and weather serving ; and if any shall contravene these, I will take it as a sufficient proof that he bears me no good will in his heart ; as, to the contrary, I will respect all that reverence my commandments in the best sort I may. Farewell."

On October 22 he set sail. There was a gale or two, but the King arrived safely in the end. He went to Oslo and, romantically " booted and spurred," entered the Queen's presence to make Thulean love. He made to kiss her ; the shocked princess declined. " It is not," she might have said in the words of her husband's playwright-to-be, " the custom of ladies in Denmark to kiss before they are married." But there also " nice customs curtsied to great monarchs." " After a few words privily spoken between his Majesty and her there passed between them familiarity and kisses." They were married, by a Scotch Presbyterian minister, David Lindsay, on November 23 ; after which they went south, by a long journey, to Elsinore, and spent the rest of the winter at the Court of Copenhagen. The King drank wine and intellect. He wrote to Scotland, saying that they were, " as is our custom, drinking and driving ower." But also he talked with theologians, and went to see the astronomer, Tycho Brahe, spent the day with him in learned conversations, and composed three poems ; of which one, since sonnets by kings to astronomers are rare, and since its opening deserves a better sequence than it altogether found, may be recorded :

> That onlie essence who made all of noght
> Our great and mightie Lord the life of all,
> When he in ordour everie thing hade broght
> At the creating of this earthlie ball,
> Then made he man at last. Thy raigne it shall
> Extend (quod Jehova) in everie cace
> Over all these breathing beasts that flatlie fall
> For humble hommage here before thy face.

He also pitch'd eache Planet in his place
And made them rulers of the ruling Lord
As heavenlie impes to governe bodies basse
Be subtle and celestiall sweete accord.
    Then great is Ticho who, by this his booke,
    Commandement doth over these commanders brooke.

At the end of April the royal party returned; the Queen landed in Scotland on the first of May. Lennox, Bothwell, Hamilton, and a crowd of lesser lords, received them at Leith and took them to Holyrood. The land had been remarkably peaceful while the King had been abroad, the person and seal of royalty being out of reach. But with his return disputes began to appear. There was trouble about the coronation. The King fixed it for a Sunday; the ministers objected. He demanded that the Queen should be anointed; they objected. The King overruled them on the first point and threatened to import one of his few bishops into the ceremony for the second. The ministers grudgingly gave way. Oil was less papistical than episcopacy. The Jews had oil, but not bishops, being in this respect closer to the pure Church of Christ than Catholics. The harlequinade swept up to the altar of marriage and majesty—" the Countess of Mar, having taken the Queen's right arm, and opened the craigs of her gown, Mr. Robert Bruce immediately poured forth upon those parts of her breast and arm of quhilk the clothes were removed, a bonny quantity of oil." It is necessary to remember that Mr. Robert Bruce, a great man of God, must have loathed doing it. Mr. Andrew Melville delivered a speech, in Latin and in verse, which the King tactfully, and probably in real admiration, at once insisted should be printed. Melville modestly assented, and received the congratulations of learned Protestants abroad upon his achievement.

The coronation was followed by a triumphal entry into

Edinburgh, also with a Latin address by Mr. John Russell. Little Master John Russell was enclosed in a silver globe affixed to the top of the gates, from which at the correct moment, dressed as an angel, he descended to her Majesty's feet, and laid before her the keys of the city. Within, forty-two young men received her, in white taffeta, black-vizarded like Moors, with gold chains dangling about them, who went dancing before her Grace all the way. Thus the Queen of Scotland came home.

It was not an unhappy marriage, though it could hardly be called happy. The Queen, like so many people, wanted to enjoy herself, and had to make the best of such opportunities as Scotland provided. She liked as much festivity and dancing as she could get; she liked as many splendid masculine courtiers as she could get; she liked, or would have liked, more of her own way with James than she ever got. James, who was never beguiled more than he chose by his Favourites, was even less beguiled by his wife. There were, of course, scandals; there were certainly quarrels. The King developed a habit of making the Queen ask him to advance any one whom he wished to advance, thus preventing any complaints against them afterwards. The Queen developed a strong tendency towards Catholicism, with which the King, except when it inconvenienced his politics, did not interfere. His later friend, Bishop Goodman, wrote: " The King of himself was a very chaste man, and there was little in the Queen to make him uxorious, yet they did live as well as man and wife could do, not conversing together. . . . He was never taxed or tainted with the love of any other lady."

Certainly, though he wrote one or two sets of verses, it is not ladies who have been in question. It is the gentlemen who have clouded the King's fame. Yet, when it comes to the actual question, it is extraordinarily difficult to feel sure of this homosexual reputation. It is clear that

he liked masculine Favourites rather than feminine.   It is
clear that he derived a strong emotional satisfaction from
the presence of masculine beauty.   He was always leaning
on it and patting and stroking it, embracing and kissing it,
sipping at its richness as he sipped continuously at his
strong French wines.   But, much as he sipped the wines, he
never drank deep and was never drunk, and it is not impossible that, much as he sipped at this other deep strength
of emotion, he never cared to get drunk on that either.   He
was certainly abnormal, and the tales may be true.   He was
a spiritual homosexualist if not a physical, and if it were not
physical it was his taste or his secret guard that kept him
from it.   But, for what they are worth, there are three
chief points against it : (i) the continual evidence of the
general report of his chastity ; (ii) the inclusion of sodomy
among the sins against which in the *Basilikon Doron* he
solemnly warned his son (it is true this proves nothing,
except in so far as James was too intelligent and too egotistical at once to offer the world such a joke as the world—
and his son—would have found the warning, on the other
hypothesis) ; (iii) the extreme friendship which grew up
between the last and greatest of the Favourites—George
Villiers—and the highly moral Prince Charles.   It is difficult to believe that Charles would have accepted Villiers
so profoundly and intimately if he had supposed that he
was serving, or had served, the King so.   But it is more
difficult to suppose that, had it been so, some enemy of
Villiers would not have seen to it that the Prince was told.
Villiers might have explained that it was all over.   But . . .
and so the argument can go on.   In effect, we must admit
an unusual delight in masculine beauty accompanied by
loose behaviour and wanton speech.   Beyond that James
locks up his coffer.   It is one of the most annoying things
about James that in everything it is the very last secret
which he hid so carefully and so finally away.

The " hot and holy matter " of his marriage, as the
English agent called it, having been safely established,
James turned his attention, while yet his country was in
moderate peace, to those who had sought to stay her
journeys. For his safe return with her had been a spiritual
triumph as well as an earthly, and now there were to be
proper reprisals upon the King's enemies. The pardon
which James was often willing to extend to the leaders
of earthly treason must not reach to the leaders of those
who had denied their God. In this he need not fear the
hostility of the Kirk ; long before he had laid any but a
baby's hand on sword and sceptre, the witch hunt had been
raised in Scotland. Now in his years of discretion, the
King headed it. Witchcraft was an abominable sin. " I
have been occupied," he said in the June of the next year,
" these three quarters of a year for the sifting out of them
that are guilty herein." His activity had been quickened
by the activities of the sorcerers against him and his bride
at sea. By December certain of them—one warlock and
three witches—had been sought out and set in ward. John
Fian was a schoolmaster, and it was he who was first
brought to trial ; the other three followed him—Agnes
Sampson (" matron-like, grave, and settled in her answers ") in January, Barbara Napier in May, Euphemia
M'Calyan in June. The last two certainly were of good
family ; all of them were of education and standing.
Between them they revealed all that had happened that
summer when they were working against the King.

In all some thirty-nine persons were chiefly concerned :
three companies or covens. In a bakehouse in North
Berwick one day there gathered eight or nine of the devoted
crew, with John Fian their leader, and sent to other wise
women at Leith a letter, directed to a certain Marion
Lenchap, which said : " Ye sall warne the rest of the sisteris
to raise the wind this day, att eleavin houris, to stay the

Queen's cuming in Scotland " ; it assured them that the
others also would do their part, and when they all met there
should be a universal storm over the sea.   To achieve this
they received from the hands of the Accursed One a cat,
which, going down to the shore in procession and singing,
they flung far into the sea, whereupon the storm indeed
came up and the Queen's ship was almost cast away.   Also,
when the King's Highness himself set out for Denmark, the
Accursed One promised his servants that he would raise a
mist so that the King would be driven to England, but this
promise was never fulfilled.   He bitterly inveighed against
the King one night when the hateful assembly was con-
vened in the Kirk of North Berwick, and being asked by
certain in that dark gathering the cause of this especial
hatred against the person of his Highness, answered : " By
reason the King is the greatest enemy he hath in the world."

Since these and other attempts upon the royal voyage
failed, further means had to be used.   The whole three
covens gathered together " on Lambnes-evin " in the year
1590, between Musselburgh and Prestonpans, and the
Devil himself came to them in the likeness of the Black
Man.   He gathered out of the whole a certain nine, choosing
those most meet for the abominable service, and set them
in one company, leaving the other and inferior persons in
another company.   Then that wise and brave matron,
Agnes Sampson, propounded to him and to all the destruction of his Highness's person, saying : " We have a turn
to do, and we would fain be at it if we could ; therefore help
us to it."   The Devil answered that he would do what he
could, but it would be a long work, for he would be thwarted ;
but he bade them make an image of wax, and bring it to
him that he might lay enchantment on it ; also he bade
them hang and roast a toad, and gather its excretions, mix
other poisons with it, and lay the complex venom where it
might drop on the King's head or body at his going out or

coming in. Also he commanded them to procure linen belonging to the King—whose name was pronounced always in Latin—in which the magical image might for a while be wrapped, that when it in its turn was roasted and melted before the fire the King might more easily waste with it.

This they did, and in another night delivered a waxen image, wrapped in a royal linen cloth, to the infernal high priest, who having pronounced words over it returned it to Agnes Sampson, and she to her next neighbour, and so round the circle, each saying as it was passed from hand to sacrilegious hand : " This is King James the Sixth, ordained to be consumed at the instance of a noble man, Francis Earl Bothwell." For the purpose of all the conjuration was that another might rule in the King's place and the ward of Scotland pass into the hands of the Devil's man. But by some misadventure, from which, it would seem, even the hosts of hell were not free, the image was never used, and indeed at a great meeting on All Hallows Night there was tumult among the sorcerers. Then, in the churchyard by the same Kirk of North Berwick, there was music and dancing, when Gelie Duncan played on a trump, and with muffled face John Fian led the ring, and after him, endlong through that place of graves, went the springing Barbara, and Agnes, and Agnes's daughters, and all the plighted company to the number of seven score. Afterwards they gathered within the Kirk, and there started up in the pulpit the black and mighty figure of the Apostate, holding a black book, crying to them to be good servants to him and he would be good master to them. So strong was the spell of the solemn Kirk and the hellish music and the dreadful dance, and the knowledge of the eternal perdition over which all the revel went on, that the poor human creatures grew even wilder than their Master who stood there, calling on them. The image had been given back to him at the previous convention, and now they cried

for it.   Effie M'Calyan remembered it, and Robert Grierson
shouted for it—the image, the image that should have
been roasted, the image that should have been roasted and
melted for the melting and undoing of the King's person.
And in the wild lit darkness the covens cried and shrieked
and wailed that they were beguiled, and the High Master
in the pulpit soothed them and promised them they should
have it the next time, and for that reason the next time
should be the sooner, but it was not yet ready, not quite
ready.   The women especially entreated him : " four honest-
like women were very earnest and instant to have it." At last
the monstrous black answering promised that it should soon
be got into the hands of Barbara and Effie, and with that the
assembly were content.   But, it seems, before ever the Devil
kept his word, the King's servants laid hold on those four
lesser leaders to carry them to the justice of the King.

Such, at least, with much more, was the tale that in
their separate examinations—two after grievous torments
—they told.   James himself came to be present, not un-
courageously to his own feeling.   His curiosity drove him
to experience exquisite thrills of danger and fear by causing
Gelie Duncan to play the dance of the witches in his
presence.   John Fian was brought first to trial, in the
course of which a strange thing happened.   He was examined, he was tortured, he confessed ; he was relegated to
solitary ward.   The next day he was full of a tale that the
Devil had appeared to him to tempt him—clothed in black,
carrying a white wand.   Fian renounced him : " I have
listened too much unto thee."   The Devil answered :
" Once ere thou die thou shalt be mine," snapped his
white stick, and vanished.   All that day Fian was left in
solitude to recover from the torment, and called much on
God, with great penitence and prayers.   The darkness of
the night came down on his cell, and in the morning when
the guard came to him—in the morning of the Holy Inno-

cents, when in the wilds of the North some few masses
were still said for the conversion of the King—he was gone.
James heard the news, and ordered " a hot and hard pursuit," by which, in due course, the fugitive was discovered
and brought in. But he had changed. In the King's
presence he was examined touching his escape ; he would
say nothing. He was re-examined concerning points in
his earlier signed confession ; he utterly denied and renounced it. " Everything he had said was false, and now
he would say nothing." The King, sitting there with the
lords of the Council about him, looked on the wretch and
knew what had happened ; in that supernatural absence
he had met again the supernatural Prince of the abyss and
made new covenants. The supernatural evil that James
feared and defied lifted itself in that moment in his own
soul ; vividly it lived in the chamber, no more about John
Fian, broken schoolmaster, but in the hearts and faces of
his judges, achieving its end (as the habit of supernatural
things, good or evil, is) by the apparent rejection of itself.
The King called for more torments. In that presence they
brought them, they pierced and twisted and rent him, " and
notwithstanding all these grievous pains and cruel torments,
he would not confess anythings." Silent and devoted he
remained, like that Iago for whom Shakespeare, if he
read *Newes from Scotland* (it was published in 1591), where
the tale was given, might from him have taken a thought :

> Demand me nothing ; what you know you know,
> From this time forth I never will speak word.

He was put to death. Agnes Sampson, also tortured,
confessed ; Effie confessed, apparently without torture.
Barbara Napier, by an extraordinary chance of justice or
injustice, was declared innocent. The King was not
present at her examination, and he caused most of the
jurors to be tried for giving a false verdict ; they put
themselves into the King's will and were pardoned.

CHAPTER SIX

The Falling and Rising

PLEASANT as it is to think that Barbara Napier escaped
the slaughter, it is necessary to understand that the King's
anger had a mortal as well as an immortal cause. By the
time the trials were finished, if not before, he felt himself
in the presence of witchcraft certainly but also of sedition,
and he suspected that the jurors who declared her innocent
were her deliberate partners in the lesser, if not in the
greater, sin. The means of the conjurations might lie in
the courts of hell, but their cause walked in the palaces of
Scotland, and its name was Francis Hepburn, Earl of
Bothwell. Barbara had hinted at him ; Agnes Sampson
had named him. The absolving jurors were likely to be
art and part of the same conspiracy ; clients of Bothwell,
secretly standing for him against the King. He came to
their trial, and from his seat of judgment he made a speech
in which he denounced the want of political virtue in Scotland. Men (he said) set themselves more for friend than
for justice. " This corruption here bairns suck at the pap."
Whatever evil was charged upon a man his friends sought
first to keep him from arrest and then to secure his escape.
He asserted his own innocence in such things ; he dared
accusation and judgment. " And as I have begun so I
mean to go forward ; not because I am James Stuart and
can command so many thousands of men, but because
God hath made me a king and judge, to judge righteous
judgments." Witchcraft was an abominable sin ; it was
maleficium or *veneficium*, worthy of death if practised
against any of the people, and the like, at least, if against

the King. " Not that I fear death, for I thank God I dare
in a good cause abide hazard."

He seems to have let the erring jurors escape. His
eyes were fixed on that other figure behind them, and he
had other evidence. Another dealer in witchcraft had been
seized, a man called Richard Graeme, who also had made
confession involving the earl. Another waxen image had
been shaped for the King's destruction, and hung in
magical ceremonies between the body of a fox and the head
of a young calf. Grotesque and imbecile as the antic is,
it is also bestial and malevolent. The King's body was to
be envenomed by the spiritual power of evil, and to waste
with the wasting image. It is, no doubt, laughable. The
King, in that age, with his own convinced beliefs, did not find
it quite so laughable. " In this year," wrote James Melville,
nephew of the great Andrew, in 1591, " Bothwell lost the
King's favour, the quhilk being excessively indulgent towards
him divers years, turned at last in implacable hatred."

The dance of strong and beautiful figures around the
person of the King becomes, therefore, during the next
few years, a more sinister thing. The points of the swords
are directed towards him, and wave dangerously near his
heart. Still he avoids them. He retreats, and they lose
direction ; he advances, and they give way. The two chief
figures, besides his own, in the whirl of steel, are those of
Huntly and Bothwell. The murmur of Latin rises from
the prayers of heaven and hell about him, but either way
meant to snare him in alien and invisible cords. The
induction of that dance had taken place in the brief rebellion
ere James had set out for Denmark ; it was now resumed
and prolonged. Gordon and Hepburn had been allied,
and were opposed, and were to be again allied, in the strange
movements of that curious dance. But the aim of Hepburn
and Gordon, allied or opposed, was always the same—the
prisoning of the person of the King

It is to be remembered that such a seizure was not necessarily regarded as an act of rebellion. Rebellion and dethronement were unconstitutional and sinful. But the capture of Majesty and its control were almost constitutional. The King highly disapproved of it, but rather as a solecism than as a sin. Part, perhaps, of the scandal caused, later on, by the execution of Essex in England, and part of the blame laid on Francis Bacon, was because general opinion thought that a constitutional act had been treated as unconstitutional. It was one of the disadvantages of single person government that whoever held the person held the government—supposing the person could be dominated as well as detained. Detention and domination were just permissible ; rebellion was not. Essex had intended one, and suffered for the other. In England the attempt was rare ; in Scotland, frequent. It was therefore natural for James, however ungraciously, to recognize such attempts as part of the dangers and difficulties of his exalted office.

James and Bothwell and Huntly were not the only dancers in that complex measure. The General Assembly of the Kirk looms on one side ; the Catholic might of France or Spain—but mostly Spain—on the other. Other visible and invisible partners slide in and out—devils and wizards and spies and Jesuits. The crowned and ageing person of Elizabeth appears sometimes ; more often the small hunchback person of Robert Cecil. The figures of the dance become more and more complicated as intrigues multiply, but always in the midst is the solitary figure of the King. Little by little, the King lost almost everything. He is at his nadir—he is all but a continual fugitive, without safe possessions or sure rest or anything but his own ghostly vision of the double crown. And then, at first so softly, and then so suddenly, there comes the change. The King is King of Scotland. His enemies fly or fall ; the feuds die down ; the King's writ begins to run. There is one final

spectacular outrage, and all becomes still. Out of that
stillness there rises at last the sound of the trumpets
announcing the departure southward of the King of England,
Scotland, and Ireland, while Cecil waits for him at Theobalds.

The dark course is lit for us by certain incidents ;
certainly the whole can be traced, but the cartography
would need volumes. Without such length we can see it
lit up here and there, by torches in Holyrood, a burning
house near Edinburgh, the sun shining on a ship hidden
among islands or an army marching northward or on
crowds thronging in the streets of Edinburgh. The murder
of the Earl of Murray, the affair of the Spanish blanks,
the triumph of Bothwell, the royal conquest of Edinburgh
—these are the chief moments in which the life of those
years is seen. After the trial of the sorcerers, the King
caused Bothwell to be seized and warded in Edinburgh
Castle, that he might answer to the accusations of witchcraft. The brief while that he remained there is like the
pause before the dance begins. Soon, and certainly by
treachery, he escaped as John Fian had escaped ; more
fortunate than his tool, he fled to his Border holds and there
for some months remained. In the December he returned.
The Court had retired when, on a winter night of 1591,
two days after Christmas, he came with a band of Border
ruffians and of broken men whom he had been entertaining
in his southern holds. They got into the palace at first
almost unobserved ; then one of the captains lost time in
attempting to set free certain prisoners, and the alarm
went out. The Chancellor Maitland heard a boy at a
distance calling something about a tumult of men, and
barely in time barricaded himself in an inner room. The
King took refuge in a tower. The doors of the royal
apartments were locked and barred. The Borderers surged
on ; an attempt was made to burn down the King's door ;
hammers crashed upon the Queen's. By then it was too

late. A gentleman of the Court had already hastened to
the Provost of Edinburgh. The common bell was rung—
that sinister sound which peals out again and again during
these years. The citizens, led by the magistrates, came,
and the raiders found themselves attacked from the rear.
Bothwell called them off, cut through his assailants, and
was away, leaving behind him a few prisoners who were
promptly hanged. The King, going later to St. Giles to
return thanks, was warned by the preacher, John Craig,
that as a warning against his religious negligence, " God
had made a noise of crying and forehammers to come
to his own doors." James wanted to get in an answer ;
he tried to keep the congregation by beginning to speak.
But by accident or deliberation Craig did not notice. His
duty was done ; he went his way, and the irritated James
returned to Holyrood, to make use of Huntly by sending
him with a commission against Bothwell, with " letters of
fire and sword."

It was ostensibly from this commission that James
was immediately involved in an outrage upon the other
side. There was between the House of Huntly and the
House of Murray a bitter feud. The Earl of Murray was
young and beautiful—" the bonnie Earl of Moray," " comely,
gentle, brave, and of a great stature and strength of body."
He was the son-in-law of the Regent Murray, who years
before had lowered the pride of the Huntlys and executed
the present lord's father. Other great clans supported one
side or the other, subject always to the needs of their chieftains at any moment. In December, Murray had left his
northern princedoms and ridden south to his castle of
Donibristle, near Edinburgh, for one or more or all of
various reasons. It was said, with truth, that his friend,
Lord Ochiltree, also a Stuart, was engaged upon an effort
to achieve a reconciliation between him and Huntly. It
was said, possibly with truth, that he was in touch with

Bothwell, and ready (if necessary) to carry off the King to safe keeping, once Bothwell had seized him in that Christmas raid. How far he and Bothwell would have agreed over the disposal of the sacred person is another matter. It was said, finally and with least possibility, that he was a favourite with the young Queen, and that this was known to the jealous mind of the King. Huntly, still to the anxiety of those of the pure religion, was known to be in close attendance upon the King in Edinburgh. It was not then known that he had already signed a bond with Maitland (now Lord Thirlstane) for the destruction of Murray and three others, including Argyle. The Chancellor was to have lands ; the earl was to have blood.

Bothwell was foiled ; Murray, still suspected, lingered in his house. The Chancellor was said to have procured a warrant from the King for his arrest, and the appointment of Huntly to execute it. It was folly or wisdom, if it were so ; and if wisdom, then the greater folly. On February 7 the King went out hunting ; the Lord Huntly, with forty horsemen, went with him. On the way he rode up to the King, telling him he had news of certain accomplices of Bothwell near at hand and was to seize them. The King forbade him to pass the ferry. Huntly promised obedience and immediately disobeyed ; he and his men rode fast to Donibristle. Murray and his Stuarts saw them come ; they shut themselves in, were summoned to surrender, and refused. About the house the battle opened. The Stuarts, firing from within, slew some of Huntly's people. The February night came down upon the besiegers piling corn ricks against the house and firing them. The fire took hold. Murray came charging out with his men. The Sheriff of Murray was slain. The earl, though one of his hands was so burnt that he could not hold a weapon, burst through his enemies and ran down to the shore. His helmet plume was burning ; it is said his long hair also

caught. The men of Huntly rushed after that dreadful
comet. They caught up with him ; they stabbed at him.
Huntly hesitated ; one of his men cursed him and bade
him strike and be part of the deed. On the edge of the
water, in the darkness lit by the burning house, Huntly
struck with his dagger at the beautiful face under the
burning plume. Murray, already mortally wounded, panted
out, " Ye have spoiled a better face than your own," and died.

When the murder was known, the outcry was dreadful.
Within short distance of Edinburgh itself the Papist earl
had committed slaughter, nor could any one tell how
deeply the King was involved. He took the deed very
heavily, but again the shadow pursues him. It was
rumoured that he had forbidden boats to cross the ferry,
lest Murray should be forewarned ; tales went about of the
favour that Anne of Denmark had shown to the dead
man. James, with his Council, removed Huntly from all
his commissions of lieutenancy. Huntly by now had
ridden north. The bodies of his victims were exposed in
Leith Church, and the mother of the earl appealed for
vengeance. His bloody shirt, raised on a spear, went
through the north. The King was loth to act. He had
no reason to feel Murray's murder more than any other of
the outrages that daily filled the land ; in fact, though
it would be unfair to say he felt it less, it is probably true
that he never cared overmuch about the slaying of one of
his mighty nobles by another. He had brought them
peace and they would not have it. He was the King, and
Murray was but one of those many subjects who suffered
in life or goods because of the weakness of the King. That
he was a great person made little difference to James, who
could harden his heart well enough, and in fact had had
to do so often enough before. Nor did he care to please
Pure Religion by attacking Huntly, while Pure Religion
refused to censure its own friend Bothwell. Huntly entered

himself in ward ; there was a mild investigation and he
was pardoned. He was compelled, however, to remain in
the north, and the King was left to face his enemies alone.
The unpopular Chancellor (though no one yet knew of the
bond) was thrown over, and retired from Court. It was
not enough. The Queen, who hated Maitland, the Kirk,
who hated Huntly, Bothwell, who wanted power, Argyle,
Atholl, and others, who wanted blood, were massed against
him. He soothed the Queen and (more reluctantly) the
Kirk. He assented to all the extreme demands of the
ministers. The Estates met in April, and defined the
Church of God in her power and apostolic beauty. All acts
against her discipline and liberty were to be repealed ;
her jurisdiction was to be completely enforced. Religion,
heresy, excommunication, deprivation, were delivered into
its hands. Bishops, in so far as there were any, were to
be utterly abolished. Idolatry was to be utterly rooted
out. Christ, through his ministers, was to be imperial lord
of Scotland, walking on the blood of the ministers' foes.

Bothwell was formally forfeited. In June with a
hundred men he raided Falkland, again to be driven off
by the country folk. The King dared hardly sleep twice in
the same place. He was exhorted to humble himself. He
was not sufficiently humbled to admit his responsibility
for Murray's murder or intermit his laughter at the ridiculous in Christ's Kirk. One day, as he was going to look at
his hounds, he was intercepted by a young woman, the
daughter of a saddler of Aberdeen. Her name was Helen
Guthrie, and she was much oppressed by a sense of Scottish
sin. She could get no peace for brooding on the iniquity
that was abroad—swearing and Sabbath-breaking and
worse. She had a paper full of it, and she thrust it
upon the King. James took it. He began to read, and
then he began to laugh. He laughed so much that he could
hardly stand, and yet in the midst of laughing he cursed

—horrible oaths, or what seemed so to Helen Guthrie. Shocked and religiously indignant, she rebuked him. He controlled himself sufficiently to ask her if she were a prophetess. She said she was a poor simple servant of God, and wished to make him a servant of God also ; it was his duty to punish vice—especially murder—and her duty to remind him of his. Still laughing and still swearing, James caused her to be taken to the Queen.

Such incidents are not so significant as they would be in the case of a monarch more removed from his subjects ; there was always something of the patriarchal " father of his people " about James, even in his youth. He desired to be open to approach, to judge, like the king in Browning, " sitting in the sun." He found gaiety as he could, once in a singular small idyll of love. John Wemyss, younger of Logie, a gentleman of the Bedchamber and a favourite servant of James, had been discovered in dealings with Bothwell, and promptly put under guard. But he and the Queen's principal Maid of the Chamber, Margaret Twinstan, herself a Dane, were wonderfully in love. One night, when the King and Queen had retired, Margaret came to the guard and told them the King wished to question their prisoner ; they were to bring him. Thinking no ill, they obeyed. They all came to the door of the royal chamber, and there Margaret bade the guard wait. She and John disappeared within. She took him stealthily to the window, and showed him a rope hanging without. Their Majesties slept ; the lovers parted. John escaped down the rope, and the waiting maid stayed to wait for the day. In the morning the guard discovered the trick ; Margaret was haled before the King. But James laughed and forgave her ; he forgave her lover also ; happily, in that mirth, they were married. The less romantic result was that every one felt a King so easy to lovers was not to be feared, and many of all classes became friendly with Bothwell.

It is, therefore, the other picture that is more central—the King on his way to his hounds, with his few gentlemen, intercepted by the saddler's daughter. James might wish to listen, but he did not wish to have no alternative to listening. The saddler's daughter rebukes him, and in angry laughter he is compelled to hear her. Around them an anarchy of brigandage and murder fills the country, and over it loom the awful pulpits, from which by November a more sinister conclusion was sounding. The King heard it, and was still helpless. " The King," they said, " might be excommunicated, in case of contumacy and disobedience to the Will of God." And none of the faithful need pay allegiance to an excommunicate King. He was all but an exile in his own land. It seemed that there was nothing he could do—except avoid Bothwell. The double crown existed in his heart but there was hardly a shadow of one upon his hair. Yet at the end of the year, rising from an incident which looked at first as if it would cause the complete overthrow of his temporal kingdom by the Presbyterian, the crown began gently to shine once more.

That incident was the affair of the Spanish blanks. On December 27, 1592, Mr. Andrew Knox, minister of Paisley, " acting on information received " (from English agents), set out with a band of Glasgow students for the Cumbrae Islands, which lie in the mouth of the Clyde. There they found a ship, upon which, when they had entered, was a certain George Ker, brother of Lord Newbottle, with his baggage. The baggage was seized and searched ; it held letters from the Catholic earls to Spain, and—what appeared more shockingly dangerous to the Presbyterian champions —a number of blank sheets, signed by Huntly, Errol, and Angus.[1] The blanks were to be filled up with the terms

---

[1] The Angus of the Raid of Ruthven, " the ministers' King," as James called him, had died in 1588. The new earl was a Catholic. So the weight of religion swung from year to year.

of a treaty between Philip of Spain and the lords signatory. Mr. Andrew Knox was thanked—and on behalf of Elizabeth thanked by Sir Robert Bowes, who all this time was indefatigably supporting the cause and assisting the conspiracies of the Protestant party. Ker was brought to Edinburgh. The King sent orders that he was to be made to confess, even by torture if necessary. At least a beginning of torture was applied. Ker admitted that there were negotiations proceeding for the descent of a Spanish army and for its support by the Catholic Scottish lords. The King's person was to be held at the disposal of the Spanish Majesty.

But there was also found among the letters and the blanks a paper in James's hand—a memorandum on the possibility of Spanish aid. He had noted down its advantages and disadvantages ; he had leaned, as might have been expected, to the view that a much better method would be for himself, when sometime in the future he had got Scotland settled, to do something by himself, with the aid perhaps of some small number of men, certainly of some money. The King and the Catholic earls were personally sympathetic. But Huntly was not a king, and what he called Spanish counsel James called Spanish captivity. Nor was James ever quite certain how far the ardour of the True Faith (as of the Pure Religion) might go in dispossessing him. It was why Ker was put to the question—besides the satisfaction so stern an inquiry caused to the Kirk.

This document, by some intelligent person, was at the time suppressed. Angus, who was in Edinburgh, was put into ward. Huntly and Errol were ordered to put themselves in ward. They did nothing of the kind ; presently Angus escaped to join them. It was this continual escape of suspected persons that raised more suspicions between Kirk and King. James interviewed Andrew Melville and

other ministers, and came to a kind of understanding that
if he were firm with the Catholics, the Kirk should be firm
with Bothwell. He gave audience to Bowes, and told him
harshly what he thought of Elizabeth's harbourage of
Bothwell. He marched north to Aberdeen, rather against
the will of the great nobles who were with him, who might
have their own feuds among themselves but, in a general
way, never wanted the Prince to interfere, and were wholly
opposed to royal confiscations, which set undesirable
precedents. The Catholic lords retreated to Caithness.
James, after a show of firmness and confiscations, came
back to Edinburgh to interview a new envoy from Elizabeth,
Lord Burgh, whom he warned that if the Queen went on
supporting Bothwell, " I shall be enforced to join with her
greatest enemies for my own safety." He had, to a very
small extent, had his own way.

Between February and July the surge of the restless
ocean continued. Maitland came back to Edinburgh and
retired again. The Master of Gray came back and was
half in favour. Even Arran was called to secret interviews.
In the Parliament Mr. David Makgill, the King's Advocate-
General, presented reasons why the northern earls could
not be prosecuted by law—insufficiency of evidence, etc.
On July 22 in the pulpit, Mr. John Davison, a notable
preacher, entreated the Lord that " the King by some
sanctified plagues might be turned again to God." On
Tuesday, July 24, the Lord, working in a mystery, graciously
acceded to the prayer ; whether Mr. Davison knew of the
answer before he made his prayer we cannot say.

On that Tuesday morning Lady Atholl brought two
men down a private passage that led from the Gowrie
house in Edinburgh to the palace. One was Bothwell ;
the other was a Mr. James Colville—one of the secret
agents of Cecil. The three slipped into the palace and up
to the royal apartments. Lady Atholl led the way to the

King's antechamber, went across and locked the door
that led to the Queen's room, and hid the two raiders
behind the arras. There they stayed while in the courts
below guards were set by their confederates, Lennox and
Atholl himself. A curious conjuncture of motives had
brought the new plotters into harmony. Lennox hated
Maitland and feared his return to power. The Atholls were
bent on vengeance for Murray. Bothwell was bent on
glory and power. Colville was acting for the English
government. The whole clan of Stuart were up, with the
English, to seize and master the royal chief of the clan.

James woke. Moved by distressed nature he got up
and went into his retiring-room—half dressed, his hose
loose, and his points undone. He heard suddenly a noise
in the antechamber and came out, clutching at his clothes.
Bothwell, his sword drawn, sprang before him, Colville at
his side. Bothwell (so he said) exclaimed mockingly : "Lo,
my good bairn, you that have given out I sought your life,
it is now in this hand." James, sending out a cry of
" Treason ! " made for the door into the Queen's room and
found it locked. He turned back on the intruders. The
memory of something more than rebellion shook him—the
thought of North Berwick and the black man. He shuffled
forward—the absurd creature in his absurd disarray—and
he cried out : " What do ye seek ? do ye seek my soul ? Ye
shall not have my soul. Strike, if ye dare, false traitors ! "
It was one of those not infrequent moments when the
King ought to have lost his head ; he had wept when he
was sixteen—he was meant to weep and to cower now.
But he had wept from rage then, and now he raged without
weeping. Lennox and Atholl came into the room ; Bothwell and Colville knelt down, a mocking homage. The
King verbosely stormed on. " Kneel not, kneel not . . .
ye pretend ye are come to stand trial for witchcraft ; look
ye like suppliants ? . . . Am I not your anointed King ?

. . . I will not live a prisoner and dishonoured." He sat himself down on a chair. " Strike, if ye dare." Bothwell protested loudly ; he was loyal, he asked but for a fair trial. He flung his long hair back, and offered his sword-hilt to the King. The lords interceded for him. The King rose, and led Bothwell apart to a window. In the court below some of the citizens began to gather ; a few gentlemen of the Court cried up to the King to know how he did. James told them all was well ; they could retire, and return later. He came to an agreement with the earl. Bothwell should be brought to trial immediately ; all his offences to be forgiven ; his enemies to be dismissed. Meanwhile, however, he should retire from the Court. He did. He rode hastily to Berwick, where he interviewed the English warden, to whom, with messages of gratitude to Elizabeth, he announced his expectation of becoming Lord-Lieutenant of the whole country. He then rode on to Durham, arriving at the Deanery about three on August 2, where for a few days he made himself a guest of the Dean, Dr. Tobie Mathew, the father of Bacon's friend.

To the Dean the exultant free-lance poured out his story, his hopes, his certainties. He gave him a long and extraordinary description of how he had assured the King of his own devotion to Elizabeth, " the ornament of the Christian world." With Elizabeth's help, he was certain he could " manage the estate about the King." Splendid and voluble, " nothing dainty to discourse his humour or any good quality he hath," he poured the flood of his talk over the English dignitary. The Dean was a little unhappy ; he wrote Burleigh a long account, but added " that in case it be not lawful (as in mine own poor opinion it is nothing convenient) for me to have talk with him or any from him " he hoped Burleigh would tell him so. Bothwell himself wrote a voluble letter to Elizabeth, beginning "Most Renowned Empress," and went back to Scotland.

But if Bothwell was voluble, so was James; if Bothwell was arrogantly confident, James was sublimely certain ; if Bothwell was overbearing, James was unyielding. To be attacked by two parties at once left him still with the single, but important, advantage that if he were taken by the one he could, sooner or later, look to be rescued by the other. By his agreement with Bothwell certain lords were dismissed from Court, among them the Catholic Lord Home. Bothwell returned and was triumphantly acquitted of any connection with witchcraft. But meanwhile the King had secretly arranged with Home a plan of escape. It failed ; there was a fierce interview between the King and the earl. It lasted, with intervals, for two days. The King refused concessions. Sir Robert Bowes came in, and made speeches of innocent astonishment ; the King snubbed him. The preachers were brought in, and made efforts at mediation. The King at last consented to pardon Bothwell and his accomplices, and to bar his own friends from the Court till the Parliament in November, on the condition that Bothwell also withdrew.

James, in those two days' obstinacy, came very near to victory, and it is notable that it was precisely against Bothwell that the victory was won. Bothwell was an adventurous and popular figure. But he had no beliefs from which he drew strength, and more than natural violence was needed to override the King. Andrew Melville could shake, if not terrify him. But Andrew Melville believed—probably erroneously—that he stood for Christ. So, also probably erroneously, did the King. They fought in another world as well as this, a world in which Bothwell had never entered, and the resources of which the King felt to be at his disposal. No doubt, had he chosen, he could have dissembled and procrastinated

longer with Bothwell. But he did not choose. The memory
of Satan was too vivid. He got rid of the earl, and in
a month had called a convention of lords at Stirling, at
which he declared all his promises to have been extorted
by force.

In some hour or two during the process of the affair,
James put his anger and his desire into three sonnets.
Two of them do but lament the triumph of " perjured
infamous foxes " and the infection of the heart of Justice.
Somewhere within this decade Shakespeare was shaping
similar ideas, also in a sonnet—" Tir'd with all these, for
restful death I cry." But the King's other poem inquires
into his own state of mind, and reflects what he hoped was
happening : courage and wisdom were united within him.

A faschious [troublesome] fight does force my freest minde
Betwixt two valiant champions I persave—
The one trewe courage, rightlie is defin'd ;
The other wisedome, temperat and grave.
Thy selfe undanted showe, quoth courage brave,
Bot wisedome wishes for a while to staye.
Quoth courage, rather die then live a slave.
Quoth wisedome true, if so should be for aye,
Bot wracke thee not upon thy selfe, I praye,
Since keeping up thy selfe bot for a space
On others sine thy courage kithe [show] thou may ;
Quoth courage, lingring is a great disgrace.
    Of all these straits the best is out of doubte
    That courage wise, and wisedome shoulde be stoute.

By the end of the year he could feel that, through wise
courage and stout wisdom, he had checked the Catholics
and thwarted Bothwell. He pursued his devious way
between the two religious hosts, both of them angry that
for all his soft words he seemed no nearer their separate
desires. The Catholics saw him always hovering just outside the fold of Papist lambs ; the Kirk saw him always
straying dangerously near the lair of Papistical wolves.
Fold or lair, he never entered it. He produced an " act of

abolition," by which all his subjects were to become Presbyterians or to leave the realm, in which case, however, they were still to enjoy their lands and revenues.   Jesuits were to be sent away ; orthodox chaplains to be received into the Catholic households.   The matter of the Spanish blanks was to be dropped.   It pleased no one.   Bothwell made a final attempt on Edinburgh and failed.   He was thereafter thrown over by Elizabeth, and compelled to turn to intrigues with the northern earls.   The Kirk was shocked and alarmed by this news.   The King saw his opportunity. With the assistance of all true King's men, he would make an end of one party.   He called on the Kirk for support, which the Kirk reluctantly gave.   They heartily distrusted the King, but when the King was doing as they had begged him and definitely marching against the Scarlet Woman, they could not very well hold back.   Anxiety nevertheless possessed them.   The King collected Andrew Melville and carried him off to see the fighting between Christ and Antichrist.   The fighting, however, was mostly over before James, Melville, and the royal army arrived.   Argyle had advanced and been defeated by Huntly ; he brought the news himself to the King.   The annoyed James, still more annoyed at finding from the usual intercepted letter that Huntly had been calling his advance " a gowk's storm " (=an April shower), pushed on.   The earls, as usual, fled.   But this time James did more damage : he blew up a number of strongholds ; he appointed Lennox as his lieutenant ; he even left a small body of troops in the north.   He took oaths from all the northern lords who came in, and at last returned to Edinburgh, leaving a broken north behind him.

Huntly and Errol, despite the appeals of the Jesuit fathers, fled to the Continent, where, for some months, they remained.   But either they found the going up and down others' stairs too bitter, or the wilds of Caledonia called them too piercingly. They turned; they returned. Quietly, without any show or tumult, they slipped, in 1596, again into Scotland. Lady Huntly bore their submissive petitions to the King.

The King by now must have been growing exhilarated by his victories. He had overthrown the witch-consorting Bothwell, and mastered the Jesuit-befriended Huntly. There remained the greatest, the noisiest, and the fiercest of his enemies—the Kirk of Christ. He was thirty. He had become less and less inclined to be preached down. A prospective master of two realms, an actual master of theological learning, must occasionally have his own way. He was friendly enough with some of the ministers, but at last he had begun, wrote the English agent, " in severity to rule like a King." Mr. James Melville, the great Andrew's nephew, tried to conciliate him, but in vain ; he had to record that " as I was thus about to win the King as in me lay to the Kirk, so was he in winning of me to the Court ; and when on other side all meanes was usit and bathe keppit our groundes, without grait vantage, ane of another, we relented and fearlie reteired."

The uncle was of less sympathetic mettle. He preferred the roar of the Lion of Judah, and James had heard enough of it. When the Papist earls were known to be again in the country, and the King still showed a wicked disinclination to root them out, the Kirk appointed a kind of Committee of Public Safety, consisting of four ministers from the four quarters of the country, who were to sit in continuous session with the Presbytery of Edinburgh. They were to be watchful against " the farther dealing of the adversary," and to consult with the " best affected noblemen and burghers " concerning " religion and common peace." Unfortunately, there were no longer many well-affected noblemen. The generation of Presbyterian stalwarts, such as Murray and Morton, had long ago passed, generally by

violence. James Melville lamented that there were none
among the nobility with whom he could " communicate his
mind anent public affairs, let be to have a dealing with in
action." The nobility found that lands and the secure
holding of lands depended more and more on the jest of the
King, and less on the oratory of the Lord's people. Great
families had weakened each other by their feuds. James
could still, perhaps, do little, but he could, at any moment,
strike for the moment. He could call on the lesser gentlemen
and break the greater, as he had broken the Catholic North.
He turned his attention, perhaps without any lucid intention,
to Presbyterian Edinburgh. When that fell, he was King.

In September the General Assembly sent a deputation
to James to beg him to take measures concerning the Popish
lords. It was known that the King liked to be approached
mildly and smoothly, and James Melville was therefore
appointed to speak. James Stuart interrupted him irrit-
ably. He " crabbitly querrelled " their meeting ; he
accused them of spreading fear where no fear was. The
other James began to answer, still mildly ; but the roar of
the lion drowned him. Andrew burst in—" in so zealous,
powerful, and unresistable a maner, that howbeit the King
used his authoritie in most craibed and cholerick maner,
yett Mr. Andrew boore him doun." Fanatic raged against
fanatic. Andrew spoke, " as from the most mighty God."
He caught James's sleeve ; he cried out that the King was
but God's silly vassal ; he overbore all the royal interrup-
tions—" There are two kings and two kingdomes in Scotland ; there is Christ Jesus, and his kingdome the Kirk,
whose subject King James the Sixt is, and of whose kingdome not a king, nor a head, nor a lord, but a member. . . .
And, Sir, when yee were in your swedling clouts, Jesus Christ
raigned freelie in this land, in spyte of his enemeis . . .
will ye now, when there is more nor necessitie of the con-
tinuance and faithfull discharge of their duetie (drawin to

your owne destructioun, by a devilish and pernicious
counsell), beginne to hinder and dishaunt Christ's servants,
. . . yee must be served with all sorts of men, to come to
your purpose and grandour, Jew and Gentile, Papist and
Protestant."

" Yee must be served with all sorts of men, to come to
your purpose and grandour, Jew and Gentile, Papist and
Protestant." It was true ; James desired that all men
should live peaceably under the rule of the King. The civil
power was to bridle and harness the twin religious lions
that—too often—sought their living meat from God. In
Falkland Andrew Melville, as later as in Rome Bellarmine,
denied it ; the King ruled by permission from God through
the prophets or the priests of God. We have become so
used to James's prattle that we have forgotten that toleration is a thing that exists dangerously. The Dictators of
Europe to-day thunder back the roar that breaks out of the
sixteenth century, proclaiming the mastery of the power of
their curious gods.

The King pulled himself together, and managed to
dismiss the deputation pleasantly. He was always more
inclined to laugh than to rage at his spiritual adversaries,
and perhaps it was what chiefly annoyed them. Andrew
could never quite rid his mind of the idea that James did
not take him seriously. At heart James took him seriously
enough, but his seriousness involved a capacity for laughter
which Andrew's did not. The King therefore could put up
with a good deal of shouting, and even, after a momentary
irritation, be good-tempered over sermons, in or out of the
pulpit. Only there was always likely to come a moment
when the exposed nerve of his convictions was touched, and
then he could snarl and bite like the leopard he sometimes
seemed to be.

In November a minister of St. Andrews, Mr. David
Black, succeeded in touching that nerve. He preached.

He extended his survey to England as well as Scotland. He said that the Queen of England was an atheist, that its bishops were lords of an empty idolatrous pageant, that James was a traitor to God, that Satan was at the head of Court and Council, that kings were devils' bairns, the nobility cormorants, and the council miscreants. With much more. Even the English ambassador, who was always tender to the ministers, protested. Elizabeth, whose name was given that month to the second child of Anne of Denmark (in whose time, said Mr. Black, it was impossible to hope for good), would not endure to be called an atheist. James ordered Black to be summoned before the Council. He told the ministers he did not think much of the matter—only " take heed, sirs, that ye decline not my judicature ; if ye do so it will be the worse."

It was too late. Black, enthusiastically supported by the brethren, loudly declined the judicature. In the pulpit, he said, he was subject only to Christ, unless he exceeded his commission, and only " the prophets " could judge whether he had done so ; James was not among the prophets. All efforts to soften the incensed points of the mighty opposites failed. The pulpits were ordered " to sound mightily " ; the drums of them called to a spiritual war. The King's letters demanding submission were laid before the Lord. The Lord, for once, did nothing. Black was again summoned and again declined. Between James's party and the ministerial party there went busily to and fro the " cubicular courtiers," men who were anxious to overthrow the Government because of the economies it had been trying to effect. At that time James had appointed eight gentlemen, known as the " Octavians," who were to the cubiculars a stumbling-block and to the Kirk foolishness. But they had been straightening the finances and increasing the authority of the King.

The King caused the trial of Black to be pressed in the

K

absence of the accused.   The Kirk proclaimed a general
fast and protested that, whatever happened, " they were
free of his Majesty's blood."   The King from the Tolbooth
commanded twenty-four zealous burgesses to leave the
city, and was answered by a deputation from a great
Presbyterian convention in the Little Church, who came to
beg him to avert the dangers that threatened them.   He
threatened them in turn, and then was compelled by the
increasing crowd to retreat.   The crowd poured back to the
church, where one of the ministers had meanwhile read
aloud, and loudly, the history of Haman and Mordecai.
Cries broke out of " Armour, armour ! bills and axes ! "—
it is said raised by an agent of the cubiculars, in hope of
treating the Octavians like Haman.   The riot grew loud
and fierce about the Tolbooth, where James had shut himself
up.   He sent the provost to quiet the people, and the Earl of
Mar to negotiate with the ministers ; as soon as the tumult
was a little lulled he escaped from the Tolbooth to Holyrood.

From there, however, he struck a Jacobean blow.
Early the next morning he removed, with all the Court, from
Edinburgh, and sent a message by a herald to the market
cross declaring that the capital was no longer fit to be the
capital.   The courts of law were immediately to leave ;
noblemen and barons were to leave ; strangers were to
leave.   He himself would for ever abandon it, unless when
he came to execute judgment.

Dissension broke out in Edinburgh.   The ministers
made mighty efforts to incite in the citizens a spirit of
defiance or, alternately, martyrdom.   The citizens failed
to respond effectively.   The ministers declared that the
King had once been possessed by a devil, and now was
possessed by seven worse devils ; he was in a state of frenzy,
and it was lawful for his people to bind him.   Unfortunately
it was clear by now to the lay folk of the city that James
himself, in frenzy or not, was likely to do all the binding.

He was known to be summoning men—Highland and Border clans. The wildest rumours of destruction shook the city; the citizens saw for their only prospect death on their own thresholds. The chief ministers, fearing to be handed over as the vicarious and sole martyrs, fled. On January 1, 1597, the King returned, entering a humbled and anxious city, and imposing on it such terms as he chose.

But the submission of Edinburgh was only the sign of the double victory of James Stuart. He struck again—against Papist and Presbyterian at once. He wrote to the northern earls, saying that they must now, for the last time, decide: either to leave Scotland or to accept the religion of the Kirk. He summoned, himself, at Perth, away from the fierce spirits of the south, a General Assembly, from which he demanded an assent to the King's final authority. " I must love myself and my own estate better than all the world," he wrote to Huntly; " and think not I will suffer any professing a contrary religion to dwell in this land." " I claim nothing," he said to the Assembly, " but what is due to every Christian king . . . the civil government is committed to me." The Catholic lords submitted; the General Assembly submitted. The Lord Francis Stuart Hepburn, Earl of Bothwell, fled from Scotland to Normandy. Small demonstrations on both sides in odd places were suppressed. Huntly and the rest forswore their errors, and in solemn ceremony were relieved from excommunication and received into Presbyterian communion. There appeared, among the ministers of the same communion, certain nominees of James who were to be called Bishops—unordained as such certainly, and unmitred, but otherwise dreadfully like the Romish episcopate of England. The True Faith and the Pure Religion lay down, each now more lamblike than lionlike, and there went securely over a quietened Scotland the padded feet of the royal Cat that walked by his lone.

CHAPTER SEVEN

THE KING ON THE KING

IT was the year 1599. There was a little peace in Scotland. The young Prince Henry was a child of five ; his sister Elizabeth a baby of three. Henry had been born just before his father set out against the lords of the north. The expedition indeed had been delayed for his baptism, on August 30, 1594. Elizabeth's ambassador had carried the child to the chapel at Stirling, as, twenty-eight years before, the French had carried his father. After the ceremony the baby had been knighted, touched with a ducal coronet, and proclaimed : " The Right Excellent High and Magnanimous Frederick Henry, Henry Frederick, by the Grace of God, Knight and Baron of Renfrew, Lord of the Isles, Earl of Carrick, Duke of Rothesay, Prince and Great Steward of Scotland." In the pageants and masques the King himself had taken part, in the clothing of a Knight of Malta. Three lords, in women's attire, had presented three armed and mounted amazons.

The spiritual amazon, however, was the Queen. And she was defeated. James appointed the Earl of Mar guardian of the child. It was an hereditary office ; his family " by three descents together have had the custody and governance of the sovereign princes of the realm." But the Queen had been very angry, and had plunged into intrigues. She let herself become the head of yet another faction. But neither she nor the faction would break James's will or baffle his capacity. He heard she was ill, rode to see her, and found her with his enemies. He drove them away and imposed his will upon her. He would, he

told her, be master in his kingdom.   Against her will she
yielded, abandoned the conspiracies, and allowed herself
to be exhorted and directed by certain ministers of the
King's party.   " The King caused Mr. David Lindsay to
travel with the Queen . . . and in the end the Queen said :
' Let the King be plain with the Queen, and the Queen
should be plain with the King.' "   They were reconciled,
but James had his own way.   " For your behaviour to your
wife," he later advised the Prince, who had unknowingly
caused the trouble, " treat her as your owne flesh, command
her as her lord, cherish her as your helper, rule her as your
pupill, and please her in all things reasonable ; but teach
her not to be curious in things that belong her not."   Unlike
Papists and Puritans, Kirk and Commons, the unfortunate
Anne of Denmark had from the first to submit.

There was a little peace in Scotland.   The King had
time for thought and for composition.   He contemplated
the young Henry, his eldest-born, his successor ; he determined, like so many fathers, to give his son the full benefit
of his own experience.   Henry should have a book to tell
him how a King ought to behave.   It is a mark at once of
his good intentions and his limited mind that he took himself
quite seriously in the unceasing, and unceasingly comic,
part of the father advising his son.   Had Henry asked for
it, though from mere courtesy, there would have been
excuse.   But the Prince was only four . . . too young then
to understand the joke.   The King sat down to begin
Basilikon Doron.

It was not the first royal essay in prose.   There had
been one or two religious *Meditations*—on the Apocalypse
in 1588 (a suitable year), on *Chronicles* in 1589.   In 1597
there had been *Demonology.*   In 1598 there had been a
serious effort in political service—*The Trew Law of Free
Monarchies ; or, The Reciprock and Mutuall Duetie betwixt
a Free King and his Natural Subjects.*   This had been

published anonymously, addressed to " my dear country-men," with a civil protest—" I would be loath both to be faschious and ferthlesse. And therefore, if it be not sententious, at least it is short." As an unusual matter of fact, it was ; running only to about ten thousand words. That had been for all ; the new book was chiefly for the Prince. It was written and set up, and it is said that only seven copies were printed : if that were so, it is one of the worst examples of James's extravagance, though not that most usually quoted. But misfortune followed. The book, or extracts from it, came into the hands of Andrew Melville and of another preacher named Dykes. The extracts were produced before the General Assembly, who heard with horror the " Anglopiscopapistical " conclusion expressed in them. They professed not to know the writer, though every one was talking of the reputed writer. Dykes was compelled to flee ; the King, knowing himself accused, determined to defy the accusation by accepting it. He commanded the formal publication of the book. It appeared, and the whole of the faithful went into a strict two days' fast in order to avert the judgments of God from the Court and country, especially the country. It would have been simpler, could they have borne it, to wait upon time and that inevitable antagonism which God has so persistently set between one generation and the next.

In effect those who did read the book might have noticed in it not so much the advice to the young as the memory of the mature. For as we turn the pages of either the *Trew Law* or the *Basilikon Doron*, unsympathetically scornful of a political system alien from our own debased oligarchy, it is the personal reflection of the life of James that appears and appeals. He was, by now, approaching, in spite of all fasts and feuds, the supreme power in Scotland. Bothwell was wandering in Europe, to die poor at last in Naples, a year before his King. Huntly was a subdued

Presbyterian. Elizabeth could not live much longer ; already the great Queen's great favourite, Essex, was writing letters to James, as if to the living lord of the future. The preachers were still prophesying, but the shadow of the mitre lay over them. The great nobles, exhausted and baffled, were yielding to the accumulating power of the King.

He was already beginning the imposition of his authority over even the Highlands and the Hebrides ; the full work took him all the rest of his reign.   He was as inflamed, as merciless, as vicariously bloody and unscrupulous, towards the inhabitants of those remote lairs as towards any closer rebels or traitors. " His Majesty was very merciful," it was said of him, " but must be rubbed with a fomentation of his own oil to make him more supple." No fomentation soothed him when he was aroused by the wild deeds of these outer lords and clans.   The MacGregors especially offended him continually, by invasion and massacre, and against them especially he aimed a justice which too soon became first anger and then cruelty.   Later, he caused the Privy Council to pass an act abolishing their very name, commanding all who bore it to change it for some other, and forbidding any who had once borne it to meet in greater numbers than four at any one time.   They became known through the Highlands as " the clan that is nameless by day," and even of those nameless creatures James hardly left four to meet.

But that was not yet ; and now, far south of such horror, in a little peace, he saw his enemies failing. He knew he had come through. It gave his active and propagandist mind pleasure to sit down and explain why he ought to have come through ; why, through the years of flight and capture, threat and denunciation, pursuit and peril, there had dwelled in him the perfect right to come through. Both in the *Trew Law* and the *Basilikon Doron* he did so, both obviously and less obviously. The exposition is there, but so is the opposition, even though disguised. His past lives in the doctrinal pages of the two books which are, so, but one. And there also is that first act of self-preservation so necessary to every believer, so amusing to every sceptic, and so just if the gospel, whatever it may be, is true. For James knew very well that he might not have come through. He provided for that once possible, and now impossible, alternative ; in the pattern he was making he closed that opening against objection. Victory does not always prove the justice of the cause ; rebels may succeed, and then they are God's scourge and play the devil's part. " It is ofttimes a very deceivable argument to judge of the cause by the event." Heads, the King's cause won ; but tails, it did not lose. The irony, however, loses something of its strength when we reflect that it ofttimes is.

However, not even ostensibly had he lost. God had spared him and the country that bitter scourge of their sins, and James went on to explain the greatness of His work. All those years, though Gowrie's leg might be thrust in the way, or Arran be received with royal salutes, or Bothwell leap from behind the arras ; though Huntly might plot to keep him for the King of Spain, or Andrew Melville catch him by the sleeve, or Durie bid him send back the horses of the Duke of Guise, through all those years the King had had power to exalt low things and abase high things, and "make of their subjects like men at the Chesse : a pawn to take a Bishop or a Knight, and to cry up or down any of their subjects as they do their money." Even the coronation oath (which Morton had taken for him : was he a little hurt by the knowledge ? No ; it was his oath : Morton only served) had been taken to God, not to the people, and the people must not therefore invoke its clauses for their protection. They ought

not to have discussed the Prerogative; it is Mystery.
They ought not to have sought to press into the *arcana*
but to " rest in that which is the King's revealed will in
his Law." Many had desired to " take away the mysticall
reverence that belongs unto them that sit in the Throne
of God "; too many, in his past years, had audaciously
" waded into the weaknesse of Princes "—again as when
Bothwell mocked with his sword out before the startled
King clutching at his clothes.

It had been sacrilege, all that riot, and the Lord had
justly overthrown it. As convinced as his opponents were
of the workings of that Justice, he wrote steadily on, laying
down the everlasting conditions of mortal government.
Because they had been so broken in his own past, he took
care in his own mind to reason them out as unbreakable.
It had often been held that kings were made royal by their
crowning and anointing, not by their mere birth. He
himself had been crowned and anointed by the lords. But,
as he knew, the lords might not have crowned him; they
might have found some other method of ruling Scotland.
Would their choice have invalidated his right? No
certainly, he answered himself. The King is king in
himself, and by no assent of his subjects. The King is
their " heritable overlord; and so by birth, not by any
right in his coronation, cometh to the throne." The duty
of obedience never lapses; it is due to the new monarch
as soon as the old dies. It is Mystery.

It is Mystery, this royal dignity and divinity, " between
the civil and the ecclesiastical," sacerdotal in its office and
nature. He who had come so late to his kingdom and
so often had nearly lost his kingdom, knew now that kings
were established before all laws; all power flows from
them; none may rise against them. It is monstrous and
unnatural for sons to rebel against a father and " control
him at their appetite." The physical word expressed

something of the physical horror he felt. Night and
terrible things happening in the night oppressed him—the
night from which he woke to see Gowrie's outstretched
leg, or that which was broken by the shouts of the raiders
trampling on the son of the Master of Mar, or even some
earlier night of which he retained no memory when murder
was done under the torches in Holyrood. He defended
himself against that evil spirit with his spiritual dogma ;
once more he slew the slain. No rebellion ; no sedition ;
only " sobs and tears to God," such tears as a boy had been
compelled to shed, such sobs as Cuthbert Armourer had
heard from a forlorn youth.

His own appetites had been mild enough, but that
was of his goodwill. So far as his right went, he could
have had all ; yes, even when he had actually nothing of
his own, he had a right to all. Samuel had declared it, in
the prophecy of the evil king who " will take your fields
and your vineyards and your best olive-trees and give
them to his servants. And he will take the tenth of your
seed, and of your vineyards, and give it to his eunuchs
and to his servants, and also the tenth of your sheep."
This was as much as to say : " Your persons and the
persons of your posterity, together with your lands and
all that ye possess, shall serve his private use and inordinate
appetite." He had demanded no such tribute. The
children of James had been far more fortunate than the
children of Jacob, though they were too stubborn or too
foolish to know it. His own royal honour forbade ; he
had a duty towards God and his honour which he meant
to try to fulfil. Obedient subjects should thrive under
him in peace. But if he had chosen—— Had Samuel
lifted a weapon against Saul, had David or Elias ? Yet
if they had willed, no doubt but they could have raised a
rebellion as well as any preacher in Scotland ! He laboured
the contrast, growing " somewhat satiric."

When, in explaining to Henry, he came to the nature of the Scottish crown rather than that of universal monarchy, he had no such unconscious need to conceal his difficulties. He spoke of the nobility and their great faults : one of which he had publicly declared ten years before. They drank them in with their nourish-milk— the desire to oppress and enthral poor neighbours, the boldness to support their own following in any wrong, the haste on any provocation to begin feuds, " and bang it out bravely." The King's laws suffered harm by the heritable sheriffdoms and regalities ; let his son, so far as possible, dispossess hereditary rights. It was the business of the King to be open and affable to all honest persons, that suits should come to him, not to the great Houses. The nobles must obey the Law as much as the meanest hind, and the King is the Law. " Be awful to beat down the hornes of proud oppressors ; embrace the quarrell of the poor and distressed."

He turned off for a moment to merchants. It is natural to be grateful to James when we find him remarking as a fault in merchants that " albeit the victuals rise or fall of their prices, according to the aboundance or skantnesse therof, yet the prices of their wares ever rise but never fall, being as constant in that their evill custom as if it were a setled Law for them." James had not so many economists about him as we have, and he had not understood that this strange mystery, which every one has observed, must certainly be a law. He proposed to alter it, to put it right, fix each year a settled price of all things, taking into account the price in other countries, and if the native merchants sold at higher prices, foreigners were to be free to import. It was a wild enough dream, meant to help the consumer. We, knowing that it cannot be done and the consumer can never be helped, can only regret his pedantic mind.

But how rare even in pedantry to find a Prince who desires to help the consumer !

It had not altogether been his fault that he had failed to control nobles and merchants. Looking back, he noted with a kind of humble self-deception that when he came to the throne he had been too gracious at the beginning, and thought he would win all men's hearts. It does not seem as if, between Buchanan and Morton and the Ruthven lords, the King had had much opportunity to be gracious. But perhaps he dimly remembered, as he wrote, that wonderful maturing of his affections when the Lord D'Aubigny was in Scotland ; when the King—then a boy of fifteen—rode from town to town with masques and splendours and dances to welcome him, and with the beauty and wisdom of the beloved Lennox by his side. " I thought to win all men's hearts," the solemn, grotesque creature wrote. O visionary dreams of childhood, perhaps he did !

The *Basilikon Doron* ended—let us give James his due —with Virgil. " Let it be your chiefest earthly glory, to excell in your owne craft : according to the worthy counsel and charge of Anchises to his posterities, in that sublime and heroicall Poet, wherein also my dicton is included. . . .

> "Tu, regere imperio populos, Romane, memento
> (Haec tibi erunt artis) pacique imponere morem,
> *Parcere subjectis, et debellare superbos.*"

The italics, egotistical and honourable, are the King's.

The two books, in their principles and in their details, cover an infinity of James's writings and speeches, before and after. It is not surprising that he was obstinate in his beliefs. Others had been put before him, but never very persuasively, never as a matter of amiable or academic discussion. They had, all his life, come violently, vocal with physical noise, from Buchanan to Bothwell, Durie to Melville, Ruthven to Ruthven. For all his obstinacy

James had a very real tolerance ; he wanted to argue as much as to win. True, he wanted to win as much as to argue, but he had not been wisely trained to endure intellectual defeat and the beautiful grace of thinking one may be mistaken. He had spent all his life among those who were sure they were not. He had had lectures from preachers who prayed for his conversion, and quiet interviews with Catholic priests who did the same. His conversion to something or other was always looming on the horizon of the garden where otherwise he could have happily sauntered and disputed. In public or in private he was prayed to and prayed for. Between sermons and Masses it is not surprising that the Will of God which they all invoked kept him where he was, only much more obstinate than before.

He could understand that people differed from him ; so much his sense of actuality taught him. But how it was that they differed, how strong their sense of truth, how plausible their arguments—that he could not understand ; there his imagination failed. His own outraged system of beliefs returned to outrage others. It was deplorable, but it was a little the fault of all those vehement propagandists the smoke of whose petitions ascended to heaven round the person of the King. He had been " persecuted . . . not from my birth onely, but even since four moneths before my birth."

But through all this equally determined, though on the whole less vehement, assertion of the Prince in his royalty, there is one surprising omission and one continual tendency, and the two are related. The omission is that nothing anywhere is said, or suggested, of the propriety of the substitution of the heir to the Throne for the occupant of the Throne. The heir begins to reign as soon as the monarch dies ; yes, but what if the monarch has not died and still the heir begins to reign ? Where in all the high textual arguments is the explanation of how it came about that James, for twenty years of his reign, was there at all ? the exposition, however concealed, of his defence against Mary his mother ?   It does not seem to exist. She herself is there occasionally ; those loyal to him are favourably noticed as having been loyal to her ; her slanderers are contemned. But the profoundest disloyalty of all, if loyalty is to be brought in at all, is not excused or explained. He seems simply to have forgotten all about it.

She had abdicated, it is true.   Neither she nor Elizabeth her sister, nor the Kings of France and Spain, nor Scottish lords and preachers and priests had treated that instrument very seriously. She herself had revoked it. The abdication and the revocation had been cards in the perilous game, and had been played as and when necessary. It may be that in one mind alone of all Europe was that abdication seriously taken, and that mind her son's. Fate, it seems, had given her in her son the single solemn simplicity that took her at her word, forcibly extorted though the word was. She had thought he would unite the crowns of Scotland and England, and so (by his choice and at her cost) he did. Fate took her at her word.

Or else, more probably, he forgot her ; merely and naturally forgot. It would accord with the limitation of his mind. He had never seen her ; he had never been aware of her as anything but a phantom—at first a perilous phantom, which presently, becoming a phantom indeed, ceased to be perilous. She was not, therefore, as vivid to him as that other phantom which still possessed the English Crown. She was not actual, and had not been for twelve long and busy years. He had nothing of that lofty imagination which, brooding over the radical principle of monarchy, would have seen inclusively all alteration and overthrow. If he had not been a King, he would never have written upon monarchy. His honourable anxiety to do right by his people, his not dishonourable desire (given his mind) that his people should do right by him, reflected the pattern of his own wishes and fear. And there Mary had never been quite so important nor so dangerous as Elizabeth ; nor her northern Catholics so fierce and possessive, at least in seeming, as the ministers, the Ruthven lords, and Robert Bowes. She was less actual to him ; his actual substitution for his mother less than his hoped succession to his god-mother. As long as he could remember he had been the King. He wrote laboriously on, in that style which, shrewd and effective enough—and more amusing than he altogether intended—rises nowhere to any greatness of imagination or any sudden passion of spiritual truth. " The concised shortness of my style," he called it in the preface to the *Basilikon Doron* ; but, though it is by no means as long as might be feared, it is not concise. There are no arrows ; there is no marble. It is a rippling stream.

Yet that concern with the Mystery of kingship had its own mystery. He felt that the King was a mystery, and that he was the King. He himself then was a mystery, and something of that sort he really did feel. The style itself is aware of his physical nature. Its lack of great philosophic scope, its natural shrewdness, its flexible vitality, when they come to the Mystery he was trying to express, approach a material mystery. His body, from its birth, had been royal ; his body had been the subject of plots and captivities ; his body had been the centre of his own imaginative life, such as it was. His intellect returned constantly to unillumined actuality. Therefore in learning he was something of a pedant, relying only on meticulous exactitude. In law he was a precisian of the past. In statecraft he recognized facts but not ideas, until they were forced on him as facts. In monarchical doctrine he was a physicist ; he half identified royalty with his material flesh.

There is something significant about the phrase " prying into the weakness of princes," when it is considered in what state of helpless disarray Bothwell caught him.

He was saved from any madness of megalomania by his intelligence and love of good-fellowship. But when he hung on his Favourites' shoulders, when he stroked their cheeks, and played with their hands, it was James Stuart in his monarchy who did so. It was the creator " of all but their breathing and their soul," a physical mystery of all but omnipotence which, however thwarted, could never agree to be thwarted. He gave himself, in maudlin tears and sentimental embraces, and yet the inner mystery of himself remained intact, for his nature was the King's, and the King was subject to nothing on earth. He dissembled (they say) in love as in hate, but the dissimulation was inevitable, for his nature, mental and material, was aware of both kinds of motions—the general motions of mankind and the solitary motions of majesty. Only at the very end—bullied and thwarted and sick—he lost the interior crown. His continence of mind and his chastity of kingship were violated in the house of his loves. There, if at all, he sinned.

CHAPTER EIGHT

GOWRIE

HISTORY, which is shaped by all men's actions at all moments, allows us at odd moments the fanciful delight of observing some common creature like ourselves exhibited among the lords and princes, resolving their ironic comedy by his own. Such a moment occurs with the apparition in the history of Scotland on Tuesday, August 5, in the year 1600, during a bright summer afternoon, in a turret chamber of the Ruthven house in Perth, of Andrew Henderson, chamberlain to the Earl of Gowrie. He does so very little ; he stands in his steel plate, irresolute and trembling, sometimes springing into frightened motion. He is so absurdly inadequate that he tempts us to make the moment more important artistically than, historically, it actually was ; to pretend, with what excuses we can raise, that the history of England and Europe also has been what it has been, that, for instance, the Protestant Catholicism of the Church of England, and her daughter churches throughout the world, is what it is because of that single man's hesitation and inactivity.

He did so little. He was a servant of that strange house over which the shadow of necromancy lay. Its lords were said to be deep scholars, and some of them learned in forbidden things ; they wrote magical characters and talked with familiar spirits. But though this was a common rumour, yet they also had been friends and servants of the Kirk, and champions of the pure Gospel. Between them and the Stuart dynasty lay almost an hereditary feud, as if Destiny had determined to fulfil the threat that had

L

broken from Mary Stuart after the killing of Rizzio:
"Well, my lord, it is within my belly that will one day
avenge these cruelties and affronts." It had been the
Lord Patrick Ruthven who had come into the privy
chamber, returned from overseeing the fifty-three wounds
of the stabbing, to provoke and receive that cry. He had
died in exile ; his son, the Lord William Ruthven, had
succeeded to his title, and then after being raised to the
Earldom of Gowrie, after being pardoned for his share in
the Raid of Ruthven, had been slain by the craft of Arran
and the assent of the King. Two sons succeeded ; in the
year 1600 the second, John, was Lord of Ruthven and Earl
of Gowrie. He was a young man of twenty-two, living
with his brother Alexander, the Master of Ruthven, in this
great house at Perth on the river Tay. From under those
windows the Tay flows on into the Firth of Tay, on the
southern side of which, protected by a dangerous coast,
there then stood Fast Castle, a lonely fortress belonging
to Robert Logan, Laird of Restalrig, a friend of the
Ruthvens. It was a castle convenient for the holding of
a notable captive—even a royal one ; and the way to it,
down the river, was convenient also, private and swift.

The preliminary movements of Andrew Henderson are
known now to all the world, though they were hidden then
until on that Tuesday afternoon he became visible to its
astonished eyes. On the previous evening he had been
called to the Earl's presence, and asked what he was doing
the next day. He said he had business with some of the
Earl's tenants. His lord bade him leave that, and be ready
by four in the morning to ride to Falkland with the Master.
They went, the Master, Henderson, and one other servant,
and in the town Henderson was sent to watch near the
palace till the King came out. He saw the King's train
gather for hunting ; he saw the King coming to join them ;
he hurried to tell the Master, who passed up to meet the

King. After this interview Henderson was told to ride back to Perth and say the King would be coming. He obeyed. His lord questioned him at some length about their reception, and what noblemen might be expected with the King. He answered, " None but my lord Duke." Later on the Earl told him to put on his mail—there was a Highlander to be seized. He obeyed. Then it was dinner-time, but while he served the Earl's dinner the other servant returned, and presently the Master also. The Earl spoke with them, and thereupon went out with a company. Henderson followed ; some distance from the house he saw King James riding up with a group of gentlemen. The Earl met him, and turned back with him to the house. Then there was a bustle, and long delay in getting together a dinner for the King. At last it was ready, and while it was being served the Earl slipped out for a few minutes, and sent Henderson to an upper room called the Gallery Chamber, where the Master was, himself following. The Earl bade Henderson hold himself at the Master's disposal. The Master said, " Let Andrew Henderson gang in to the round of the chalmer, and I will lock him in, and tak the key with me." Which was done. There he was left— locked in. He knew nothing of what was purposed, but he was alarmed by this secret preparation ; he knelt down and prayed to God to shield him from the evil that he feared was approaching. He rose and waited, not so very long before the door opened, and there came in two men, the younger bareheaded, holding the elder by the arm. The younger was Alexander, Master of Ruthven, the elder was James, King of Scotland. Through the opening of the door as they entered, Andrew Henderson becomes visible to all future generations, by his agitation determining our politics and our creeds.

Such (he swore) was all he knew of that strange morning's activities. Had he known all he might have had more fear.

He had stood out of hearing when the Master, in the fair August morning, went up to James. The King was with his train ; they were all about to mount when James found the Master genuflecting by his side, begging for a private word. He good-humouredly assented, and the two stepped aside. They paced up and down talking, for about a quarter of an hour, James's hand lying familiarly on the other's shoulder. The Court waited ; there were present the Duke of Lennox, the Earl of Mar, James Erskine and Thomas Erskine, Sir John Ramsay, John Murray, carrying the King's hawk, Sir Hugh Herries, and others. The King could see them as he walked, while he listened to the curious story the Master was telling. It was a story of how, on the previous evening, he, the Master, walking in the fields near the Ruthven house in Perth, had seen a man muffled in a cloak, slinking past him. He had stopped him, and after some questions had pulled away the cloak— discovering a pot of gold. Thereon he had seized both man and gold, taken him to the house, and left him bound in a remote room. He suggested humbly and loyally that if the King would come there he could investigate the whole affair and probably take over the gold. The King, with his persistent and (they say) pedantic feeling for exact law, said he could not see how he was concerned. No man's treasure, that was a free and lawful subject, could appertain to the King, unless it was hidden in the earth, when it would become treasure-trove. But this was not. The Master answered that the stranger had confessed that he intended to bury it, so it was in effect treasure-trove. The King said there was a good deal of difference between doing it and meaning to do it ; his intention was not alike as if it had been found already hid. The Master said he thought the King overscrupulous ; if he deferred to meddle with it, the lord his brother and other great men might meddle, and make his Majesty the more ado. This remark suggested to the King's mind that it might be foreign gold, brought to help stir up sedition ; he asked what kind of coin it was. The Master said it seemed to be foreign coin. The King, confirmed in his guess, proposed that the magistrates of Perth should take charge of both stranger and treasure ; the Master urged that if the magistrates (and necessarily the Earl) came in touch with the gold there would be little left for his Majesty. The King saw the truth of this, and considered. But he saw also his train mounted and ready, heard the game started, and bidding the Master follow him, went back, mounted his horse, and began the chase. The Master still protesting that the King would not find every day such a choice of hunting, and that all might have been finished while the Earl was at church, dispatched Henderson back to Perth, and obeyed.

James meditated at intervals, until they killed at eleven, on the story. He spoke further with the Master while they rode. It was fantastic, but it was not quite impossible. Strange muffled creatures with foreign treasure did sometimes haunt Scotland. Wild stratagems of treason flickered about the land. But the question now was—whose was the stratagem, the stranger's or Ruthven's ? It was impossible that the King should entirely trust Gowrie or any of his house ; he trusted hardly anybody, and he knew, by old experience of Morton and the elder Ruthven and Francis Bothwell, the value and danger of his person. But he was not a coward, and forewarned, he had an obstinate confidence in the power of his royalty—the divinity that hedged and protected him. By the time they had killed he had determined to go to Perth and find out the truth. The pot of gold might be faerie, but it might not, and a pot of gold, in whatever coins, would be useful to the privy purse. Besides, there was a mystery, and the King would as soon hunt down a mystery as a deer. He

was " apt to search into secrets and to try conclusions."
He would not stay for the " curry of the deer." He sent
for another horse to follow him. His gentlemen, seeing
this, sent for their swords and fresh horses. The Master
urged that a few ordinary servants would be enough, the
King, " half-angry," replied that he would not mistrust the
Duke or Mar in such a matter; he saw no reason for such
extreme secrecy—he spurred upon this other thrilling chase.
As he rode he called Lennox privately to him, saying, " Ye
cannot guess what errand I am riding for ! I am going
to get a poise (a hoard of treasure) in Perth ; " and told
him the story. Lennox, though he knew no harm of the
Master, said it all sounded very unlikely. The King told
him to follow closely after when the Master was about,
and, " between trust and distrust," on they went.

Near Perth, the Master rode on before, to bring the
Earl his brother out to meet the King, which he did. The
whole party arrived at the house, and Gowrie apologized
for the lack of immediate dinner. He had actually been
warned by Henderson, but he seemed to be surprised.
Some kind of a meal was got ready—a moorfowl, a shoulder
of mutton, a chicken, strawberries. The King was kept
waiting a good while, but at last sat down in a private
apartment on the ground floor ; when he had nearly
finished, his gentlemen went to dine in the great hall on
the same floor. After dinner they wandered out into the
gardens, eating cherries, waiting till it should please his
Majesty to be ready. Gowrie went with them. Only one,
the young John Ramsay, was not with them. He had
relieved Murray of the King's hawk, that he might dine
the easier, and had met with a gentleman of Gowrie's who
had taken him away to admire the Great Gallery.

His Majesty meanwhile had been expecting and asking
the Master to open the secret. The Earl had been going
in and out ; as the King finished dinner, the Master at his

back whispered that it was time to go ; let the King send
his brother away. James, rallying the Earl on his gloom,
sent him off to drink a royal health with the train. The
Earl went ; the King rose, and bade the Master bring Sir
Thomas Erskine. The Master said he would call privately
whoever the King wished, but let there be nothing public.

They went together—out of the room, through the end
of the hall where the train were at dinner, up a great staircase, down a corridor, the Master locking the doors behind
them. He smiled now ; he said several times he had the
fellow sure and safe enough. The King, alight with
curiosity, greed, caution, and majesty, went shuffling on ;
the young Master, in growing agitation, carrying his hat
in one hand and holding James by the arm with the other,
went beside him. They came at last into a large room in
which was a door leading to a smaller turret chamber.
They passed into the turret, and the King saw before him
not a bound prisoner but a man free and half-armed.
The door was thrown to behind him.

Immediately the Master, with an outrageous gesture,
flung his hat on his head, sprang to Henderson's side, and
pulled out the hanger the man wore. Naked weapon in
hand, he turned on the King, crying, " Sir, you must be
my prisoner ; remember on my father's death." James
began to speak. The excited Master exclaimed, " Hold
your tongue, sir, or by Christ ye shall die ! " James did
not hold his tongue—he never could ; he went on speaking.
He began, " Mr. Alexander, you and I have been very great
together——" and talked on, defending himself over
Gowrie's death, putting it on to his Council of the time, since
he himself had been a minor (which was true), warning the
youth to be careful, for if his life were touched, " there are
men in this town and friends who will not leave it un-
avenged." The Master declared with oaths that he desired
neither life nor blood, and the King answered him sharply,

" What traiks albeit ye take off your hat ? " The apparent anticlimax was a real climax ; the Master, confused and defeated, took off his hat. In that revocation of his first gesture, he consented to the presence of the majesty of the King. An older and stronger man might have done it in irony ; that it was not irony there but obedience is shown by what happened next. The King had re-established his Court. He went on, " What is it ye crave, man, an ye crave not my life ? "

" Sir," the Master answered, " it is but a promise."

The King said, " What promise ? "

The Master did not clearly know ; he gave way again. He said, " My lord my brother will tell you."

The King answered, " Fetch your brother here."

In those few moments everything had gone wrong. The distracted Master said, " Sir, you will not cry or open the window whiles I come again ? " Was ever so rare a fantasy—the captor begging the captive not to let his whereabouts be known ? James consented ; there was the doubtful figure of Henderson in the background, and he did not intend to drive the two of them to immediate extremes. The Master went out of the room, locking the door. Henderson said afterwards that he thought he remained against it, and did not go downstairs. We do not know. Either in his own mind or after speaking for one wild moment with the Earl, he came to frenzied resolution. The plot must go forward ; they were already condemned and could not afford delay. He put his hand to the key again and unlocked the door.

Away beneath him, in the gardens of the great house, which lay to the right of the dining-hall, as one looked down it from the street, the entrance court lying on its left, the Earl had been engaged on his part of the business. He had to get rid of the throng of gentlemen the King had brought with him. Had James, as the Master had suggested, come with but two or three lower servants, all would have been easy. But there were noblemen on duty ; the plot had had to be hastily revised, under the peril of their attentive eyes—in a whisper or two. The best had been done that could be. Gowrie was waiting. As he loitered with the rest in the gardens, there came out to them suddenly from the house a gentleman of Gowrie's, calling out that the King had already privately mounted and ridden away. It seemed his servants must follow in haste. The Earl began immediately to shout, " Horse ! horse ! " But Lennox, already uneasy, went hastily from the gardens, through the hall, and across the courtyard, to the front gate that gave on the street, where, finding the porter, he asked if the King had gone. The porter denied it. Mar, coming up, said, " Tell me, in verity, has the King gone out ? " The porter answered, " In verity, no." Gowrie had caught them up ; he heard this, and said he would go and find out what had happened. He went back into the courtyard, and disappeared up the great staircase that led to the gallery at the other end of which the turret chamber lay. He may, somewhere there, on the staircase or in the gallery, have met his brother, or he may have turned back before he came to the door against which the Master leant. By hasty agreement or by separate decision he turned and came swiftly back, to say angrily to the porter, " Thou liest ; he is forth at the back yett and through the Inch."

The innocent and ignorant porter stuck to his facts. He said, " That cannot be, my lord, for I have the key of the back yett, and of all the yetts of the place."

The other courtiers had come up ; they were all standing in the street, outside the gate. At the porter's words there fell upon them for a moment a pause of irresolution. If the King had gone, and the Earl said he had, their duty was to get their own horses and follow. But if the King had not gone, and the Earl said he had, then the Earl was lying and the King was in peril. They could go—it must have occurred to one of them—and look in the stables for the King's horse. But even if the horse were not there, it would not be conclusive ; horses can be moved. Yet to challenge the Earl of treason on the word of a porter would be the most violent of insults. They paused, uncertain. From the windows of the houses nearby faces looked down on the grand folk ; all about them townspeople were passing or pausing, including one of the bailies of the town. Gowrie stood with them, for that moment, waiting. Above them, suddenly, a window was dashed open and a voice cried out.

When the key of the door of the inner chamber had been turned upon the two within, the King had turned his attention to his companion, who, hovering all this while in the background, had taken the hanger from the Master's hand. He said, " How came ye in here, man ? "

" As God lives, I am shut in here like a dog," Henderson said.

" Will my lord of Gowrie do me any evil, man ? " the King asked, and with a spasm of fearful loyalty the startled man said, " I vow to God, sir, I shall die first."

The King looked at the windows ; he had promised not to open them. Keeping his promise to the letter, and keeping the dignity of his estate, he bade Henderson open one, which he did. It was no use to them ; it looked out only on to the courtyard. " Fie, the wrong window, man ! " James cried ; and then suddenly Alexander was in the room again, shouting, " By God, sir, there is no remedy." He rushed upon James, clutching at his hands, trying to bind them with a garter he had in his own. The King, calling out, " I am a free prince. I will not be bound," tore his left hand loose, and jumped clumsily aside ; the Master sprang after him, clutched his hand with his own left hand, and thrust his right against the mouth. Henderson, still following up the pair, not daring to attack his lord, not daring to allow his lord to injure the King, pulled at the Master's right hand, leaving the King's mouth free. They were all up against that other unopened window. The King had his back to it ; Henderson reached over the King's left shoulder and thrust it open, and as he pressed towards it, the King, between him and the Master, was slewed round, and able to lean out with head and shoulders. His eyes fell on the group in the street ; he called out. Lennox, below, exclaimed to Mar, "That is the King's voice, be he where he will." They all turned ; they looked up ; they saw James's face, red and hatless, one hand up to his cheek and mouth ; they heard him cry, "I am murdered ! Treason ! My lord Mar, help, help ! "

As in one great rush they went back through the front gate, across the courtyard, and up the great staircase in the far north-western corner, the King disappeared from the window. For within, understanding from the shouting and running below, that the King's men were on their way and all was indeed lost, the Master "trembling," cried out to Henderson, who had so helplessly thwarted him, "Is there no help with thee ? Wo worth thee, villain ! we all die ! " and desperately laid hold on the hilt of his sword. The King's hand caught at his and held it ; they reeled, struggling, into the outer chamber. Henderson, following ("doing nothing but trembling all the time," the King said afterwards), slipped across and unlocked one of the other two doors in it, for his own escape and for entrance to any of the King's men. This door led to a little turnpike staircase ; the other to the Great Gallery, and so to the great staircase. As he did so, there came running up the turnpike stair, Sir John Ramsay, still holding the King's hawk on his wrist. He himself was but twenty-three years old, four years older than the unhappy Master, who was still struggling with James. But now the King had forced the Master down, with an arm over his head ; the Master's upstretched hand, however, was still clutched over the King's face and mouth. The King, wresting his mouth free, called out, " Strike low ! He has ane pyne doublet " (a secret coat of mail). Henderson slipped away down the turnpike. Ramsay, letting go the hawk, drew his dagger, and struck. The wounded Master released the King ; James, " with his own hand," flung him off down the stair. He stepped back ; he saw the hawk Ramsay had released as he drew his sword flying loose. The King set his foot on the leash. Ramsay, running to the window in the inner chamber and looking out, saw two of the King's men below—Sir Hugh Herries and Sir Thomas Erskine. He called to them. They ran up the turnpike stair, a servant of the Erskines with them, passing the body of the wounded Master. Herries thrust at him again ; he cried out, " Alas ! I had na wyte (blame) of it ! " and died.

The three gentlemen now with the King had come there by different chances. Ramsay coming down from the Great Gallery into the court had heard—apparently before the others who were still in the gardens behind the house—that the King had ridden off, and without further inquiry had gone off through the front gate to the stable to get his own horse. While he was at the stable door he heard behind him the King's voice crying out, but could not understand what was said. He rushed back, through the gate, passing several confused groups on the way, into the quadrangle, and saw near to him—what the others had not observed—the open door of the turnpike. He ran up the stair, just as Henderson opened the door at the top.

Herries and Erskine had been with the other courtiers, but while these hurried after Lennox and Mar to the great staircase, they turned their attention to Gowrie himself, perhaps with the idea of holding him hostage for James's safety. Gowrie, like his brother, had lost control of events ; if indeed he dealt in necromancy, his spirits had deserted him. James Erskine caught hold of him as he stood there, so did Thomas Erskine. The Earl, disengaging himself, ran a short distance off, drew sword and dagger, and cried, " I will either be at my own house or die at the gate." A number of his men ran up, calling out to know at whom they should strike. At their head he passed back into the quadrangle. While this confusion raged, there was a cry that the Master was slain—the news coming either from Ramsay calling to Herries and Erskine from the window, or (more probably) from Henderson, who by now had slipped down the stair and was making his own escape through the press. He was spoken to by one of the Earl's servants, and answered as he went. The town was stirring, arming, hurrying. The bailie, Andrew Ray, who had been at the gate and heard the King cry out, was running through the streets, calling out, " Treason, treason ! For God's sake, all honest men, haste and release the King ! " giving command that the great bell of the town should ring, and then with such force as he could gather, setting out on his way back to the house.

There were, therefore, by now four parties, or indeed five, if the townspeople be reckoned as two. The King, Erskine and his man, Ramsay and the hawk, were in the turret chamber, with Herries at the door. Gowrie and his men were in the court at the foot of the turnpike, where also lay the body of the Master. Lennox and Mar, with a confused following of King's men and Gowrie men, had by now reached the great door of the turret chamber and were trying to burst it open. There had been a ladder by it, which they had broken in driving against it ; they had then sent for hammers. The townspeople without, many of whom were for Gowrie, were shouting abuse of the

King : " Come down, come down, thou son of Seigneur
Davie ! " The bailie with the other officials and townsfolk
were hurrying back to the King's aid. The unarmed King
looked round for the Master's sword which had fallen from
him by the door ; his friends thrust him into the inner
chamber. The King could hear heavy blows, interspersed
through the window with the screaming of women, the
shouting of the crowd, and—very soon—the tolling of the
bell. But he had no time to attend ; there were angry
voices at the other door. Gowrie and some five followers
were there with swords drawn, one of them calling out
challenges to Herries, who with his own sword out held the
entry. Then Ramsay and Erskine and the servant Wilson
joined him ; there was a confused scuffle. The royal
hawk was there to fly about the room like Pallas beating
her wings above the fated suitors of Penelope. Gowrie
broke out as they fought, saying something—appeal,
defiance, explanation, invocation—no one understood.
Ramsay struck at him, as at his brother ; the blow was
again fatal. The Earl stood still, leaning on his sword ;
one of his people caught at him and managed to hold him
up for a little, then he fell dead within the chamber. His
men at first fled ; the door was thrown to and locked.
But a certain Alexander Ruthven soon rallied them,
and they attacked again, thrusting swords and hal-
berts through the door chinks. Meanwhile hammers had
been battering against the other door, and none among
the King and his four friends knew who was there—true
men or traitors. Voices could not be recognized through
the heavy door and in the general tumult. But a certain
Robert Brown, one of Lennox's party, left them, passed
again round the fatal circle, along the gallery, down the
great staircase, across the court, up the turnpike in the
momentary flight of Gowrie's people, and coming into the
Presence gave assurance of good news. Those within

hastened to help those without, but it was not till a hole had been smashed in the door, a hammer passed through, and then the door battered open from within, that at last the two parties could unite. Lennox, Mar, and the rest poured in; the King's men were again together. Alexander Ruthven, hearing new voices, cried to Lennox, " For God's sake, my lord, how does my lord of Gowrie? " Lennox answered, " He is well; get you away. You are a fool; you will get little thanks for this labouring." The King and all of them kneeled down, and the King thanked God.

Even so, they were not yet free or safe. The riot without the house was increasing. The Ruthven women were screaming to the crowd that the Earl was dead; that there had been enough to take meat and drink from him living, and there were none to avenge him dead. Alexander Ruthven rushed out of the house, calling out that the town was unworthy of its provost, and that the Earl was slain. He pushed his way into a shop near at hand, wildly demanding " Powder! powder! " There are a hundred glimpses of other figures: William Rynd, a fletcher, who was " slaying flesh " when the tumult broke out and came hurrying, having caught up his sword; Michael Baxter, a tailor, who had been " shaping a cloak," and came without weapons; James Bower, a notary, in his armour; George Forest, another tailor, with a halberd; William Duncan, a skinner, with a sword; John Brown, a webber, with a staff, and so on. These were all called up by the turmoil. From a room above them in one of the houses looked out Alexander Peebles, who, by the discretion of his household, had been locked in. Some of the crowd were shouting that they would see the Earl, that the green coats (the colour of the royal train) were traitors and thieves who had slain the Earl, that they should all pay for it, that they were murderers and butchers who had slain an honester man than any of themselves, and the taunting cries of " Seigneur Davie " barbed the shouts. The bell was tolling, the town was up ; the King's men knew that the Ruthvens were popular lords of all that country, and a storm of rage was already beating round the tower where the head of the Ruthvens and his brother lay dead. But presently there was a new sound, for the bailie with his force had arrived, forced a passage through the mob, and taken stand under the windows. Those within, listening, heard a voice calling up, " How is the King ? " Lennox and Mar looked out and answered, " The King is well, praised be God." " Then," said the bailie afterwards, " I cried up to his Majesty, and showed him that the bailies and township were come in all haste to supply and relieve his Majesty ; and therefore besought his Majesty to command what was his Majesty's will and best to be done." James came to the window and showed himself ; he waved his hand to the throng, bidding the magistrates, since all was well with him, cause the people to disperse to their own homes. In the end this was done, some having to be hustled and even knocked out of the way ; others going willingly, like Thomas Eve, who testified that he was " half-dead when he heard the King was slain, but hearing his Majesty was well and safe he praised God and passed home." One of those who was not in his own home was the perplexed Henderson, who after going home and telling his wife that but for him the King would have been twice stabbed, went out, and walked up and down the bridge for about an hour. After which he took to flight and went into hiding.

Gowrie House was put in charge of the magistrates of Perth. The bodies of Gowrie and the Master were reserved for presentation and attainting before the Parliament when it should meet. (It met in November.) Close and immediate inquiry into all the circumstances of the day was

ordered. At last, about eight in the evening—the day
had turned dull, and it was raining—the King did indeed
mount his horse and rode out again for Falkland.

It was the end of his most flagrant day of peril and of
triumph ; also, it was the last day of its kind. There
were other plots, but the King's person was never again
approached so nearly and so dangerously. Crisis had
come upon him ; he had met it, and now he passed from
it towards another kind of life. He rode away from the
dusky house of the conspiracy of revolting sorcerers ; he
rode gently back towards Falkland and on towards security
and relaxation ; towards correspondence with Cecil, towards the coming of Carey and the succession, towards
the end of abduction, towards the ancient councillors and
open houses of England, towards the peace which with the
good and the ill in him he loved and sought, which was
to be his delight and danger, and after his death to be in
part the cause of his ill-fame. He rode also towards the
cruelty of his vengeance—the hunting after the two
younger brothers of the dead men, the dismissal of their
sisters from the Queen's service, the oath to root out
" their whole house and name." The Queen, then pregnant,
took the dismissal of her ladies badly ; there was irritation
and anger in the household.

This tragedy also had its harlequinade. Religion came
as a pantaloon to argue with the clown of royalty. James,
piously aware of the goodness of God in preserving him,
commanded that the preachers of Edinburgh should dilate
upon it in their sermons. Belief in God's goodness in this
particular involved, of course, belief in the accuracy of the
King's account. But the whole story had hardly been
published, when rumours grew up that the King's was but
half the truth ; that not the Ruthvens but James had
planned an evil day of surprise and blood ; that the subtle
Stuart had determined to root out the obnoxious house,

M

and that the bodies which lay so horribly waiting their
final mutilation and exposure on the scaffold at Edinburgh,
were those rather of the deceived than of the deceivers.
There was a whisper of the love of Anne of Denmark for
the younger Ruthven, as there had been of her delight
in the young Murray. It was, men said, the revengeful
James who had conceived destruction, and thrust himself
into the chambers of Perth, and lured the Master aside,
and cried to his servants falsely, and when he knelt with
his men in the room by the body of the Earl it was for the
success of his schemes that he gave thanks. His evidence
was perjured, and Henderson had been bribed to support
him with other perjury. As in the other actions of his life
there has been from that day to this a flickering shadow
of James thrown out behind him, with other uncertain
shadowy heads nodding grotesquely towards his own as if
in horrid whispers and obscene gestures until they rush
together in the darkness, which leaves when it rolls away
the blood of the innocent dead crying to God for vengeance.
So far then the ministers in general did not go ; so far not
even the obstinate minority of five that refused to give
thanks for the King's salvation. These five were brought
to Holyrood, and James argued with them. He was eager
that they should accept his view, not merely as the royal
but as the rational explanation, while they in effect refused
the rational because it was the royal.   The King expounded,
explained, and argued, and at last said, " Are ye yet fully
persuaded or not ? " Mr. Robert Bruce, he who had
anointed the Queen, said, " Surely, sir, I would have
further light before I preached it to persuade the people."
The other at first agreed ; afterwards, what with argument,
what with threat, they were brought to believe the King.
But Bruce remained obstinate. He refined upon kinds
of act and kinds of belief. He hinted that he could not
believe that part of the tale which concerned the Master.

"Then," said James, "you could not but count me a murderer."

"It followeth not, if it please you, sir, for ye might have some secret cause," Bruce objected. The King, patient and persistent, went over the whole story again. Bruce offered to sign his acceptance of the articles containing it. James asked him if he trusted it. "Yes, sir," said Mr. Robert. "If ye trust it, why may ye not preach it?" said the King. "I can tell you, sir," said Mr. Robert. "I give it but a doubtful trust, for I learn this out of Bernard—in doubtsome things to give undoubted trust is temerity, and in undoubted things to give a doubtsome trust is infirmity." "But this is undoubted," said the King. "Then bear with my infirmity," said Mr. Robert.

They wrangled over his infirmity through four long conferences. Mr. Robert said he more or less believed, but he could not answer for what he might believe or say in the pulpit. "I know not certainly what God may suffer me to speak. I may stand dumb. Therefore, sir, leave me free, and when I shall find myself moved by God's spirit, and to have the warrant of his Word, I shall not fail to do it." Dumb, the ministers were hardly ever caused to stand. The vexed King said, "That is plain Anabaptistry! that is, cabal and tradition." Bruce said he should altogether believe if Henderson, who had been taken, were brought to the scaffold for his part in the plot, and at the moment of death remained faithful to his story. The King declined to take this extreme method of convincing Mr. Bruce, and instead banished the minister to commune with his own soul abroad.

Eighteen months later he was allowed to return, but they still could not agree. "'Ye must subscribe my innocency,' said the King. 'Your own conscience, sir, can do that best,' said Mr. Robert. 'It is very hard for me to do it.' 'Why is it hard?' said the King. Loth was

Mr. Robert to answer, lest he should irritate him, but he insisted. Then said Mr. R., ' Your Majesty will not be offended if I speak freely ? ' ' Not,' said the King. ' I was reading,' said Mr. Robert, ' upon Ammandus Polanus, touching the slaughter of the magicians, when the King of Babel commanded to slay. Ammandus disputeth the question whether the King of Babel did well or not. First, he saith, *animi gratia*, it would appear that he did well, for he had the plain law of God for him in many places ; yet he concludes against the King that he did not well, for, howsoever he had the law, yet as he looked not to the law, nor had regard to God not His glory, he is a murtherer. Now, sir, I pray, what can I or any man say what your Majesty had before your eyes ? or what particular ye had ? ' ' It is true,' saith the King ; ' and therefore I will give you leave to pose me upon the particulars.' ' Then, first, if it please you,' said Mr. Robert, ' had ye a purpose to slay my lord ? ' ' As I shall answer to God,' saith the King, ' I knew not that my lord was slain till I saw him in his last agony, and was very sorry, yea, prayed in my heart for the same.' ' What say ye, then, concerning Mr. Alexander ? ' said Mr. Robert. ' I grant,' said the King, ' I am art and part of Mr. Alexander's slaughter, for it was in mine own defence.' ' Why brought ye him not to justice,' said Mr. Robert, ' seeing ye would have had God before your eyes ? ' ' I had neither God nor the devil, man, before my eyes,' said the King, ' but my own defence.' Here the King began to fret. He took all these points ' upon his salvation and damnation,' and that he ' was ance minded to have spared Mr. Alexander ; but being moved for the time, the motion prevailed.' Farther, Mr. Robert demanded of the King if he had a purpose that day, in the morning, to slay Mr. Alexander ? The King answered, upon his salvation, that day in the morning he loved him as his brother. Mr. Robert, by reason of his oaths, thought

him innocent of any purpose that day, in the morning to
slay them ; yet, because he confessed he had not God
nor justice before his eyes, but was in a heat and mind
unto wrong, he could not be innocent before God, and had
great cause to repent, and to crave mercy for Christ's
sake." So the dance of theology closed

On November 19 in that year the Queen was delivered.
Charles, afterwards King of England and Scotland, was
born at Holyrood. In the twilight, one evening, the nurse
saw the cradle of the Prince rocked by the apparition of
a little old man, who vanished from before her, leaving
behind him only a black cloak.

CHAPTER NINE

THE SUCCESSION

THE King, riding back with his gentlemen along the road from Perth to Falkland, seems to the spectator to be emerging from heavy northern clouds along the highway of a clearer and lordlier world. The rainy August night closes upon him, in no more than a natural and transitory darkness. He is already on the last stage of his journey towards the double crown. The nobles are silent about him ; any clamour of the preachers that breaks the silence is a babble out on the wild. War and danger have fled underground. As the evening and the morning succeed each other through those brief thirty months, the very country about him changes. The Tay he has left behind becomes a mirage of the Thames ; the great house upon it grows larger still and takes on a cloudy shape of the greater Tower upon the Thames, where the King's enemies are shut securely away from his harm. Through the changing landscape the King rides, along that highway which descends from the north, across the Borders, through the counties of England, on towards the mighty English house that is to close another day's journey, the tryst of Government, Theobald's. The name of the highway is the name of a man ; it is Cecil.

The princes of England had already been in correspondence with him ; letters had been received even from the lordliest of them all, the old Queen's younger Favourite, Essex. But neither in his magnanimity nor in his mischief was Essex the person to bring peace into any life, as Elizabeth and Francis Bacon could have told James. He

168

laid all his future devotion, and as much of his present as
he indecently dared, at Scottish feet, but he also urged
that Scottish feet should themselves be active. He proposed armies and demonstrations. He had warned James
that Cecil was dangerous, and James to his own disquiet
had believed him. Essex drew up a paper for the Scottish
ambassadors in which he pointed out that Cecil was in
close relation with Raleigh (who in the West commanded
" the uttermost province, where he may assure the Spaniard
his first landing . . . being also Captain of the Isle of
Jersey, there to harbour them upon any occasion ") and
the Lord Cobham (who possessed " the Cinq Portes, the
keys of the realm . . . as likewise the Countie of Kente,
the nexte and directest waye to the Imperiall citie of this
realme ") and Sir George Carew (who in Ireland held " that
province, which of all others is fittest for the Spaniard's
designs "). Essex was capable of believing anything of
anybody. But James did not know the nature of the
Favourite, and he had always mistrusted the natures of
the Cecils, father and son. He grew more nervous of the
succession as Elizabeth grew older ; he and she had understood one another very well—it was for both of them merely
a question of how little either could give and how much
they could get for it. She at any rate was another Majesty,
and James could think in terms of thrones. But he was
not certain of the terms of Cecil, until Cecil taught him.

At the request of Essex he agreed to send, at the beginning of 1601, two ambassadors southward—the Earl of
Mar and Mr. Edward Bruce. Before they arrived Essex
had attempted in England the same violence which the
Gowries had attempted in Scotland, with as much ill-
fortune. The person of the Sovereign was not even
approached, and Essex died in February, soon after the
ambassadors had started. They discreetly delayed on
their way, reaching London in March, after having received

new instructions from the King, very hostile to Cecil; " who is king there in effect," James wrote gloomily.

But now at last Cecil himself began cautiously to take gentle steps northward. Essex having been cleared out of the way, it was time that the King of Scots, if he were to come in, should be shown who was capable of bringing him in. There were to be no more demands for armies or demonstrations or stern diplomatic messages : "in quietness and confidence shall be your strength," and the quieter the better. Cecil quietly met the ambassadors. They reported hopefully on him to the King, who himself, though at a pinch capable of demonstrations and even arms, much preferred quietness. *Beati pacifici.* He sent a careful letter, half excusing, half blaming Essex, promising Cecil future favours in return for future favours, assuring him of love and secrecy. He received a reply—apologetic, obsequious, but extremely firm : let the King be at ease, let him follow " clear and temperate courses," let him not worry the Queen, let him trust very few among the English, in fact practically none but Cecil and the Lord Henry Howard. There was no need for James " to be busy, to prepare the vulgar beforehand." Cecil could do all that. And let the King take care not to use Cecil to make up a party for himself.

It was, under all its polite phrasing, an offer and a warning. The King might have Cecil—if he would have no one else but Cecil, except those whom Cecil chose. He should have the Throne—if he would have it from Cecil. The answer was easy. If Cecil, who was king there in effect, would do his duty to the King by divine right, then the King by right was willing to accept that duty, to embark on it, to ride on that broad and solitary road to the great city of dominion which awaited him, and presently to take care that the sides of the road were decked with such titles, houses, and estates as the road might think convenient. His next letter began : " Richt trustie and well-belovit," and the third " My dearest 10 "—ten being Cecil's cipher number in the correspondence, as Henry Howard's was three, and the King's thirty.

The correspondence is a little dull because of the infinite leisure of the sentences (one—not the longest—of James's runs to 356 words), and because of the perseverance with which the high contracting parties emphasize their goodwill. But as the prelude to the induction of a King, and that King James Stuart, it is not at all dull. Cecil stresses, not without cause, the jealousy of the Queen ; he touches with a fatal hostility the activities of Sir Walter Raleigh and of the Master of Gray ; he soothes James with assurances that all will certainly be well in the end. James was unable to conceal his longing for the kingdom—partly for glory and reputation, but partly also for ease and quiet. " It is a far more barbarouse and stiff-nekkit people that I rule over. Saint George surelie rides upon a towardlie rydding horse, quhaire I ame daylie burstin in daunting a wylde unreulie colte." He was at first troubled when he heard of the proposed peace with Spain, but his concern was dynastic rather than theological. If the peace were made (he wrote) it would no longer be thought odious to dispute upon a Spanish title ; and the King of Spain would be able to send agents, laden with golden arguments, for the advancing of his ambitious and most unjust pretences ; and lastly Jesuits, seminary priests, and all that rabble, would enter in swarms like the caterpillars or flies into Egypt, no man abhorring them, because the Spanish practice was the greatest crime they were ever attainted of, which would by the peace be utterly forgotten. Cecil, in his reply, drew distinctions between ordinary priests, of whom he said, " I confess that I shrinke to see them dy by dozens," and the Jesuits, and also between some Catholics and other Catholics ; the last distinction being necessitated by the variable religion of the Lord Henry Howard, who (besides being sometimes a Catholic) was a strong Cecilian. He also was writing letters—" Asiatic and endless volumes," the King, who preferred a simpler literary style, called them. James drew the old distinction : he would never allow in his conscience that the blood of any man should be shed for diversity of opinions in religion ; he would never agree that any should die for error in faith against the first table, but they should not be permitted to commit works of rebellion against the second table. He reverenced the Church of Rome, as " our mother Church," and held persecution as one of the infallible notes of a false church. But he would be sorry if Catholics multiplied, and by the connivance of the Government so increased that they became masters.

At long intervals the correspondence proceeded over two years. James had had to wait long, but now, when the Howards, and still more when Cecil, began to write, he knew the end was coming. It was spoken of everywhere except in the presence of the Queen of England ; there none hinted at her successor or glanced a doubt of her life. She refused to know that eyes, letters, horses were turned otherwise than to her ; or to hear, except in fatal reverie, the flight of her courtiers to the new sun, as other courtiers had come galloping to Hatfield when, forty-five years earlier, she had waited as a girl of twenty-five for the news of her sister's death. Up to the very end then she might have found herself in the Tower, destined for death. And now indeed she was destined for death.

It was Friday, March 25, 1603. The Queen was very ill. Holyrood was in a state of expectation such that even now we can feel the suspense. James refused to go any-where, waiting, always and only, for the final news. The final news lingered yet for days as it had lingered for years. He had been comforted, on the one hand, by a draft of the

proposed proclamation which Cecil sent him ; on the other,
he had been seized by a torturing thought. Suppose the
Queen lived for years in this state of semi-imbecility,
what then could be done ? He was on fire to be gone ;
thirty years of vigil burned in him towards the dawn, and
what now if the dawn still delayed ? He sent for Edward
Bruce, who was in the secrets of the royal letters to Howard
and Cecil ; he bade him write and ask. Bruce obeyed,
inquiring, approving, applauding. At six in the evening
he ended his letter, fastened it with two turns of green silk,
and sealed it twice—a saltire, on a chief three crowns. It
was hardly done when the King sent for him again ; another
messenger had arrived with many letters from gentlemen
of good account. The King and his servant read them
hastily ; they held all one tenour ; they all signified
Elizabeth's " near approach to her everlasting rest."
Many English were reported to be already on their way
north, " such as have not known us heretofore." Night
fell ; the March darkness was alive with the faint echo of
those multitudinously approaching hooves. It was sixteen
years and a month since the other news of Mary Stuart's
death had been brought to her son. Bruce sat down to
write once more to Howard—a brief note. " Take care of
the main point . . . have a care that the city be made
sure." He was weary ; he ended ; he pressed on the red
wax a more magnificent seal—a shield ensigned with the
Scottish crown, containing a lion rampant in a bordure
charged with eight fleurs-de-lys. The Queen of England
at Richmond had already for forty hours lain dead.

The Friday night, the Saturday, passed. Holyrood
heard no more certain news. As Saturday closed the King
retired ; he was already in bed when he heard that yet one
more rider had halted there, a man known to him, the
messenger who had once been stopped at Berwick by royal
orders when he bore the official tidings of Mary's death,

Sir Robert Carey, the English Warden of the Middle March.
There was no delay now, and little need for orders. Carey
was hurried to the bedchamber. He came in, exhausted
by riding, bruised by a fall, his head bloody with a hurt
from his horse's hoof. By the bed he kneeled stiffly down ;
his voice saluted the King of England, Scotland, France,
and Ireland. To the sound of that full title James stretched
out his hand ; Carey touched it with his lips, the first kiss
of the completed royalty. Godmother and mother had
unwillingly released their proper crowns. The King of
England lay quiet and composed, asking a few questions
about the Queen's illness, about her death, whether Sir
Robert brought letters from the Council. Sir Robert had
not ; he had slipped away without the Council's leave and
against their will ; he had indeed narrowly escaped detention. But he knew that everything in London had been
quiet and he was not without a token. He drew out a
blue ring, a ring taken immediately and secretly by his
sister from the dead Queen's finger, a ring once given her
by James. The King looked at it, recognized it, said that
Carey was a true messenger, and dismissed him with
promises of favour. Indeed, he needed them, for his
present office was done—the Marches existed no more.
He went out, leaving the first King of England and Scotland
to taste the knowledge. For three days it was kept more
or less secret ; on the third an official embassy arrived, and
the homage of England was laid publicly at James's feet.

On the following Sunday at St. Giles there was an
exchange of orations. A sermon was preached lauding the
King and the goodness of God ; afterwards James took
voluble leave of his people. He assured them of his care
and providence ; many (it is said) wept. At the palace
he signed the Act of the Council abolishing the very name
of the Clan MacGregor. On the Tuesday, so much were all
things in readiness, he set out. The Queen and the children

were to follow. Lennox and a number of Scottish lords accompanied him, with all those English gentlemen who had so lately poured into Edinburgh. The intolerable romanticism of Life arranged one other theatrical incident. Near Musselburgh the grand progress was interrupted by meeting the funeral of Lord Seton, one of the oldest and truest servants of Mary. The royal company halted ; the King himself, dismounting, sat down on a stone by the wayside till the dark procession had disappeared. It vanished ; the King rode on. He himself, later, did what he now could for his mother ; he caused her body to be brought from Fotheringay and buried, in high ceremony, at Westminster.

At the great English fortress of Berwick the guns saluted their new lord with such a thunder as had never in that place been heard before. From Berwick he entered his new world. Leisurely he came ; vistas opened before him, and within them happy vistas of the mind. Behind him lay the harsh castles of Scotland ; around and before him the open manor-houses of England. Behind him died the riotous shouting of the crowds of Edinburgh and Perth ; around him the country-folk thronged from their work to see and cheer him. Behind him stood the Presbyterian ministers of pure religion and his few titular bishops ; towards him came the robed and orthodox bishops of the tradition of Christendom. They bent to him and blessed him, the keys of cities were laid before him, the country gentlemen welcomed him with feasts and shows hitherto unimaginable ; the most magnificent hospitality was shown him by Sir Oliver Cromwell, a landowner of Buckinghamshire. Savouring it all intensely, from actual food to spiritual homage, he passed slowly through. He had had shows and pageants before, but never like this, never with such ostentation of loyalty and delight. He was much in the press of people and things, and so were the gentlemen of his household. Sir Thomas Erskine, at one stopping-place, was approached by a London lawyer who bore official letters for the King ; his name was Francis Bacon. Nearer, through that happy month, they came to London, and first, one night, the lordly cavalcade stopped at Theobald's. Riding slowly, the King came up the great walk ; before him the trumpets sounded, and the sheriff of Essex rode with his men. About him were the nobility of England and Scotland, bareheaded, observing no special order, now one, now another, coming up to the King's side and falling back again, according to his Highness's pleasure. At the entrance to the first court the whole glorious company dismounted, all but the King. Four nobles stepped to his horse, two before, two behind, and ceremonially laying their hands upon it, brought him forward into the second court. There he himself dismounted ; a young man knelt to present a petition, which the King graciously received. He went forward ; he came into the court. He saw before him a gathering of the great ones who had invited him : the Chancellor Egerton, the Treasurer Buckhurst, Henry Howard the Privy Seal. At their head, smaller and greater than any, deformed and decorous, stood the Secretary Robert Cecil, the lord of that house and, under the King, of England. The storm of shouting and cheering went on ; the great folk genuflected ; on the soft pawing hand of Majesty rested the soft-spoken lips of Cecil. The King raised him ; together they passed into the house. The two extraordinary figures disappear—the loutish King and the dwarfish Secretary. The multitude throng across, filling the courts, roaring applause. At that point rather than in the later ceremonial entry into London the accession of James was accomplished.

The cheering crowds had seen passing through them a man of a trifle over medium height, well set, and inclined to fullness of figure. He was high-coloured, with large and staring blue eyes ; his hair brown, his beard thin and

scattered. He held himself better on horseback than on
foot ; " in the whole man he was not uncomely," but his
weakness and awkwardness were enhanced by the famous
quilted doublets and stuffed breeches which he wore as a
protection against a sudden dagger-thrust ; they have been
the only fact commonly remembered about the King.
He was given to much talk, in a Scottish accent ("the full
dialect of his country," Bacon called it), and to being much
among men. Serious observers, however, remarked that
the large, quick talkativeness could, at need, be brief enough
and to the point, just as the going abroad into the press
did not mean that he allowed the press into the secrets of
his heart—the *arcana* of kingship, as he loved to call them.
Circle within circle of servants, councillors, and favourites
left the last sphere of his spirit still unopened. But that,
at the moment, his new statesmen did not know. There
was, indeed, no deeper secret in it than he made known :
it was but his own conviction of his own double nature—
an immortal man and a mortal god, sinner and king,
creature and creator. Cecil and he went in.

He had met Cecil, and in Cecil's mind was the point at
which the Stuart monarchy and the English gentry were
to become aware of each other. But that point, the point
at which he himself held them and at which he supposed
them to exist, did not quite coincide with the actual point
at which they did in fact make contact. It was infinitesi-
mally off the true centre, for there was one thing Cecil had
not taken into his calculations. Perhaps he could not, he
who never relaxed, he the admirable Civil Servant whose
work, whose interests, whose religion, whose patriotism,
whose selfishness, were so entirely one and unresting. He
did not allow for the natural inclination of mankind to
enjoy itself. It was an unfortunate thing for the English
monarchy, and perhaps for the English people, that both
the King of England and the gentlemen of England decided

to relax at the same moment.　It is understandable enough. The King had achieved his desire ; he was mounted on St. George's towardly horse, and he looked forward to happy canters through wide, peaceful, and agreeably obedient fields.　His person would be safe, and his wishes fulfilled, and his doctrines respected.　There would be plenty of money.　The month-long journey confirmed him in everything.　He would be able to loll comfortably on the throne, and there would only be tiny troubles from now on.　He would bring peace wherever it did not exist ; he might bring peace to the warring Churches of Europe ; but, above all, he would know peace himself.　He relaxed.

All over England the great majority of the country gentlemen also relaxed.　Elizabeth had been an experience, glorious, terrifying, sometimes enjoyable, sometimes disagreeable, but unique.　She had been wearing to her immediate servants ; Burghley's tears and Walsingham's moans testify to it.　Even to a wider circle she had been— and almost to the end of her reign she remained—unexpected.　It had been unlikely that she could succeed to the Throne ; more unlikely that she could succeed on the Throne ; most unlikely that she could succeed without a husband.　She had done all three.　There had been continually two expectations—she would be assassinated or she would be married.　Both expectations had been continually disappointed.　Gratifying or not, these disappointments had, for the most of her reign, kept her interesting.　New every morning was the sun.　Towards the end of her life the apparent defeat of the Spanish fleet, the disappearance of the marriage problem, the pressure of taxes and monopolies had combined to make her more tiresome and less interesting.　But by then she was a tradition ; she was also something very like a disagreeable genius ; and the moment of the succession loomed uncertainly.　She became suddenly not so much an unexpected fact as an historic fact. She united opposites. In that sense she is not unlike the Church of England, of which she was asserted to be the Governor (but not the Head) ; which for three centuries has been about to perish (so they assert) and still amazingly remains. It is called a *via media* ; it is about as much like a *via media* as Elizabeth herself, unless indeed the meaning of the *via media* is that it contains both the extremer ways at once. The Church of England, incredibly Catholic and impossibly Protestant, is not unlike the Queen, who was incredibly royal and impossibly *vulgar*—in the original sense of the word. Something in the genius of our nature combines opposites. The ablest of the Queen's Men was himself impossibly poetic and incredibly commercial. The tale of our armies is of men incredibly sceptical and impossibly heroic, as in that most marvellous of all the battlecries of the world when the English troops moved into battle calling : " Early doors, this way." An army of passionate mystics might have sent up that shout as a hymn to heaven, but heaven has created only one people who are mystics in irony and martyrs in unbelief ; the people over whom the tragic splendour of Elizabeth made her littleness a blazon of royalty and her falsity a glory of devotion, who was indeed Perfidious Albion, and lost nothing of either by being wholly the other.

Elizabeth was gone to the exposition of herself before the Cause of irony and scepticism and heroism and belief ; and James, her godson, reigned in her stead. Once he had been crowned in peace—except for one imbecile device— the whole body of English gentlemen relaxed. The great emotional scene in the great Queen's last Parliament had summed up the whole reign, and now both reign and moment were passed. From London throughout the kingdom there was exhaled a sigh of satisfaction at the succession, which became almost unnoticeably a sigh of relief at the change and a sigh of anticipation of enjoyment.

N

It was less conscious than James's own sighs of satisfaction, relief, and anticipation, but it was none the less deep-drawn. At one and the same moment, and, as it were, in one and the same place, James and the gentlemen of England decided to relax, to spread themselves, to be comfortable. Nothing is more devastating than for two innocent hopes of comfort to find that they contradict each other. Both James and his new gentry felt that now there need be no more talk of money. Unfortunately, both of them had the capacity—almost the right—to draw cheques on the future's banking account. The future, however, keeps only one account, and that not a very large one. When it arrived, therefore, it was already bankrupt.

There were a few already who, in minor things, doubted the solvency of the future, but even they hardly visaged the complete bankruptcy. The admirable Mr. John Chamberlain, that intelligent gossip to whom ages owe so much, wrote to Sir Dudley Carleton at The Hague, exactly a week after James had left Edinburgh : " These bountiful beginnings raise all men's spirits, and put them in great hopes, insomuch that not only Protestants, but Papists, Puritans, and the very poets with their idle pamphlets, promise themselves great part in his favour, so that to satisfy or please all, *hic labor hoc opus est*, and would be more than a man's work." But *labor* and *opus* were the last words the royal immigrant had in mind. He was come to a land flowing with milk and honey, and had small idea but that the honey and milk would continue. It was the more venomous bees and the more obstinate cows who were to be the difficulty in the new Canaan ; until the sharp stings and bitter horns of the armed horsemen of Cromwell gored and blinded the Majesty of a King, and drove him into a grave which has never quite seemed a martyr's.

The contented illusions, however, in which both parties

existed were not to be thoroughly dispelled for some years
yet. Meanwhile there occurred an affair hardly worth
mentioning except that it affected one of the few flamboyant
Elizabethans left—Raleigh, and that it shows the mind of
James in one of its more foolishly offensive moments.

It was the last and most futile of all the plots, futile
or effective, that had been laid to seize his person since,
thirty-six years before, the Lord Bothwell had summoned
the Earl of Mar to surrender his charge. There was,
certainly, to be one other plot, the Gunpowder, but the
professed object of that was the exact opposite of the
possession of his person ; being rather the entire dissipation
of his person. But here a strange mixture of causes and
persons came together in an absurd effort to do something.
There was a Roman priest named Watson with certain
co-religionists of his own, including a gentleman called
Sir Gervase Markham ; Lord Grey of Wilton, a young
Puritan and leader of Puritans ; there was George Brooke,
brother-in-law to the Secretary, and brother to Lord Cobham, Warden of the Cinque Ports ; there was Cobham
himself ; there were other odds and ends ; there was,
remotely on the outskirts and knowing very little about it,
Raleigh. There was an intention to seize the King and
force him to grant concessions to Catholics ; and an intention to seize the King and force him to do something else ;
and an intention to dethrone the King and substitute
Arabella Stuart ; later on, there was an intention (on the
part of Father Watson) to tell the King and rely on his
gratitude. Cecil, of course, knew about it. That charming
man, Bishop Goodman, attributed a large portion of the
whole wandering lunacy to George Brooke—" he knowing
well the practice of former times, that statesmen did make
plots and then discover them, he being brother-in-law to
the Secretary, thought he might run the same course, and
that it should be done by way of trial and temptation."

The other part became known to the Jesuit Gerard, who sent some kind of warning. Arrests and examinations followed ; at last all the conspirators were gathered in, and the trials followed. Cecil and the Howards went down to Winchester to take part in the commission which would destroy Raleigh, and carried out their part. He, eventually, was sent to the Tower. Sir Edward Coke, the Attorney-General, conducted the case for the prosecution. Never before—it was one of the advantages of England— had James had so loyal, so fierce, so effective a legal servant as Sir Edward Coke : until, years afterwards, Sir Edward shocked him profoundly by turning Parliamentarian.

The accused were all found guilty and sentenced to death. The sentences came to London for the King's approval. About the priests there was nothing to be said : the sentences were ratified and they were executed. George Brooke, if he had thought to use Cecil's distaff, found the web break ; he was beheaded. But the others were treated differently ; and the mind of James is seen in action.

For some days all sorts of rumours went about the Court. Some lords were said to be pressing the King to pardon ; others, to execute. At last, in a full setting of the Court, the King made a speech. He enlarged on the difficulties of his problem. He expanded the peculiar dilemma of justice. They were all guilty, and he was merciful. Some one ought to be executed, yet " to execute Gray, who was a noble young spirited fellow, and save Cobham, who was as base and unworthy, were a manner of injustice." Yet again, " to save Gray, who was of a proud insolent nature, and execute Cobham, who had showed great tokens of humility and repentance, were as great a solecism." The royal speech went on, comparing and contrasting, " travelling in contrarieties," emulating Plutarch ; no one could guess what the end would be till it came, " and therefore I have saved them all." Even after such ratiocination his Majesty at first sent off the pardon unsigned, and had to recall the messenger, a Scottish groom of the bedchamber, named John Gill, to add the indispensable name.

But this was not the end. The King had kept the Court in suspense to hear the full exposition of his mind ; he was also minded that there should be a proper suspense elsewhere. At Westminster, on the morning of Friday, December 10, three gentlemen were to be brought out, one by one, to die—Markham, Grey, Cobham. It was a dark and rainy day ; there was the usual crowd of spectators about the scaffold, even though the execution would be by simple beheading and not by hanging with the dreadful accompaniments of treason. John Gill, barely arriving in time after the extra delay over the signature, tried to fight his way to the scaffold and failed ; he found himself thrust back. He saw Markham was already on his way, and, calling out desperately to one of the gentlemen present, managed at last to reach the sheriff. He passed over the pardon, and with it his instructions—things were to be done indecently but in order. Markham, turning from his last devotions, found the sheriff at his side, who said that since he was so " ill prepared " he should have two hours respite, and ordered him to be taken back to the great hall of the Castle, where he was locked in and left to meditate. Meanwhile Grey came to the scaffold with a crowd of young courtiers waiting on him, playing his part gaily, Puritan as he was, but (unlike the Catholic Markham) spending long at his devotions with the religious aid of the ministers—keeping every one in the rain, as a spectator commented, more than half an hour. At last he made an end ; he, too, turned towards the axe to find the sheriff intervening. The order of death had been altered, he was told ; Cobham was to die first, and so he in his turn was taken back to the Hall. Cobham, a nervous unreliable creature, had managed to resolve himself into steadiness ; he made short prayers and a short speech. The sheriff for the last time intervened—he was to be confronted with the other prisoners. In the rain they all waited, executioners and spectators, till the helmets of the guard were seen bringing back Markham and Grey. They mounted the scaffold ; the three looked strangely on each other, " like men beheaded and met again in the other world." Between earth and sky, in a slow tasting of the prolonged expectation of death, they stood listening while the sheriff's voice rehearsed their crimes once more, the necessary justice of the King, and the execution of it which was to come upon them. He paused, waiting ; they assented— it was their business and perhaps their belief. The sheriff accepted their assent, and then in an outbreak of admiration proclaimed the King's pardon : pardon ? no, but amelioration : they were not to die. There was a burst of wild cheering. The prisoners were removed again to prison, and the horrible display of mercy was done.

It was the King's plan ; no other would have dared it, and hardly any other could have managed it. Nor is it mere tyrannical cruelty ; his words must be allowed their weight. The unreal dilemma in which he felt himself involved, the too real agony in which he involved others, the desire to be terrible and the desire to be merciful are all his, and his the grotesque result. When he gave himself up to the Devil he often did it sincerely from the noblest motives, but it is hardly possible to believe that he did not enjoy doing it. He sipped the rich wine of cruelty and was never drunk. He knew it was not only wrong but unwise to be drunk, for then he was off his guard. Through the division between caution and intoxication the Devil, on these occasions, slid into his senses, as when he listened to the music that Gelie Duncan played for the dance of lost spirits and was at once fascinated and appalled.

CHAPTER TEN

THE KING AMONG THE CHURCHES

JAMES in his Scottish years had had experience of the Presbyterian, the Roman, and the necromantic Churches; he had now one other to find. The Romans he still had, and the Puritans instead of the Presbyterians, much the same thing as they were, in spite of the difference in ecclesiastical organization. The Presbyterians in Scotland were a Kirk of their own; the Puritans in England were but a part of a greater Church. He was free now from any need of conciliating, and he hoped he was free from any difficulty in controlling, those mutual enemies. " Na, na, we'll have no need of the Papists now," he was said to have cried out in the surety of his succession, and he felt the same about the Kirk. He need no longer use Huntly to threaten Melville or Melville to defeat Huntly. The covens of witchcraft had faded; their nearest image in England was the House of Commons, but he had not yet discovered that. The leisure of his relaxation had not yet elbowed theirs, or not more than with a mutual condescension of apology might be passed by. Politically, he was more firmly seated then ever before, and theologically he had found a new thing, he had discovered the Church of England.

The Church of England has nourished and inspired many poets, saints, and martyrs. It has, however, had few royal children who have taken so intelligent an interest in it as James Stuart. At first that interest was largely self-preservative and tutorial. He delighted to take refuge with his new Bishops under the pretext of allowing them

to take refuge under him.   Of all classes of men the Bishops
of the Church of England were least likely to form conspiracies against his person, as Jesuits and Presbyterians
had done.   He was in good hope they would not even
preach at him, or seize him by the arm and call him " God's
silly vassal," or attach their titular signatures to blanks
meant for the King of Spain.   Yet they were at once
Bishops of as true a faith as those of Rome and of as pure
a religion as superintendents in Fifeshire.   He and they
mirrored themselves in each other.   He was disposed to
benevolence as they to obedience.   Occasionally a Calvinist
or a precisian or a textual maniac might appear among
them, but the general episcopal mind was as loyal as he
was royal.   The doctrine of the two kingdoms began to
disappear and leave the much pleasanter landscape of the
one kingdom of God, the King, and the Bishops, dispensing
a single supernatural authority.   He had had quite enough
of the doctrine of the two kingdoms.   In the end, if it were
examined far enough, it always meant the same thing
whether enunciated by Jesuits or Presbyterians.   It meant
that in the very last analysis there was something which
the King could not and ought not to control, and which
could and ought to control the King : the operation of the
Holy Spirit, formally declared by the many concordant
mouths of the General Assembly or by the single mouth of
the See of Peter.   The double kingdom of this world and
the other was invariably one in which he existed on suffer-
ance, even in this world.

It was therefore not surprising that he relaxed happily
into the cushioned throne which the Church of England
appeared to provide.   *Beati*, they might responsively
murmur, *pacifici*.   Yet it would be unfair to James to
think that he stayed there.   He desired very earnestly,
with a limited but actual mind, to be the son as well as the
defender and governor of the true faith and the pure

religion. He might be the lord of ecclesiastics, but in his curious simple soul he wished to be the servant of the servants of God. He could not traverse the spiritual distances which lay within the gate ; *doctor legalis* perhaps, but no *doctor seraphicus*. But the legal and moral dues he paid. He explored as far as he could. On his death-bed he made confession and received absolution at the hands of his priestly subjects, and surrendered himself to doom as under the protection of the Church militant upon earth.

But now, at the beginning of his new reign, he examined with curiosity and pleasure this new organization of religion. He had had, as he came south from Berwick, every hope and even every expectation of renewing the long vanished desire of his boyhood, though touched now by the less innocent selfishness of maturity. He looked again " to win all men's hearts." There would be exceptions ; at Newark he had ordered a thief to be hanged, rather against the strict legal habit of England as (it seems) was explained to him, and the thief's heart must have been hard to win. But he indefatigably expected affection. It was why whenever he found it, exhibited in becoming detail, he always reciprocated. Men in general were slow to surrender their hearts ; it seemed to him rather the fault of their lethargy or perversity than of his own incapacity. He was kindly and reasonable, but they were stubborn and greedy. He was anxious to extend toleration to the Catholics—so long as they were not intolerable. He was willing to let the Puritans go their way—so long as their way was properly conformable. As a result of his utterances all parties had heard good things of him, all parties expected good treatment. The Pope had suggested that if James would not himself become a Roman, he might at least consider the Romanization of the young Prince Henry. The King had declined, but he said he would always listen to reason. The Puritans had presented

a Millenary Petition asking for the abolition of such superstitious practices as the sign of the cross in Baptism, the
rite of Confirmation, the ring in Marriage, the words
" priest " and " absolution," lay-baptism (in cases of
danger), and other such monstrosities ; they begged for
better financial, academic, and ecclesiastical provision for
" a preaching ministry." The King, doubtful but not
hostile, was willing to hear all they could say in their
favour. He proposed to bring his own learning to bear on
the matter, and for that purpose he caused a conference to
be called at Hampton Court in January 1604. *Beatus
pacificus*. The Bishops—nine of them, with nine of the
lesser clergy—and four leading Puritan divines attended ;
so did Cecil and other lords of the Council. It was an
innovation. Elizabeth had never wished to spend three
days disputing on theology, and the Council had already
differed from James on the question of recusancy fines.
James had momentarily given way, and the fines had for
a month or two been reimposed. But it was obvious that
he had given way with reluctance—the Watson plot notwithstanding—and that in religious matters he was to Cecil
an unreliable (because an expert) quantity. The fines
were again suspended, and now he was determined to hear
the other dispute.

On the first day, a Saturday, the King took his place,
but the Puritan doctors were not called. James wished
to find whether on several points he and the Bishops were
agreed. He looked round on them, and could not contain
his pleasure at seeing these robed and reverend elders
instead of the fierce and suspicious gospellers of the north.
Here was discussion and apprehension rather than challenge
and conflict. Already half-contented, he began ; he
inquired of doctrine and of custom ; as they answered him
in full, he broke into the benign words : " I exceedingly
well approve."

Here and there they differed a little; the Bishop of London was earnest and the Bishop of Carlisle learned, but all was taken well on both sides. For almost the first time in his life, the King had taken part in discussion which was really discussion. The Bishops had found a King who knew what the Apostles and Fathers had or had not really said. In this state of high good-humour they parted, and came together again on the Monday to hear the Puritans.

There was not now quite the same pleasant feeling. The King intended to be impartial, but he could not entirely rid himself of the warm interest which he and the Bishops had shared on Saturday. Nor was he wholly at ease when, as from a distance, he heard again that dangerous phrase, " the purity of Christ's Church," resounding through the chamber. But he checked the Bishop of London—who interrupted Dr. Reynolds, the chief objector—and he showed a willingness to urge the Bishops to make small concessions. The question of episcopacy itself loomed, but there the King was decided: " I approve the calling and use of bishops in the church, and it is my aphorism, No Bishop no King." He was equally firm over a proposal to insert more negatives in the Articles. What was the good of telling men what they were *not* to believe ? His mind went back to Mr. Craig of Edinburgh, who had multiplied " detestations and abrenunciations." No, no ; let us have a creed we can hold in our heads and need not keep in our table-books.

Dr. Reynolds spoke again: " May your Majesty be pleased that the Bible be new translated."

The Bishop of London was scornful, but the King approved. " I profess," he said, " I could never yet see a Bible well translated in English ; but I think, that of all, that of Geneva is the worst. I wish some special pains were taken for a uniform translation ; which should be done by the best learned in both Universities, then re-viewed by the bishops, presented to the Privy Council, lastly ratified by royal authority, to be read in the whole Church, and no other."

It is a climax rather for us than for them ; they had not experienced the centuries. It would be but a just recompense for the laughter and scorn that has been spent on James Stuart to speak usually of the Authorized Version in the old phrase as " King James's Bible." They all assented and passed on—to trouble. In that single brief interlude they had created immortality.

The King, as the hours went by, grew more and more fretted by the desires of the Puritans. Mr. Knewstub took exception to the cross in baptism ; he spoke of " weak brethren." The King had had experience of " weak brethren " before, when Mr. Robert Bruce had attributed his incredulity of the Gowrie plot to his " infirmity." He totally disapproved of such weakness. Mr. Knewstub began to talk of Christian liberty. The King's mind flew to the beardless boys who had braved him to his face, telling him that every man was to be left in ceremonies to his own liberty. His temper began to rise—" I will have one doctrine, one Discipline, one Religion, in substance, in ceremony. Never speak more to the point, how far you are bound to obey." Mr. Knewstub took exception to the surplice ; Dr. Reynolds to the words, " with my body I thee worship." The King said, smiling : " If you had a good wife yourself, you would think all worship and all honour you could do her were well bestowed on her." They took exception to the Churching of Women. The King said that he approved it—" Women being loath of themselves to come to church, I like this, or any other occasion, to draw them thither." But in spite of his good intentions, his patience was by now wearing thin, and Dr. Reynolds unexpectedly broke it. He demanded meet-

ings of the clergy every three weeks, " with prophesying."
The King felt all his past rush back on him ; the sacred
body throbbed with the approach of danger. " If you aim
at a Scottish presbytery, it agreeth as well with monarchy
as God and the devil. Then Jack, and Tom, and Will,
and Dick shall meet and censure me and my council.
Therefore I reiterate my former speech, *Le Roy s'avisera* :
Stay, I pray, for one seven years, before you demand, and
then if you find me grow pursy and fat, I may, perchance,
hearken unto you, for that government will keep me in
breath, and give me work enough."

He rose from the Conference in something like a rage ;
he touched his hat to " my lords the bishops," the servants
and images of monarchy and himself, " a mortal god."
He turned to the Puritans—" If this be all your party hath
to say, I will make them conform themselves or else I will
harry them out of the land or else do worse." He went
abruptly out of the room. It was a great day's work for
the future. Between them all they had promised the
Authorized Version and determined the inevitability of
the Nonconforming Churches. Two obstinacies had allied
themselves, and the third obstinacy was to grow into a
separate thing. The King wrote jestingly about the discussion to the Lord Henry Howard. There was a third
day's meeting, but it was mostly concerned with other
things. The King's temper was fixed ; the Bishops declared that he spoke by the inspiration of the Spirit of
God. " Then the Spirit," said Sir John Harington, " is
something foul-mouthed." Yet the admiration of Majesty
in action stirred in equally cool minds ; the Chancellor
Ellesmere said he had never before understood how *Rex est
mixta persona cum sacerdote*. The sacerdotal Majesty of
James and the Catholic episcopacy of the Church of England
were united in the bonds of affection for ever.

The Conference appeared to James not unsuccessful,

but there dwelled in his mind the vision of himself presiding at an even greater gathering of peace. Invincibly convinced that reason, elucidated by authority, must in the end persuade all sincere men to holy union, he allowed himself to dream of a General Council, where the Pope and he might lead the warring churches, and with double oratory persuade them to the formation of a single Church of God. The Catholic sovereigns would be there to assist—the King of France, the King of Spain, the Emperor. The heaven-elect of Christendom would reform Christendom, largely on the theological plan of this Thulean scholar, though no doubt the plan might be amended in detail. He was not obstinate. The Reformed Churches would be his especial care ; as their effectual, if not nominal, patriarch he would embrace the other patriarch of Rome. At once Pope and Emperor of Protestant Europe, he would discourse with the Pope and Emperor of Roman Europe—all generations should call him blessed. Pitiful and grandiose, yet not ignoble, the dream haunted him. It would be God's work ; that it would also be his own did not diminish its glory. He lost his head in those mists of peaceful ambition. But when he emerged from them to the details of his royal labour he always found his head again—and his head, so far as actuality went, always screwed on the right way. The Catholic envoys, Roman or Spanish, naturally never understood his dream. It seemed to them silly, which it was. But it also seemed to them that any one who could entertain it must be approaching conversion, which James was not. It is not the only time that the wild speculations of the minor poets of these strange islands have misled the more classic poets of ecclesiastical Europe.

In fact, however, the King did achieve a European reputation, though not the kind he most desired. There was never a General Council, but there was a general controversy. When one considers James's historical reputa-

tion, it is astonishing to remember that he took a leading
part in a mighty dispute which shook the studies and lecture-
rooms of Europe. It had begun before he took part, but
he became the symbol of an intellectual war. The Breves
of the successor of Peter were answered by the successor
of Plantagenet ; a Cardinal in Rome contradicted ; the
King replied ; a Cardinal in Paris preached against his
doctrine before the assembled Estates ; and again the
King replied. Certainly he had help ; he had Lancelot
Andrewes. Arguments and abuse spread everywhere.
Books (and the size of them ! the number of them !)
thundered for and against. The doctrine of the Cardinal
Bellarmine and the doctrine of James, King of England,
contended in a multitude of publications. So far had the
" son of Seigneur Davie " come from the lonely and slandered nursery of Stirling. There had emerged from Thule
an intellectual pattern of Church and State which the
powder of the Fifth of November had blown spiritually
into the high places of the world. Under other names,
in other terms, it is a problem which still vexes us—this
relation of the civil and religious powers. Still in our
streets the morning telegraph throbs and the evening star
glimmers with the arguments of James Stuart. Only we
say the State where he said the King.

It was not his original intention. He desired to win
all men's hearts. In 1603, despite Cecil and the Council,
he suspended the recusancy laws. He assured his Roman
subjects of goodwill. Priests were allowed to enter the
country ; lay households went unfined. Informal communications passed between the hunting-lodge of Royston
and Rome which did not touch the underlying question :
had the deposing power of the Pope a moral value for
Catholics ? Did it, to a Roman and English gentleman
of estate or to the least of his servants, *matter*, if the Holy
See deposed James ? James wanted an arrangement by

which troublesome Catholic subjects would be excommunicated.　The Pope declined, and hinted again at the formal
conversion of Prince Henry.　James declined.　The number
of Catholics increased as the priests returned.　The Queen,
though not openly Catholic, refused to receive communion
in a Protestant church.　The King began to find the results
of toleration intolerable.　He reinforced the laws against
the entrance of priests and deported all that could be
found.　By 1605 the whole attempt at peace broke down.
James's verbosity in conversation had spread in Europe
the idea that he might be converted.　It came to his ears.
He was as angry as Newman when it was rumoured that
he might return to the Church of England.　He heard
that the angels of the Court of Rome were preparing to
return thanks over one sinner—or, at least, heretic—that
had repented.　Nothing more annoyed his immovable
mind.　The rumour had arisen partly because he had
assented to the expulsion from their posts of the extreme
Puritans.　He now assented to the reimposition of the
recusancy fines.　Death he did not permit, but money
had its useful side; already the Crown was in straits.　It
was February 1605.

Months went by in the persecution, and at the beginning
of November—it was Sunday, the third—Cecil, by now
Earl of Salisbury, came alone to the King.　The Secretary
had already tested the King's temper, though he was never
quite sure of him.　He never understood the King's intellectual consistency, nor the King's courage.　But he did
understand his pedantry and his conceit, which were far
more noticeable, and he submitted a paper which aroused
both those qualities.　Much as we may allow to James's
real intelligence, it seems unlikely that he would have
interpreted the paper so adequately unless either God or
Cecil had inspired him.　He himself attributed it to that
share of the Divine Wisdom which lodges in kings; we may

prefer (even according to the King's own account) to attribute it to Cecilian prescience. This was the letter, sent to the Lord Mounteagle by his kinsman Francis Tresham :

" My Lord : Out of the love I bear to some of your friends, I have a care of your preservation : therefore I would advise you, as you tender your life, to devise some excuse, to shift off your attendance at this parliament. For God and man have concurred to punish the wickedness of this time. And think not slightly of this advertisement, but retire yourself into your country, where you may expect the event in safety. For, though there be no appearance of any stir, yet I say, they shall receive a terrible blow this parliament, and yet they shall not see who hurts them. This counsel is not to be condemned, because it may do you good, and can do you no harm, for the danger is past so soon as you have burnt this letter ; and I hope God will give you grace to make good use of it ; to whose holy protection I commend you."

The King read it, considered it, and (as he told the tale), though he was the least suspicious man alive, said it seemed to him more weighty in its style than most idle letters of the kind ; he thought it should be taken seriously. The Secretary's literary judgment differed. He went into a long explanation of why he thought it was negligible, basing his argument on the curious phrase : " the danger is past, as soon as you have burnt this letter." Cecil argued that if the danger was past when the letter was burnt, then the warning was useless since at the burning of the letter the danger would no longer exist. James, feeling that this reading was silly—which it was, as Cecil must have known—looked for another and found it. He said that " as soon " might mean " as quickly." The danger, whatever it was, would be as sudden and brief as the burning of a letter, it would be aimed at the Parliament ; it would be wrought by unseen hands. He said to

o

himself : " Gunpowder," and he said it to Cecil. Cecil
took it " with a merry jest," but, being impressed (so James
said), caused the vaults to be examined. Which, indeed, he
and the lords had already determined to do.

The vision of the two men, in the gallery at Whitehall,
leaves the Secretary's face in shadow. There were suspicions
at the time, held by other than Catholics, that he was not
ignorant of the making of the plot. It was reported that
Thomas Percy, one of its chief members, was seen leaving
Cecil's apartments at two in the morning, and it was
rumoured that in the final catastrophe Percy and Catesby
and Tresham died not inconveniently. He stands there,
decorously debating with the King, explaining at length
why *this* sentence is absurd. He expounds its folly ; he
provokes the King's curiosity and subtlety. Without some
such spur it seems unlikely that James would have been
inspired to think that "as soon" meant "as quickly,"
" contrary to the ordinary grammar construction." James
showed himself a little stupefied at this amazing revelation
of the depth of Divine Wisdom hidden in kings. As on
the one side the Bishops of the Church of England praised
the Holy Spirit in him, so on the other conspirators rushed
to justify his solution of their cryptograms. It surprised
him to discover how right he always was.

So far as James himself was concerned, that was the
conclusion of his concern with the plot, nor is there any
need here to dwell on the details. The conspirators were
seized or fled ; those fleeing were pursued, surrounded, and
taken or slain. Wild rumours went abroad about the
Catholics ; quiet whispers about Cecil. It is certain that
there was a plot ; it is quite uncertain how much Cecil
knew about it. It is also certain that it made no difference
to the King's own general attitude towards the Catholics,
except that he assented to the forming of a new oath of
allegiance. If Cecil thought to frighten the King, he

failed ; if he thought to alter general principles, upon which the King endeavoured to act, he failed. James seemed still to be nursing, though less hopefully, vague ideas of amity with Rome.

The new oath had more purposes than one. There had been for years very definite dissensions between home and foreign Catholics. The admirable ardour of the Jesuits regarded the Church as the Society to which man was chiefly bound. The sincere devotion of the English Catholics, the new generation of whom had grown up in an England already Protestant, felt more acutely the strain of a double loyalty. There had been hostile passages between the two parties, of which the Government took all the advantage it could. The new oath was intended to thrust another division between them, and to that end it was carefully prepared. It had also to satisfy the King. It pledged those who took it to loyalty, notwithstanding any excommunication or deprivation put out by the Roman See, and to disallow any Papal power or authority to depose, dispossess, invade, or attack the King. But it went further. It added : " And I do further swear, That I do from my heart abhor, detest, and abjure as impious and heretical, this damnable doctrine and position, That Princes which be excommunicated or deprived by the Pope, may be deposed or murthered by their subjects or any other whatever." The kernel of all was the word " heretical." Every Catholic was to swear that the doctrine that excommunicated Princes might be deposed by their subjects at the will of the Pope was false to the Catholic Faith.

At first a number of Catholics did. Even the Archpriest in London who acted in lieu of a Bishop consented to swear, after some searchings of heart and examinations by the Council, and his example fired others. The shock of the plot had startled many (as Ben Jonson in a letter to

Cecil had declared it would). But many refused. The Pope
in a breve exhorted Catholics to abstain from the oath,
declaring that he knew how they would cheerfully undergo
all manner of cruel torments whatsoever. The Archpriest,
having been arrested, wrote a letter to his fellow-priests,
hinting that the breve was not in accord with the Pope's
intention. Cardinal Bellarmine wrote to him, protesting,
and afterwards removing him from his office. The Pope
issued a second breve, reiterating his commands. Persecution—ruin for the laity, imprisonment, deportation, possible
martyrdom for the priests—descended on the faithful.
And the King, in high and sincere indignation, produced a
book, *Triplici Nodo, Triplex Cuneus, or an Apologie for the
Oath of Allegiance.* It is said that he drew up the synopsis
and Lancelot Andrewes wrote it. But the dominating
mind and purpose were the King's, and he claimed it afterwards, although (he said) he had forborne to put his name
to it because, among other reasons, it was meant to answer
Bellarmine's letter, and he could not think a Cardinal a
meet match for a King. He was very angry. He had
tried, after his own fashion and short of any serious inconvenience, to be tolerant ; even the oath left those who
took it free to believe what they pleased, short of their civil
duty. He had discouraged the sacramental test which the
Commons were anxious to impose ; he had, it seemed to
him, after the late outrageous conspiracy, behaved in a
very mild and merciful manner. The new oath was a
milder thing than the old oath of supremacy, which rejected
the Papal authority altogether. Certainly the laws re-
garding the old oath were still in existence, but James was
not anxious to enforce them, so long as he could have his
own means of distinguishing between Papists who " though
peradventure zealous in their religion, yet otherwise civilly
honest and good subjects, and such terrible firebrands of
hell " as the Powder-men. He had wished to win even

Catholic hearts. And this was his reward ! It astonished, shocked, and hurt him.

Yet even this controversy was part of a wider one. The King's argument declared that the spiritual power, though supreme in its own sphere, must not interfere with the temporal rights of the civil government. In fact, of course, this necessarily limits the spiritual power, even in its own sphere. Bellarmine developed the famous theory of the indirect power of the Pope. The Supreme Pontiff is concerned directly with spiritual things, and with temporal only indirectly as leading to spiritual. Even in temporal things he does not act so much directly as indirectly. For God does not give temporal power directly to this man or that man, but indirectly by the intermediary consent and agreement of men. It is because the Pope has to control and direct all men that he has power to take and to give kingdoms ; it is an indirect, but effectual power.

What Bellarmine pushed out through the door, he let in through the side-window. James found the deposing power making itself comfortable in the galleries of the Kings. He appealed in a long Premonition to the second edition of his book, to all the Princes of Europe, offering it to the Emperor, and to all other high and mighty kings and right excellent free princes and states of Christendom ; " our loving brethren, cosins, allies, confederates, and friends." To whom he added, " James by the Grace of God, King of Great Britain, France, and Ireland ; Professour, Maintainer, and Defender of the Trew, Christian, Catholique and Apostolique Faith, Professed by the ancient and Primitive Church, and Sealed with the blood of so many holy Bishops, and other faithfull crowned with the glory of Martyrdome ; Wisheth everlasting felicity in Christ our Saviour." But none of them committed himself. With a wisdom which had no touch of folly they all remained silent.

CHAPTER ELEVEN

The Mortal Arcana

HOWEVER much the appearance of his Majesty had to the translators of the Bible resembled the sun shining in his strength, the physical appearance of Majesty, his habits and manners, were the subject of much gentlemanly contempt among his southern subjects. They might accept him, but they could not like him. He was a King when he came to them, and the descendant of a house of kings, but it was a house that had always been alien and often hostile. The prestige of his matured royalty was considerable, yet it was foreign prestige, and something, they felt, was due to them for accepting him ; a certain observation, if not actual humility. The King showed no signs of observation. His uncouth speech offended their ears ; his familiarity their dignity ; and his conceit their pride. They were proud, but James was not proud. He was aware of his mysterious divinity, but he was not proud of it ; indeed it would have shocked him to think that he was proud of the miraculous grace of God. He was not even proud of his learning, his theology, his Latin accent. But he was conceited. He liked to talk of them ; he plumed himself on them with a simple, obvious, tiresome, and sometimes silly persistence. To the reserved dignity of Sully, the industrious Huguenot minister of Henry of France, he seemed the " wisest fool " in Christendom. His own people observed his folly even more than his wisdom— those only excepted, who, like Bacon, beheld shining through him the lambent Spirit of majestic grace. He liked to be admired ; he liked to be told that he was admirable. But he insisted that the admiration should be exhibited at things for which he was justly admirable ; and the natural offence caused by the necessity of admiring something which was indeed admirable has roused irritation from that day to this. He was tactless in his desire to instruct and improve.

In 1604 Sir John Harington, another godson of the great Queen, was given an audience. Sir John had not rushed north with other courtiers, but he had delicately brought himself to the King's notice. He was a poet, and at the end of December 1602 he had read some verses to the dying Elizabeth. Listening, she had said not unkindly : "When thou dost feel creeping Time at thy gate, these fooleries will please thee less." Time had crept, for all of them, but another three months when Sir John sent other verses to the new King at Edinburgh. A civil little note, dated on the Sunday when James had spoken at St. Giles, acknowledged them. In May Cecil had warned him off the Court : "the King doth find scant room to sit himself ; he hath so many friends." But he was at last called for. He came, one of the infinite company of English amateurs, and found himself uncomfortable in the solemn royal presence. James, looking forward to an hour of intellectual conversation, was gracious. He also was an amateur, but a Scottish amateur, and therefore more earnest than many an English professional. They talked of philosophy ; the King quoted Aristotle, so as to remind Sir John of his examiners at Cambridge. He made Sir John read Ariosto (whom he had translated) and praised his accent. He talked of wit, asking whether a King ought not to be the best clerk in his own country, and whether the English did not, in fact, think well of his own learning and wisdom. From that they switched off on to one of the King's own particular subjects—witchcraft. James raised a question which has always proved baffling :

why the Devil prefers to work rather with old women
than with others ? Sir John, bored with patronage over
Aristotle and Ariosto and with such grotesque (but interesting) questions in speculative theology, risked a joke.
He pointed out that " we are taught thereof in Scripture
—that the Devil walketh in dry places." James took it
very well ; he was always capable of laughter, except at
the nature of the King, and he said he had heard much of
Sir John's reputation for mirth. Sir John " did covertly
answer " ; he, like a greater, and wiser, subject, thought
it was not for him to bandy compliments with his sovereign.
The King went on to speak of those who by second sight
had seen the bloody head of Mary Stuart dancing in the
air before her execution ; he admitted he had himself
sometimes sought to find, out of certain books, a way to
know the future ; he named some dangerous volumes,
and advised Sir John to avoid them. Sir John neither
knew nor wanted to know them ; he willingly promised
aversion. At last (according to Sir John's own report)
the King said : " Now, sir, you have seen my wisdom
in some sort, and I have pried into yours. I pray you,
do me justice in your report, and in due season I will
not fail to add to your understanding in such points as I
may find you lack amendment." Rather ungratefully Sir
John, having escaped, wrote a slightly mocking account of
the interview to Amyas Paulet. He saw the King as a
comic figure ; so do we. He did not, however, see himself
as comic also, and we do : the exquisite amateur of art
and learning alarmed and uneasy in the presence of the
solemn student. Rather John than James, if we must
choose a patron for our own studies, but preferably neither,
or (perhaps even more desirably) both.

The King's learning was not the only subject upon
which Sir John could be witty. He observed with humour
the degenerate amusements of the Court. The masques

and pageants in which the sovereign indulged, or was indulged, were extraordinarily expensive, but they were liable to lose something of the Elizabethan state. In 1606 Sir John beheld a gross exhibition of foolery.

" One day, a great feast was held, and, after dinner, the representation of Solomon his Temple and the coming of the Queen of Sheba was made, or (as I may better say) was meant to have been made, before their Majesties, by device of the Earl of Salisbury and others. But alas ! as all earthly thinges do fail to poor mortals in enjoyment, so did prove our presentment hereof. The Lady who did play the Queen's part, did carry most precious gifts to both their Majesties ; but, forgetting the steppes arising to the canopy, overset her caskets into his Danish Majestie's lap, and fell at his feet, tho I rather think it was in his face. Much was the hurry and confusion ; cloths and napkins were at hand, to make all clean. His Majesty then got up and would dance with the Queen of Sheba ; but he fell down and humbled himself before her, and was carried to an inner chamber, and laid on a bed of state ; which was not a little defiled with the presents of the Queen which had been bestowed on his garments ; such as wine, cream, jelly, beverage, cakes, spices, and other good matters. The entertainment and show went forward, and most of the presenters went backward, or fell down ; wine did so occupy their upper chambers. Now did appear, in rich dress, Hope, Faith, and Charity : Hope did assay to speak, but wine rendered her endeavours so feeble that she withdrew, and hoped the King would excuse her brevity : Faith was then all alone, for I am certain she was not joyned with good works, and left the court in a staggering condition : Charity came to the King's feet; and seemed to cover the multitude of sins her sisters had committed ; in some sorte she made obeysance and brought giftes, but said she would return home again as there was no gift which heaven had not already given his Majesty. She then returned to Hope and Faith, who were both sick and spewing in the lower hall. Next came Victory, in bright armour, and presented a rich sword to the King, who did not accept it, but put it by with his hand ; and, by a strange medley of versification, did endeavour to make suit to the King. But Victory did not tryumph long ; for, after much lamentable utterance, she was led away like a silly captive, and laid to sleep in the outer steps of the anti-chamber. Now did Peace make entry, and strive to get foremoste to the King ; but I grieve to tell how great wrath she did discover unto those of her attendants ; and, much contrary to her semblance, most rudely made war with her olive branch, and laid on the pates of those who did oppose her coming."

Both the King and the Queen liked shows, though Anne liked to take part and James preferred to watch. He was disappointed, when he first came to England, to find there was no play fixed for Christmas night. They told him it was not the fashion ; he answered, " What tell you me ? I will make it the fashion." But he gave way, and accepted the English habit. Occasionally, on the other hand, he was offered overmuch. At the festivities of the Princess Elizabeth's marriage in 1613, after spending almost two whole nights contemplating the dancers in the Lords' masque, by Thomas Campion, on Sunday, February 14, and the Middle Temple masque, by George Chapman, on Monday, February 15—he revolted against a third, Francis Beaumont's, meant for the next night, and prepared by the Inner Temple and Gray's Inn. He was tired and sleepy. Sir Francis Bacon, who was of Gray's Inn, protested that his refusal would " bury them quick " ; James said the alternative was to bury him quick, for he could last no longer, but he received them on the Saturday with high approbation.

In the equivalent amusement of jousts and tilting the King also preferred to watch. Prince Henry and the Duke of Lennox were more efficient tilters; the Prince in 1610 was represented as the awakener of Chivalry. Three years previously, in 1607, an unpurposed incident at one of the jousts had awakened emotion in the King. The great affection and violent passion of love which was in him (so they said—but he tasted it with his head rather than his heart; he took delight in the apprehension of devotion) had had for long no intense and permanent centre. The Lord Hay, the Lord Montgomery, pleased him, but in his suburbs; and Hay at least knew it. He was as wise as he was magnificent; he was " known to be a cunning observer," and to " comply with all Favourites." He had now a great opportunity. One of his squires, at that joust, fell from his horse, and sustained a broken leg. James, looking from his seat, was touched by the accident and smitten by the young man's good looks. He caused him to be removed and attended; he made inquiries about him. It was Robert Kerr, or Carr, cadet of a Scottish house, whose father had been devoted to Mary Stuart. The King showed an increased sympathy, called on the invalid, talked with him, found him less learned than he might be, and proceeded to enjoy himself in one of the pleasantest ways that can be—by instructing a young, docile, and handsome inferior. He began to teach him Latin; the Court, openly polite but privately sneering, said that there was need his Majesty should teach him English too, " for he is a Scotch lad, and hath much need of a better language." The King and Carr did not think so; the Scots served them for their growing affection even better than the less intimate and familiar English. James felt that here at last was a harbour " for his most retir'd thoughts "—thoughts which for long he had not shared with any, high thoughts of politics and persons; here was a subject friend.

The young Carr was not quick at Latin, but in the early days of love tardiness has a virtue of its own. He was docile to his new patron, and in things other than Latin he was quick enough. James, though he was said to be careless about his own clothes, liked to see those about him attentive to him in theirs. Carr pleased him by taking clothes seriously; when they grew ruffled the King smoothed them, just as when he was ruffled Carr could smooth him again. The handsome young creature, apart from " his breathing and soul," was the King's creature. God had made him compact, of a moderate height, fair-haired, ruddy, and golden-bearded. The King made him Gentleman of the Bedchamber, and presently knighted him. He gave him his portrait, and an income. Less pleasantly he compulsorily purchased from the imprisoned Raleigh his Manor of Sherborne. The manor, upon Raleigh's attainder, had been forfeited to James. James had given it back, or had meant to give it back, to Lady Raleigh. But an important clause had, by the fault of a clerk, been omitted from the deed. Cecil (now Salisbury) suggested that the manor would make a provision for Carr. Raleigh protested; Lady Raleigh went twice to Whitehall. The King passed her in silence the first time; on the second he said only, " I maun have it, I maun have it for Carr." But he caused a Commission, on which one of Raleigh's friends sat, to make a survey, and determine compensation. Saul (the King probably thought) would have done even less: see *The Trew Law*. He had his way —within the strict letter of the law.

Not only Cecil, but also the Howards, mockingly but swiftly, accommodated themselves to the King's love. Carr was recognized by all as Favourite. The Lord Hay was one of the first to recognize it, as, years later, he was among the first to fall away. The Lord Hay was very circumspect, and had his own thoughts to keep. By 1611 among other gifts, Carr had been made Viscount Rochester and Knight of the Garter. He had enemies, of course ; the Prince of Wales for chief. But, in spite of the *Basilikon Doron*—perhaps a little because of it—the Prince and the King tended to be at petulant jars. The Queen was hostile, but James, following the *Basilikon Doron*, did not let the Queen's wishes trouble him over much. At the Council Carr's opinion was listened to with respect, as in the Bedchamber he received the secrets of the King's retired thoughts. In 1613 he received the great English title of Earl of Somerset. He had ostensibly everything —but for the usual Court intrigues—at his feet ; certainly he made, in his lordly survey of life, one mistake—he thought he had the King there too. Arran, Bothwell, Gowrie, had all made similar mistakes, and had all paid heavily for it. In his secret heart James preserved the chastity of his divine nature undisturbed. But the Earl of Somerset could not be expected to understand that. He went on his way, and with him went his secretary, an able man, well-travelled and well-lettered, Sir Thomas Overbury. Sir Thomas was the author of a small book of *Characters* of which one has become a favourite in our prose anthologies—the exquisite little vignette of pure and homely country life, called *The Milkmaid*. The Milkmaid !

It is true that, though the Court of James did not much resemble milkmaids, the King himself had a desire for the pigeons of peace. Pigeons is undoubtedly the word ; they never succeeded in being doves. They suffer from being compelled to have their cote in the midst of a harlequinade touched with horror. And one especially of those which James had loosed brought a terrible fate with it.

He had desired, coming south, to heal the schisms between the great English houses as he had tried to heal those of the Scottish. He did not actually feast the

Howards, the Cecils, the Herberts, the Devereux, at a
table outside the Mansion House. He looked around,
however, for any reasonable opportunities, and either he
himself or the indefatigably attentive Cecil found one.
There should be a marriage between the families of Howard
and Devereux.

The proposed bride was Frances Howard, daughter of
the Lord Thomas Howard, Earl of Suffolk, great-niece of
the Lord Henry Howard, Earl of Northampton, a girl of
thirteen ; the bridegroom was the Lord Robert Devereux,
Earl of Essex, son of Elizabeth's favourite, a boy of
fourteen. The noble relatives arranged the match : to
add to the union her sister was presently to marry Cecil's
son, Lord Cranbourne. The King happily presided over
the whole affair, including the ceremonials. It was a very
great solemnity—masque by Jonson, mechanism by Inigo
Jones, ladies' headdresses by the King from his own heronries,
jewels by every one from any one, so multitudinous that
even the Spanish ambassador de Sarmiento was splendidly
outdone. The marriage over, the bridegroom went abroad ;
the bride remained at Court. The King saw her there
occasionally. The Prince saw her and was attracted.
The Viscount Rochester saw her. Four years went by
and her husband returned. After a while the Countess of
Essex (she was seventeen) was carried off by her husband
into the country, and left London for another three years.

For those seven years James had no particular thought
of her. In 1613 she was brought to his notice. The Earl
of Northampton approached him with a curious petition
which immediately aroused the King's own cerebralized
curiosity. It seemed the marriage was unsatisfactory—
was, in fact, no marriage, owing to the impotency of the
husband. There was talk—among her friends—of the
possibility of a decree of nullity. In this remote and
difficult subject the King's learning—theological and

physiological—took an immediate interest. It was hinted
to him—perhaps more than hinted—that Rochester and
the lady were deeply in love, and only anxious to marry—
could Essex be legally nullified. The King caused opinions
on the possibility of a divorce for nullity to be asked : or
rather since, strictly speaking, there could be no divorce
where there had been no marriage, for opinions on the
legality of the marriage. He began to look into the
question himself. He sent for the Archbishop, Dr. George
Abbot, and opened the matter to him. The surprised
Archbishop said, that he had heard of some discontents
in the marriage, but he had not supposed matters had
come to such a head ; if he were to be judge he begged
that other bishops might be joined with him. The King
appointed the Bishops of London, Ely, and Lichfield, with
other divines and lawyers. The Bishop of Ely, it is to be
remembered, was Lancelot Andrewes, whose reputation may
at least induce us to suppose that there was a good case
on the side for which he gave judgment. He proved to be
in favour of the nullity though he took very little part in
the proceedings, much to Abbot's irritation. The Archbishop himself was honest, Calvinistic, and carefully
judicious. He naturally approached so heavy a matter
with slow gravity ; rather to his annoyance he found
himself being rushed. The Commission had been made
out, proceedings begun, pleas put in, before he had become
accustomed to the mere idea. He was hurt ; he thought
that his warning against undue haste ought to have been
treated more seriously. Things in the pleas worried him.
The Earl was stated to be incapable *Versus hanc*—towards
this one woman ; privily consenting to the suit he had
altogether refused to be publicly certified of general
impotence. The Archbishop told the Countess's lawyers
they " had made a very narrow bridge for themselves to
go over." The Bishop of Lichfield said that seven years

would not have been too long to deliberate before such a
business was begun ; " there were not more eyes upon the
earl's father losing his head than now upon the earl losing
his wife."

The Commissioners, having begun the hearing,
adjourned from June 18 to July 2. The King heard of it
and was a little fretted. He was in one of his bursts of
energy, largely on Carr's behalf. Rumours had been cir-
culating that the Favourite was falling from favour ; their
cause lay in the offensive behaviour of Thomas Overbury.
Overbury had already been in trouble over a fancied insult
to the Queen, and since then James had heard it said that,
while Rochester ruled the King, Overbury ruled Rochester.
To the first clause, through his secret life, James had been
accustomed. He had always been thought to be ruled.
But to be ruled at one remove by one who was not even
his own direct creation was a little too much. He caused
Overbury to be offered a post abroad—the Low Countries,
France, Muscovy. Overbury refused ; he would not " in
law or justice be compelled to leave the country." James
grew angry. He royally complained to the Council of
Overbury's high contempt. The Council sent Overbury to
the Tower. On April 21, 1613 he entered it ; before the end
of the year he was buried there.

The Court waited to see if this committal preluded the
fall of Overbury's master. But James assured them the
next day that he " took more delight and comfortment
in his company and conversation than in any man's living."
In this temper of public devotion to his friend he was
anxious to push on the necessary legal preliminaries for
his friend's marriage. He talked to the Archbishop,
obscurely hinting that he wished well to the suit. In fact
he wanted it, but he wanted it justly. Like the manor
of Sherbourne, he would have said : " I maun have it ; I
maun have it for Carr " ; but, also like the manor, he

wanted it at a legal price. But also his mere interest in
the unusual thing disposed him to believe in it. It was a
physiological perversity, and he was curious and credulous.
He became more conscious of the Archbishop's obstinacy
than of his honesty.

The Commission sat again and took depositions—from
servants and others who gave evidence on such things as
the hill in the bed between the two hollows where the Earl
and Countess had slept. They received a set of ambiguous
replies from the Earl ; they had the Countess examined
by a jury of seven noble matrons. By the time all this
was done the Commission was, fairly obviously, in two
parties : the one that wanted to pronounce at once in
order to please the King, the other that in effect believed
the whole thing to be a matter of collusion and the nullity
to be unjust. The Howards were very angry with the
Archbishop, more especially as the King, with what seemed
to them a quite unnecessary intellectual concern with the
case, was not wholly reliable. The Commissioners went
down to Windsor, and before James the two parties argued.
Sir Daniel Dunn, the leader of the one, argued for *Non
potuit*, therefore null. The Archbishop allowed *Non potuit*,
but from lack of love, not from lack of ability, therefore
not null. He made a passionate appeal to the King to
release him. James was " earnest, but gracious and
moderate." He explained that he thought the Earl was
bewitched ; that, in fact, the Earl had once proposed
to go to Poland, " to have tried whether he might be
unwitched." (Why Poland ? Nobody inquired.) But,
James went on, he had himself dissuaded from that course,
and had put this in operation ; if that was an error the
King would feel he had done the Howards wrong. " In
sum," wrote the Archbishop, " I found his Majesty much
troubled what to do." It is pleasant to think what the
Howards present must have suffered, listening to the

P

sincere King and the sincere Archbishop discussing as a
profound problem what should have been a mere matter
of Court tactics.

James was disturbed and troubled. He came to his
dinner and did not eat, sitting with his leg flung over the
side of the chair. It was put about by the Howard party
that he was angry with the Archbishop. But the King's
mind was not so simply unjust as that ; he is much more
likely to have been fretted by the possibility of his having
been used to support false pleas. He was inclined to think
now that it was a case of *Vitium animi non corporis*—the
Archbishop had said so and he had agreed. But the
Countess had pleaded that *maleficium*—devilry, untoward
enchantment—had affected the Earl, and James had originally believed her. He did not know what to do. He
did not want to disappoint Carr or to offend the Howards
At the same time, if it were not *maleficium*, if the Archbishop were right ? Or if the ecclesiastical court were
unable justly to grant the nullity ?

At the precise moment some *maleficium* of intellectual
irony put it into the Archbishop's head as he jolted home-
ward from Windsor in his coach, profoundly unhappy at
the King's interest in the matter, to draw up a paper of
reasons in divinity against *maleficium versus hanc.* The
next morning, early, he did so, he took it with him to the
Commission and they argued about it, all but Lancelot
Andrewes who " sat little less than dumb." It did not
occur to Dr. Abbot that Dr. Andrewes might not see any
use in arguing divinity with his superior's fixed mind.
Besides, Andrewes had souls in mind, where the others had
bodies. After further (quite intelligent) physiological details, the Archbishop proposed to try a reconciliation
between my lord and my lady. He was astonished to
find Bishop Andrewes break out of his silence to " speak
home." Andrewes was wholly against any effort of recon-

ciliation. He said it was too late ; to bring them together again might mean only that they would poison and destroy one another. On this passionate outbreak of a dedicated mind the Commission broke up, and the Archbishop sent his paper of divinity to the King.

It was an unfortunate move. Andrewes, brooding over the whole detestable business, probably saw nullity as the best way out. Sufficient evidence had been given on oath to justify it—if the evidence, though on oath, could be believed. Bishop Goodman was afterwards clear on that point ; he said of the Bishop of London that his timorous judgment ought not to have countervailed their oaths. If there were reason to think the witnesses were perjured, the perjury should be examined ; if not, the decree should be granted. Andrewes and Goodman were neither fools nor knaves, but they had no heart for long wrangles. The Bishop of Ely had said hardly anything about the Archbishop's learning.

But the King, friendly though he always was with Andrewes, had a different mind. As he read the archi-episcopal argument, his mind regained its calm. The paper was rhetorical, illogical, irrelevant, and puritanical. It allowed nullity *propter frigitatem*, but not *propter maleficium*, which (it said) might well be a concomitant of Popish superstition. But under the Light of the Gospel. . . . It demanded whether the persons had used fasting (fasting !) and prayer, if they had given alms, if they had taken medicines. It quoted late Reformed authorities, rather off the point. The King sat down himself to answer. He was better as an amateur in divinity than the Archbishop as a professional. He rent the arguments, he destroyed the rhetoric, he refused to admit in this matter any superiority of the Reformed Church over the Roman ; he annexed the authorities and turned their points against the Archbishop—in short, he won a complete intellectual victory, and ended with the advice : *Cum conversus fueris, confirma fratres tuos.* If these were all the doubts, there was nothing to them. He had not (as he soon discovered) convinced the Archbishop, but he had certainly convinced himself. He had been rational and exact. He had, in fact, concluded the whole case.

From now on, therefore, the King and the Archbishop were at loggerheads. The King felt, with some justice, that, now he had solved all doubts, judgment should immediately be given. The Archbishop, with even more justice, felt that the King's answer (when he received it) did not touch the sinister implications of the business. Strange stories of the Countess's past behaviour reached him ; rumours that a new husband was waiting for her ; gossip and scandal of all sorts. Most of it was probably true. He heard that Overbury was dead, and of worse rumours of the cause bruited about the city. He became more reluctant than ever to pronounce the decree. But the King would not endure further delay. While the Archbishop was sincerely perplexed he would be gracious, but now he felt it was quite impossible for the Archbishop to be perplexed. Sparkles of a greater Divinity had shone. He appointed two other bishops—Winchester and Rochester —to sit. He sent his answer, with a letter saying that he thought the Archbishop prejudiced against the persons, and bidding him " reverence and follow my judgment, and not to contradict it, except where you may demonstrate unto me that I am mistaken or wrong informed ; and so farewell. JAMES R."

After this breach, the Commission with its new members had but to conclude its work. At the end of September, by a majority of seven to five, the decree of nullity was pronounced, Lancelot Andrewes voting with the majority. In November 1613 the Viscount Rochester was made Earl of Somerset ; in December he was married, with the greatest pomp and splendour, to the Lady Frances Howard. Thomas Campion wrote the masque. The King, in sincere and affectionate gratification, attended the wedding.

The most fantastic thing about the whole business is that, if James was not right, he deserved to be. For the new Countess of Somerset had been attempting as an actuality against her first husband precisely the *maleficium* which the King had defended as a possibility. Another two years were to pass before the great enlightenment took place. Then it would all be known—how Frances Howard had gone secretly to a magician's house, how she had gained from him love-philtres to make Carr love her and drugs to make Essex fail from her, how spells had been cast and wax images made, one " sumptuously apparelled in silks and satins," one " in form of a naked woman spreading and laying forth her hair in a looking-glass," how she had written wildly to her " sweet father " Forman the sorcerer, and to Anne Turner the procuress ; how she had seen Essex as one hindrance to her happiness and Overbury as another, and had struck at the masculinity of the one and the life of the other, and had been freed by invited decree from one and by incited death from the other ; and what strange cords of horror intertwine the passions of men. But at the moment she came on the Feast of St. Stephen, all garmented in white as a virgin, and with unbound hair, to the chapel at Whitehall. And it is to be hoped, for those twenty months, she was as happy as she could be.

The King was not. By the time a year had gone by, the Favourite had grown increasingly difficult. He was very much the master everywhere, except—it is the old story—over the King. The dramatic scenes between them do not take place in public, as in the old days when a younger monarch stormed down the obviously insolent Bothwell. They are hidden behind the doors of the King's chamber. There Somerset raged against Court intrigues, there—"in furious assaults at unseasonable hours" (it is the King's phrase)—he battered at that final secret thing that was the King. It is impossible to imagine what more he wanted than he had got, except on the hypothesis that he wanted something he could never get. Only one person —two persons—in James's life got that, and their time was not yet. George Villiers had only begun to appear at the Court ; the Prince Charles took no more than a formal part there. And Robert Carr was not of weight enough to control the King's spirit. He tried to bully—imbecile effort !

Overbury might have saved him from it, but Overbury was dead, and Somerset was afraid. George Villiers had begun to appear at Court. Among the rich and coarse throngs he is seen once or twice on the outskirts, a younger son of a good family ; sent out to seek his fortune. At Apchurch, during a progress ; at Cambridge, during a play ; and then pushed nearer the Person, and the eyes of the Person dwelling on him, and certain powers about the Person, for his sake and their own, taking an interest in him, and an appointment as Cupbearer—these are the first glimpses ; these and one other when one of Somerset's servants spilt soup over the new young Creature. Villiers struck him, in the King's presence, and laid himself open to the penalty of mutilation, but James pardoned him. The King already proposed to himself a repetition of his earlier pleasures : he would shape and teach and fashion Villiers. "He resolved to make him a Masterpiece, and mould him as it were Platonically to his own Idea," wrote Sir Henry Wotton. He had tried it with Somerset, but the Platonic creation had erred ; the matter was too stubborn. It had become more stubborn by now. The King conceived himself able, like God, to create anew without making any kind of alteration in his intimacy with

the old. Unlike God, he was mistaken. He caused in-
struction to be conveyed to Villiers on the proper method
of approach to favour. There was a ritual in such things,
and James delighted in it. The King's Majesty was to
be approached through the Queen's. Villiers was presented
to Anne ; his patrons—including the Archbishop—prayed
her to speak for him to the King. Anne was gloomy ;
she hated Somerset, but she found no pleasure in the
prospect of Villiers. She said he would prove more intolerable than any who had gone before him. The Archbishop afterwards said she had spoken like a prophetess,
but even the prophetess did not know how complete the
lordliness of George Villiers was to be. At last she assented.
On St. George's Day, 1615, the young beauty waited with
his patrons outside the closed door of the Bedchamber ;
opposite him were Somerset and his friends. In the
arcanum of the Bedchamber the Queen made request that
Villiers should be a Gentlemen of the Chamber. Messages
were taken in : Somerset sent, begging James to limit his
favour by making the young man a Groom ; the Archbishop sent, begging the Queen to press for the higher post.
The long ritual was gone through ; the King felt his power,
and comfortably stretched himself in it. Villiers at last
was brought in. Anne, telling Prince Charles to give her
his sword, knelt before James, beseeching him " to do her
this special favour as to knight this noble gentleman whose
name was George for the honour of St. George, whose feast
he now kept." The King blinked and shuddered at the
steel (" he did much please himself with such inventions "),
but he pretended to overcome the pretended horror, took
it, and dubbed George Villiers knight. Why could not
Somerset be gay with him ?

Almost any one and every one could have told the
King : Somerset certainly seems to have told him. Long
before, in a great phrase, Bacon had spoken of a similar

error on the part of another Favourite.   Essex had thought
he could use " necessity and authority " with Elizabeth.
In some rare relations of love that state of " necessity and
authority " doubtless exists ; they are absolute.   But
there was no such absoluteness between Essex and Elizabeth
nor between Somerset and James.   The older Creature
sought to destroy the younger and to control his Creator.
He stormed in the privy chamber.   At last the King wrote
to him : a long letter.   It need not be read, but it is a
treasure of the King's mind :

" First, I take God, the searcher of all hearts, to record
that, in all the time past of idle talk, I never knew nor
could, out of any observation of mine, find any appearance
of any such court faction as you have apprehended ; and
so far was I ever from overseeing or indirectly feeling of it
(if I had apprehended it), as I protest to God, I would have
run upon it with my feet, as upon fire, to have extinguished
it, if I could have seen any sparkle of it.   As for your
informations, you daily told me so many lies of myself
that were reported unto you, as (I confess) I gave the less
credit to your reports in other things, since you could not
be an eye-witness of it yourself.

" Next, I take the same God to record, that never man
of any degree did directly or indirectly let fall unto me any
thing that might be interpreted for the lessening of your
credit with me, or that one man should not rule all, and
that no man's dependence should be but upon the king,
or any such like phrase ; which, if I had ever found, then
would I have behaved myself as became so great a king,
and so infinitely loving a master.

" Thirdly, as God shall save me, I meant not in the
letter I wrote unto you to be sparing, in the least jot, of
uttering my affection towards you, as far as yourself could
require ; my differing from your form in that point being
only to follow my own style, which I thought the comeliest ;

so as having delivered my mind as fully to May as you
could have wished,—having written this letter,—having
quite turned my countenance from Graham,—the like
whereof I never did to any man without a known offence,—
I having received your nephew in my bed-chamber, the
fashion thereof being done in a needless bravery of the
queen, I did surely expect that the idle talk would wear
out like the pope's cursing ; especially seeing my own heart
knew it to be without a ground.   For I am far from thinking
of any possibility of any man ever to come within many
degrees of your trust with me, as I must ingenuously confess
you have deserved more trust and confidence of me than
ever man did,—in secrecy above all flesh, in feeling and
impartial respect, as well to my honour in every degree as
to my profit.   And all this, without respect either to kin
or ally, or your nearest and dearest friend whatsoever ;
nay, unmoveable in one hair that might concern me against
the whole world.   And in those points I confess I never
saw any come towards your merit : I mean, in the points
of an inwardly trusty friend and servant.   But, as a piece
of ground cannot be so fertile, but if either by the own
natural rankness or evil manuring thereof it become also
fertile of strong and noisome weeds, it then proves useless
and altogether unprofitable ; even so, these before rehearsed
rich and rare parts and merits of yours have been of long
time, but especially of late, since the strange phrenzy took
you, so powdered and mixed with strange streams of un-
quietness, passion, fury, and insolent pride, and (which
is worst of all) with a settled kind of induced obstinacy,
as it chokes and obscures all these excellent and good parts
that God hath bestowed upon you.   For, although I confess
the greatness of that trust and privacy betwixt us will
very well allow unto you an infinitely great liberty and
freedom of speech unto me, yea, even to rebuke me more
sharply and bitterly than ever my master durst do, yet,

to invent a new act of railing at me—nay, to borrow the tongue of the devil—in comparison whereof all Peacham's book is but a gentle admonition, that cannot come within the compass of any liberty of friendship. And do not deceive yourself with that conceit, that I allowed you that sort of licentious freedom till of late. For, as upon the one part, it is true you never passed all limits therein till of late ; so, upon the other, I bore, God Almighty knows, with those passions of yours, of old dissembling my grief thereat, only in hope that time and experience would reclaim and abate that heat, which I thought to wear you out of by a long-suffering patience and many gentle admonitions ; but the circumstances joined to the[m] made them relish ten times worse to my taste than otherwise they would have done, if they had only remained *in puris naturalibus* of passions.

" For, first, being uttered at unseasonable hours, and so bereaving me of my rest, was so far from condemning your own indiscretion therein, as by the contrary it seemed you did it of purpose to grieve and vex me. Next, your fiery boutades were coupled with a continual dogged sullen behaviour, especially shortly after your fall and in all the times of your other diseases. Thirdly, in all your dealings with me, you have many times uttered a kind of distrust of the honesty of my friendship towards you. And, fourthly (which is worst of all), and worse than any other thing that can be imagined, you have, in many of your mad fits, done what you can to persuade me that you mean not so much to hold me by love as by awe, and that you have me so far in your reverence, as that I dare not offend you, or resist your appetites. I leave out of this reckoning your long creeping back and withdrawing yourself from lying in my chamber, notwithstanding my many hundred times earnestly soliciting you to the contrary, accounting that but as a point of unkindness.

" Now, whether all your great parts and merits be not accompanied with a sour and distasteful sauce, yourself shall be judge. Consider likewise of the difference of the things that you lay to my charge and that I lay to yours. Here is not, ' he said,' or ' she said,' no conjectural presumptions ; I charge you with nothing but things directly acted or spoken to myself. I wish to God, therefore, and I shall both pray for it and hope it, that you may make good use of this little mirror of yourself, which herein I present unto you ; it is not like Sir Walter Raleigh's description of the kings that he hates, of whom he speaketh nothing but evil ; for this lays plainly and honestly before you both your best and worst parts.

" To conclude, then, this discourse proceeding from the infinite grief of a deeply wounded heart—I protest in the presence of the Almighty God, that I have borne this grief within me to the uttermost of my ability, and as never grief since my birth seated so heavily upon me, so have I borne it as long as possibly I can ; neither can I bear it longer without admitting an unpardonable sin against God in consuming myself wilfully, and not only myself, but in perilling thereby not only the good estate of mine own people, but even the state of religion through all Christendom, which almost wholly, under God, rests now upon my shoulders. Be not the occasion of the hastening of his death through grief, who was not only your creator under God, but hath many a time prayed for you, which I never did for any subject alive but for you. But the lightening my heart of this burden is not now the only cause that makes me press you undelayedly to ease my grief ; for your own furious assaults upon me at unseasonable hours hath now made it known to so many that you have been in some cross discourse with me, as there must be some exterior signs of the amendment of your behaviour towards me. These observations have been made and collected upon your long being with me at unseasonable hours—loud speaking on both parts—and their observation of my sadness after your parting, and want of rest.

" What shall be the best remedy for this, I will tell you, be kind. But for the easing of my inward and consuming grief, all I crave is, that in all the words and actions of your life you may ever make it appear to me, that you never think to hold grip of me but out of my mere love, and not one hair by force. Consider that I am a freeman, if I were not a king. Remember that all your being, except your breathing and soul, is from me. I told you twice or thrice, you might lead me by the heart and not by the nose. I cannot deal honestly, if I deal not plainly with you. If ever I find that you think to retain me by one sparkle of fear, all the violence of my love will in that instant be changed into as violent a hatred. God is my judge, my love hath been infinite towards you ; and the only strength of my affection towards you hath made me bear with these things in you, and bridle my passions to the uttermost of my ability. Let me be met, then, with your entire heart, but softened by humility. Let me never apprehend that you disdain my person and undervalue my qualities ; and let it not appear that any part of your former affection is cold towards me. A king may slack a part of his affection towards his servant upon the party's default, and yet love him ; but a servant cannot do so to his master, but his master must hate him. Hold me thus by the heart ; you may build upon my favour as upon a rock that never shall fail you, that never shall weary to give new demonstrations of my affection towards you ; nay, that shall never suffer any to rise in any degree of my favour, except they may acknowledge and thank you as a furtherer of it, and that I may be persuaded in my heart, that they love and honour you for my sake : not that any living shall come to the twentieth degree of *your* favour.

" For, although your good and heartily humble behaviour may wash quite out of my heart your bypast errors, yet shall I never pardon myself, but shall carry that cross to the grave with me for raising a man so high, as might make him to presume to pierce my ears with such speeches.

" To make an end, then, of this unpleasing discourse, think not to value yourself so much upon other merits, as by love and heartily humble obedience. It hath ever been my common answer to any that would plead for favour to a Puritan minister by reason of his rare gifts, that I had rather have a conformable man with but ordinary parts than the rarest men in the world that will not be obedient ; for that leaven of pride sours the whole loaf. What can or ever could thus trouble your mind ? For the exterior to the world—what can any servants expect of their prince but countenance or reward ? Do not all courtesies and places come through your office as chamberlain, and rewards through your father-in-law as treasurer ? Do not you two (as it were) hedge in all the court with a manner of necessity to depend upon you ? And have you not besides your infinite privacy with me, together with all the main offices you possess ?—your nephew in my bedchamber ?—besides another far more active than he in court-practices ? And have you not one of your nearest kinsmen that loves not to be idle in my son's bedchamber ? With this should you have silenced these news-bringers and makers of lies. For no other thing is left you behind but my heart, which you have neither cause to doubt ; nor, if it did need, could they counsel or advise you how to help.

" Thus have I now set down unto you what I would say, if I were to make my testament ; it lies in your hands to make of me what you please—either the best master and truest friend, or, if you force me once to call you ingrate, which the God of heaven forbid, no so great earthly plague can light upon you! In a word, you may procure me to delight to give daily more and more demonstrations of my favours towards you, if the fault be not in yourself."

There are few writings so fully Jacobean. Its grief, its folly, its egotism, its devotion, its sincerity, its threats— all these are James. He desired to retain his friend, but he was determined also to have his own way. Even George Buchanan had never railed at him as Somerset had done, and Somerset was railing at the King. They had been very intimate; they had had all secrets in common. But if Somerset could threaten, so could the King; if Somerset was determined to try his strength against James Stuart, the strength of James Stuart would break him.

In the high summer and autumn of 1616 the breach came, in a way they neither of them thought. Away in Flushing an apothecary's boy fell ill. Dying, he made, in the hearing of those who watched him, a confession of how he, in his small way, had been parcel of a great crime; he had carried poison to the Tower of London, by which Sir Thomas Overbury had been murdered. The tale came circuitously to the ears of the Secretary of State, Sir Ralph Winwood. Winwood brought it to the King. There were tales enough of poison in those days, and there had been such tales—as the Archbishop had known—of Overbury's death and the interest in it felt by Frances Howard, now Countess of Somerset. The King had no reason to believe such fables, but he knew why Winwood spoke. He bade him use his discretion, but not to hesitate to follow it up, if he thought well.

In a month Winwood was back again.

This time the tale was more serious. He had had the Lieutenant of the Tower, Sir Gervase Helweys, recommended to him, and had said he would be glad to be of service if Sir Gervase could clear himself of a heavy imputation, for Sir Thomas Overbury had died while in his charge. Sir Gervase, supposing Winwood knew much more than actually he did, admitted that he knew of the plot and of the gaoler Weston who was the means ; he hinted at Frances Howard ; he gave assurances of his own efforts to thwart it. Winwood was vaguely friendly, accepted the explanations, and immediately carried them to the King.

James had no kind of hesitation. Sir Gervase was ordered to write a full account of the whole affair ; presently it came. Sir Gervase, when he became Lieutenant, had found Overbury a prisoner and had had Weston recommended to him by Sir Thomas Monson for the post of gaoler. One evening he had met Weston with Overbury's soup, who had asked him " whether he should now give him that which he had or no." Sir Gervase had asked dissimulating questions, had found out the intention (" Why, sir," said Weston, " did you not know what was to be done ? "), had persuaded Weston not to administer the poison, but to tell " those who set him on " of Overbury's sufferings. " Those " took advantage of the tarts and pots of jelly which Somerset's tenderness was sending to Overbury, and counterfeited them with poisonous stuff, from which on one excuse or another—Sir Gervase saved his prisoner. At last the servant of the apothecary was corrupted by a gift of twenty pounds to bring a poisoned " clyster," which was Overbury's destruction. Weston had named but one person—a widow called Anne Turner ; in the last few weeks, since certain whisperings had begun, Weston and she had again had a secret interview, being both of them anxious to find out how much Sir Gervase knew, and in what disposition towards them he stood. That, he wrote, was all he did know.

The King read the letter. Of Mrs. Turner he may never have heard, but she was then in the Countess of Somerset's household. He could have stayed things ; Winwood would hardly have talked, and scandal was always whispering. But he did not ; he took the one step that immediately made it useless to stay things. He sent the letter at once to Sir Edward Coke, then Chief Justice, putting the affair into his hands, bidding him examine it to the bottom. There was no reason to suppose Somerset implicated. But it is likely that he thought a little healthy disturbance would do Somerset no harm. He went on treating Somerset as well as Somerset would let him. He would stand by him, but the thing must no longer be a secret.

Once Coke got hold of it, it was not. Every one— including Somerset and his wife—heard of it. The Chief Justice had Weston seized and examined. Weston—not knowing of Helweys' letter—began by denying everything and protesting that Overbury died of a cold caught by sitting at an open window. But the next day, under Coke's growls, he admitted that he had, at the Lieutenant's instance, thrown away the poison ; and on the next he told a story of an interview with the Countess in the presence of Mrs. Turner, when a phial of water had been given him for the prisoner, and he had been promised a reward if he administered it. After that his admissions became more frequent. He spoke of one Franklin, a physician, who had promised a clyster for Overbury, and of how Sir Gervase had forbidden any physician to have access to the prisoner, save only the " former apothecary " or his assistants. He denied a white powder from Somerset ; he admitted a white jelly from the Countess (which he threw away " in a homely place "). He admitted he had received £180 from the Countess.

The examinations spread wider. Davies—Overbury's servant—was examined ; Franklin and Mrs. Turner were seized. Sir Gervase and Sir Thomas Monson were examined. Coke found that the inquiry threatened to touch great persons ; he wrote to the King, begging that some of

higher rank than he might be joined with him.   James
assented ; he named the Lord Chancellor Ellesmere, and
the Duke of Lennox, and Lord Zouch as Commissioners.
To see Lennox there is to encourage fancies almost physiological.   The blood of the man whom the King had once
loved ran in the veins of the man who sat to examine the
acts of the latest of the King's loves.   Somerset was not
as wise as that Lennox ; he still attempted to carry a high
hand over the King.   In their propinquity at Royston,
the sense of a crisis was over them.   Their intercourse
had become, through Somerset's storms, a less delightful
thing.   Somerset might still have had much, but he was
recklessly flinging away all that he might have had—not
by a passionate singularity of soul, but in a less exalted
gluttony.   And now there arose upon them this other
thing.   It was, of course, nothing ; there was no truth in it.
Only Somerset wanted it hushed up, and the King would
not have it hushed up.   The Justice of the King, which was
part of his Divinity, forbade.   Somerset protested, assever-
ated, and stormed.   The King did not disbelieve him, but
he was not free to believe him.   By now, he had written,
" he gave the less credit to his reports."   But he had an
affection for him ; he did not wish to lose him ; certainly
he did not wish his friend to come under the danger of
that terrible fact which could not be trifled with, which
James dared not trifle with, the sacred Justice of the King,
the supernatural and awful quality of Majesty.   Somerset
was to go to London.   It was said that messages had come
from Coke requiring him to come for examination and that
he protested it was insolence of Coke to demand him.   The
King answered : " Thou must go, for if Coke sends for me
I must go."   Easily emotional in his loves, he clung to and
petted this love that was almost done.   He felt the crisis
upon him, he cried out that he would neither eat nor sleep
till Somerset returned.   Somerset swore the King should

Q

see him again soon. " Shall I ? shall I ? " James exclaimed,
embracing and kissing him. He went with him to the
bottom of the stairs. The Earl took final leave and passed.
The King, watching him out, exclaimed : " I shall never
see thy face more." As if aware of that conclusion, and
ignorant how to avoid it, and determined not to allow it,
Somerset, like any fool in the course of his folly, discharged
from London more bullying letters. He became more
violent in his efforts to arrest or to overawe the authority
which James would never willingly allow any other mortal
soul to seize. He wrote that James had behaved unroyally
in yielding to Coke, that the Commissioners were his
personal enemies, that Ellesmere had been concerned in the
execution of the King's mother, that the House of Howard
would be angry with the King, and in some way he got his
father-in-law Suffolk to support the last threat.

Authority answered him—the exterior royal authority
which was all Somerset could understand ; the interior
spiritual authority which the voice of James could never
quite explain and to which he had never been false. He
wrote :

" I need not to answer your letter, since Lennox hath
long before this time told you my resolution in that point ;
whereupon you have bestowed so much scribbling and
railing, covertly against me and avowedly against the chancellor. Yet can I not abstain partly for satisfaction of
mine own heart, and partly for satisfying you and your ally
with reason, if reason can satisfy you, to send you these few
observations upon your letter in a business of this nature.

" I have nothing to look unto, but, first, my conscience
before God, and next, my reputation in the eyes of the whole
world. If I can find one man stricter than another in
point of examination, I am bound to employ him in it ;
and when in my conscience I have set down a course,—to

change it at the instance of the party without any other reason, but because they will have it, is very little for my honour. That I was too faint in not resisting the supreme judge's wilfulness ; I confess I ever was and will be faint in resisting to the trial of murder, and as bold and earnest in prosecuting the trial thereof. And as my proceedings from the beginning of this business have been only governed by the rule of my conscience, as the Searcher of all hearts knows ; so must I, to my regret, confess and vow, that from the beginning of this business, both your father-in-law and you have ever and at all times behaved yourselves quite contrary to the form, that men that wish the trial of the verity ever did in such a case. And how far it is now out of time, after that the chancellor hath served me more than thirteen years with all honour and faithfulness, having ever been a regalist, to rake up from the bottomless pit the tragedy of my poor mother, I appeal to your own judgment. Then, why should I be thus needlessly vexed ? This warrant stretches only to examination, wherein no innocent person can get wrong ; and, since the chancellor sees himself so suspected, is it to be thought that he dare utter any partiality ? And if you will need suspect the worst (which is rather likely than possible) were it not a more handsome way for my reputation, that he might be privately advised to be silent, when he were there, except in yeas and noes ? Or else, in regard of his age and infirmities, and his main businesses in the term time, to make his appearance but very seldom ? and so forbear to give any opinion, as not acquainted with the course of the business. And as for the external show of my election of him in disfavour of you—first, I am sore the world should see you except against so grave a man ; and next, the more severe choice I make of persons for examination, the more it is in your favour, if honour and trial of innocence be your end.

" Now, as to your motion in putting all the judges in
this warrant (if you mean for trial in law), I never meant
it otherwise ; but if you mean for examination, it is more
than absurd. And, whereas you allege that great councillors were never employed in the examination of a thing
of this nature, I say the quite contrary is true, when as
the circumstances or articles of the trial may reflect upon
any great personages ; in which cases the judges dare never
presume to meddle without better assistance. To conclude, then, I never had the occasion to show the upright-
ness and sincerity that is required in a supreme judge, as
I have in this. If the delation prove false, God so deal with
my soul as no man among you shall so much rejoice at it
as I ; nor never shall spare, I vow to God ! one grain of
vigour that can be stretched against the conspirators. If
otherwise, as God forbid ! none of you shall more heartily
sorrow for it ; and never king used that clemency that I
will do in such a case. But, that I should suffer a murder
(if it be so) to be suppressed and plastered over, to the
destruction both of my soul and reputation, I am no
Christian. I never mean wittingly and willingly to bear
any man's sins but my own ; and if for serving my conscience in setting down a fair course of trial, I shall lose
the hands of that family, I will never care to lose the hearts
of any for justice sake.

" Fail not to show this letter to your father-in-law, and
that both of you read it twice over at least ; and God so
favour me as I have no respect in this turn but to please
Him, in whose throne I sit. And so farewell ; praying
the author of all verity, to make the clean verity to be
plainly manifested in this case.   JAMES R."

In Elizabethan and Jacobean letters there is a good
deal of prim talk of justice as there is a good deal of devout
talk of God, and often neither God nor justice, when one

discovers what the letter is actually about, seem quite to be in place. It is not by any invocation of justice that the King's sincerity is shown. But the vivid directness of " I never mean willingly to bear any man's sins but my own " is perfect James. His fear, his intelligence, his justice, his piety are all in it. If, as some have hinted, it is the phrase of a man who was himself, through his physician, responsible for Overbury's death, then style is another thing from what we have thought.

Meanwhile the Earl was burning and altering letters in London. His correspondence had to be severely purged before he could trust it to the Commissioners. But there was another correspondence of which, till now, no one but he, if he, had known anything : the letters of Frances, Countess of Somerset, to Mrs. Turner and another (now dead) behind Mrs. Turner, the magician Forman. Some of these letters, though the Earl did not know it, were already in Coke's hands. But others were hidden in a box, and that was again in the cellar of a house belonging to Weston's son. Somerset, by virtue of his possession of the Privy Seals, sent a constable, with a woman named Hind, to seize the box under the pretext that they were letters concerning Mrs. Hind. They took all they could and carried them to the Earl, who burnt them. But the action came to the ears of the Commissioner, who on October 18 wrote indignantly to the King of this " great contempt," and committed the Earl to custody at the house of the Dean of Westminster.

On the next day Richard Weston was brought to trial, charged with administering poison to Overbury. From that moment the whole Jacobean legal process becomes, to a modern lay mind, fantastically wild. James can hardly be held responsible for this ; he had handed the whole thing over to Coke and the Commissioners, and in a matter of law the Commissioners would be guided by Coke.

Coke was in his glory : he was exhibiting law, he was exhibiting himself, he was serving the King, he was hunting down iniquity, and iniquity among the high places of the earth. He had arranged the evidence, choosing according to his will among the answers given by Weston in his many examinations. The indictment accused Weston of poisoning Overbury on four separate occasions, the last being the occasion of the apothecary's boy and the clyster. But after the indictment had been read Weston refused to plead. When he was asked how he would be tried, in the formal question, he stood there, in the midst of a great crowd of people—the gentry, the lawyers, the seven judges, the servants of the court ; with, at a distance, those others waiting for his voice, the Earl and Countess, the Howards, the Court, the King—and he did nothing but ejaculate such phrases as " I will be tried by God." He would not utter five words : " By God and my country." And unless he did, all the expected proceedings would collapse. It was impossible legally to proceed without the utterance of that formula. It was impossible to try accessories unless the principal had been tried. The future depended on those five words.

The prisoner was exhorted, warned, threatened ; he was told of the horrible *peine forte et dure*, the stripping, the binding, the stretching out, the starving, the slow pressing to death. He remained stubborn or bewildered. The great show which all London expected to be a preliminary to a greater show was in danger of frustration. Coke would not let his show be so frustrated. He caused Weston's examinations to be read aloud by the prosecution. The thrilling audience heard the great names read out at last, and the guilt of the murder, so the prisoner had said, laid at the doors of the Earl and Countess of Somerset. For three days Weston remained silent. James, being asked, approved of continuing the legal process against him. But at last the unhappy creature gave way and pronounced the formula. The trial could proceed. It did, and Weston was found guilty. He had said that he hoped " the great flies " would not escape. Coke, pronouncing sentence, assured him they should not.

Weston was hanged ; Mrs. Turner was hanged ; Sir Gervase Helweys was hanged. The agonized death in the secret chamber in the Tower was avenged by these bodies publicly exhibited in their own agony before the excited crowds. The excitement had caught everybody, except the King and his Attorney-General, Sir Francis Bacon ; especially had it caught Sir Edward Coke. By the time that Franklin's trial came on, his spirit was soaring into altitudes of awful fancy. Franklin, who had no taste for being hanged, did his best to satisfy so strong an appetite for horrors. The King received letters from his Justice, telling how the Countess had told Franklin that the poisons were too strong ; " they must be prepared to lay longer in the body before they should kill." Coke was fired by the thought of a poison, which, once taken, might lie days, weeks, months in the body before it acted at last. He reported that it was a happy chance for Weston and Franklin that they had been arrested, for it had been plotted to poison both him and Franklin, " but by the goodness of God they avoided it." They avoided it only at the expense of a long mental pain and, in the end, of hanging : so strangely in Coke's eyes—as to the ministers of the Kirk— did the goodness of God operate, so recklessly did he invoke that supreme charity. Even wilder things followed. The King heard how, in the speech that sentenced Franklin to death, the Chief Justice had said : " Knowing as much as I know that if this plot had not been found out, neither Court, City, nor many particular houses had escaped the malice of that wicked crew." More letters announced that he was on the track of new mysteries of evil which he would not reveal at present. Franklin, in prison, condemned, and trying to postpone execution, was hinting at darker and darker things which were conveyed to the Chief Justice : " Next to the Gunpowder Treason there was never such a plot . . . the Palsgrave . . . the Lady Elizabeth. . . . The King used an outlandish physician and outlandish apothecary about him and about the late Prince, deceased. Therein lyeth a long tale." Further, Coke found out that the master-cook to the late Prince, deceased in 1612, had once made jellies for the Earl of Somerset, and the Earl had sent jellies to Overbury. " Our deliverance," cried Coke in court, " was as great as any that happened to the children of Israel." He examined more and more witnesses, cooks and servants. The ghost of " that sweet babe, Prince Henry," rose luridly from his grave, with the marks of venom upon him, and hung—a dreadful warning of vast iniquity—over the distracted minds of London. And still the examinations and the apocalyptic outcries of the Chief Justice went on.

Sir Thomas Monson was brought to trial. He withstood Coke firmly. The Chief Justice exclaimed : " There is more against you than you know of." Monson answered : " If I be guilty it is of that I know not." Sir Laurence Hyde, the prosecuting attorney, called : " I protest, my lord, he is as guilty as the guiltiest." Monson answered : " There was never man more innocent than I ; in that I will die innocent." He must have half-expected that he would, but a greater than Coke intervened. The King had looked at the evidence against him, decided that it was insufficient, and ordered the trial to be postponed. Monson was carried off to the Tower through a hostile crowd, clamorous against the inventors of this general massacre and against all their agents.

The notion that the King had poisoned the Prince has never quite died out ; it is too precious a contribution to

our fables of romantic darkness. But it is not necessary
to believe that James sent pestilence through the night in
order to understand the drag he was putting on Coke's
proceedings. Coke was becoming a demigod of discovery
—almost (though innocently) like Titus Oates in a later
day. But, quite apart from any rumoured connection of
the King with his son's death, which Coke as a fervent
Royalist was not likely to see, though others might, it was
James who would have to bear the brunt of the business.
For the Countess of Somerset would have to be tried, and
it seemed probable that the Earl also would have to be
tried, so high was rumour burning. Coke wrote that there
was " sufficient matter against the Earl." But it was
clear to James, looking at it, that the evidence was of the
feeblest : it consisted of not much more than one statement of Franklin's, confirmed by Mrs. Turner's maid, that
the Earl had been in the house with the Countess (then
Lady Essex) during one of Franklin's interviews with her,
and that she had gone away to consult him. The King had
given the conduct of the case into Coke's hands, and Coke
was determined to proceed. If he were guilty—and James
was not quite sure—this was all very well. But supposing
he were not, and were acquitted ?

Undoubtedly then the Majesty of the King would be
compromised. The general theory of legal trial was that
the previous examinations had already brought truth to
light, and that the public proceedings were no more than
the publication of that truth. The acquittal of a prisoner
was a severe blow at the preceding examinations, and
even at Government itself. For Government was single ;
the judges were part of it ; the unifying influence, rule,
and head was the King. If the King, through his officers,
brought a prisoner to public trial, it was assumed that
the King, through his officers, knew him to be guilty. If
then he was acquitted the King had been guilty of false

accusations, or the prisoner would not have been on trial. The King was therefore false, perjured, and tyrannical. In a matter then where the evidence was at all doubtful it became of the highest moment to get the prisoner to confess. What clemency the King might afterwards extend was another matter, and (to be fair) the King extended his clemency in a way which would startle the present age. Enormous fines were imposed—and remitted ; people were imprisoned for indefinite periods—and let out in a few months ; executions were cancelled or postponed. The Mercy of the King was a very real thing. But it only operated after the Justice of the King had been entirely justified. Nor could the King promise clemency in any agreed terms ; the guilty person must be wholly " in the King's will " before anything could be done.

It would have been much more agreeable to James if the Earl would have put himself into his hands by confession without the trouble of a trial. The whole business had assumed such immense proportions ; the rumours had become so terrifying ; the strange hints so thrilling, that if Somerset were now acquitted, it would be supposed that the King's officers—and the King—had been trying to destroy him, and that for causes unknown. It might be Overbury ; it might be Spain ; it might be Prince Henry. The prestige of the Throne, already jarred, would be seriously and permanently shaken. But an acquittal was quite a possibility. Either way, the mass of excited tempers might sway into an angry resentment against the Throne. The hunger of the public for excitement needed food ; if they could not gobble Somerset they would gobble the King. If Somerset would confess, an equal amount of harm would be saved. Of course, if he were not guilty—— But in the complications of their minds that hardly mattered. He must be found guilty in law, therefore he must be guilty in law, therefore he must be guilty in fact, and probably was.

And the King was not certain that he was not. The very tales themselves were not wholly inconsistent with his own intelligence, though his intelligence, looking at the recorded facts, saw their value. But the emotions, the passions, the quarrels of the last year left the King darkly agitated. He could believe that Somerset was guilty, but at least the whole thing ought to be made public. If only the Earl would confess—and confess without a promise of mercy; that James would not grant, for it would be against his knowledge of justice. But months went by, and he did not.

Months had to go by for another reason—two reasons. The one was personal—the Countess was about to have a baby; on December 9 it was born. She was said to have vowed not to survive; the King caused ladies to be sent to guard and watch her. The other was political. In the general change and counterchange of money and secrets which proceeded at that time, it had been discovered that some of the Privy Council had been receiving pensions from Spain. It was also discovered that secret papers had been shown to the Spanish ambassador. Coke had come across a letter, among so many letters, among Somerset's papers, from Sir John Digby, ambassador at Madrid, to the King. He rashly assumed that a pension had been paid to Somerset by Spain which he was attempting to keep secret from James. Digby was recalled, and made strong representations to the King against allowing Coke to pursue his devastating way through high matters of State. Coke was enlarging his imagination daily— pensions and poisons ran together through his mind. Digby assured the King that Somerset was innocent of the pensions, the whole matter was hushed up, and Coke was firmly turned back to his old course.

The Countess and the Earl were set to be tried by their peers. The prosecution was put into the hands of Sir Francis Bacon, who contemplated Coke's tracks with dismay. " My lord Coke hath filled this part with many frivolous things. . . . This it is to come to the leavings of a business." Between them, the King and he struck out the worse insanities. " Nothing to Somerset," wrote James against note after note of Coke's discoveries—that the man who had poisoned the Prince was a physician with a red beard, that there had been a little picture of a man in white to be used for magical destruction (which Coke took to be of the Prince) and such things. The trial was to be kept close to facts—such facts as there were—against Somerset. The case, wrote Bacon, " was of a good thread but needing to be well strung together." They were both determined to use nothing but the truth as they had it. But certainly they were both agreed that the truth must prove Somerset guilty, if it were at all possible. If, even now, he would not confess.

Somerset had known the " most retired thoughts " of the King's mind. Political and personal secrets, rash confidences, intimate talk, had been held in common between them. Very few men would care to face the prospect of their closest friends making publicly, before a fascinated and delighted audience, already full of scandal and mockery, and before a wider world full of moral and religious thoughts, an exhibition of their most secret heart. It was the risk the King had to face. Somerset was trying to say something to him secretly. He threatened the King again ; he could make revelations at his trial, he told the Lieutenant of the Tower, and would. The Lieutenant sent word privately to the King, and James answered :

" It is easy to be seen that he would threaten me with laying an aspersion upon me of being in some sort accessory

to his crime. . . . I cannot hear a private message from
him without laying an aspersion upon myself of being an
accessory to his crime ; and I pray you to urge him, by
reason that I refuse him no favour which I can grant him
without taking upon me the suspicion of being guilty of
that crime whereof he is accused ; and so farewell.

"JAMES R."

Later he gave way a little, and sent a private messenger.
" Ye know Somerset's day of trial is at hand, and ye know
also what fair means I have used to move him, by con-
fessing the truth, to honour God and me, and leave some
place for my mercy to work upon. I have now, at last,
sent the bearer hereof, an honest gentleman, and who once
followed him, with such directions unto him, as if there be
a spunk of grace left in him, I hope they shall work a good
effect." He went further ; he caused the prisoner to be
falsely threatened with his wife's confession. " Ye shall
therefore give him assurance in my name, that if he will
yet before his trial confess clearly unto the Commissioners
his guiltiness (of the) fact, I will not only perform what I
promised by my last messenger, both towards him and his
wife, but I will enlarge it, according to the phrase of the
civil law, *quod gratiae sunt ampliandae*. I mean not that he
shall confess if he be innocent, but ye know how evil likely
that is ; and of yourself ye may dispute with him, what
should mean his confidence now to endure a trial, when as
he remembers that this last winter he confessed to the chief
justice, that his cause was so evil likely, as he knew no jury
could acquit him. Assure him that I protest, upon my
honour, my end in this is for his and his wife's good. Ye
will do well likewise, of yourself, to cast out unto him, that
ye fear his wife shall plead weakly for his innocence, and
that ye find the Commissioners have, ye know not how,
some secret assurance, that in the end she will confess of

him ; but this must only be as from yourself, and therefore ye must not let him know that I have written unto you, but only that I sent you private word to deliver him this message. Let none living know of this, and if it take good effect, move him to send in haste for the Commissioners, to give them satisfaction ; but if he remains obstinate, I desire not that ye should trouble me with an answer ; for it is to no end, and no news is better than evil news. And so farewell, and God bless your labours."

It is not a pleasant letter, for the Countess never did implicate her husband. All that can be said to excuse it is that James was by now extraordinarily distressed by Somerset's persistent refusal to confess and take the fullest advantage of the hovering mercy of the King. He wanted with all his heart to be merciful for Somerset's sake ; he was anxious for his own. Somerset, in a last paroxysm of rage, swore he would not go to the Court. He said he would have to be dragged there. He was innocent ; he would not submit ; the King should submit. James was informed, and wrote one last letter to the Lieutenant :

" Good Sir George, for answer to your strange news I am first to tell you, that I expect the Lord Hay and Sir Robert Carr have been with you before this time ; which, if they have not yet been, do ye send for them in haste, that they may first hear him, before ye say anything unto him ; and when that is done, if he shall still refuse to go, ye must do your office, except he be either apparently sick, or distracted of his wits ; in any of which cases you may acquaint the Chancellor with it, that he may adjourn the day till Monday next, between this and which time, if his sickness or madness be counterfeited, it will manifestly appear. In the meantime, I doubt not but ye have acquainted the Chancellor with this strange fit of his, and if, upon these occasions, ye bring him a little later than the

hour appointed, the Chancellor may in the meantime
protract the time the best he may ; whom I pray you to
acquaint likewise with this my answer, as well as with the
accident. If he has said anything of moment to the Lord
Hay, I expect to hear of it with all speed; if otherwise,
let me not be troubled with it till the trial be passed.
Farewell.   JAMES R."

It was the end. Somerset went. On May 24 the Countess,
on May 25 the Earl, were brought to trial. The prices of
seats in Westminster Hall were high : ten pounds for two
seats for the two days. The audience had to be there
early—before six in the morning, the trials beginning at
ten. The great ceremonial proceeded solemnly under the
presidency of the Chancellor, acting as High Steward of
England Francis Bacon prosecuted on both days. The
Countess pleaded guilty and was judged. The Earl pleaded
not guilty. It was yet uncertain how far he would venture
to go, and Bacon had proposed that he should be warned
" if in his speeches he should tax the King that the
justice of England is that he shall be taken away, and his
evidence shall go on without him." Less reliably, it was
asserted that two men with cloaks stood by him that they
might, at a word, hoodwink him and carry him away.
But it is most likely that anything that was said was said
to subdue him. Whether he were so subdued, or whether
he came to a quieter mind, whether he hoped for better
favour, or whether he had nothing to say that could be
relevant, at least he said nothing. News was brought to
James that he had remained silent. He and his wife were
in the King's will. They were kept in the Tower for a few
years, pardoned, and sent into an obscure life.

All this while, the angel of George Villiers's good fortune
had set and kept him by the shaken King. He was a better
pupil than Somerset, for he was more intelligent ; " he

was as inwardly beautiful as he was outwardly," some said,
and his outward beauty was very great. Something after
the manner of the Master of Gray, he combined almost
feminine looks with a high masculine nature. He had a
lovely complexion, handsome features, " his hands and
feet seemed specially effeminate and curious," yet he had
also " a courage not to be daunted," a quick mind, and
pertinent speech. He was one of those rare phenomena in
which there almost seems to dwell a spirit who can at will
either sex assume, and with much more vital capacity than
Somerset he received the impress of the King's workmanship. He shone miraculously. He was an exquisite
dancer, very good at all bodily exercises : " he jumpt
higher," wrote one critic later, " than every Englishman
in so short a time, from a private gentleman into a Duke-
dome." It was to a more noble dance that the counsel of
Francis Bacon invited him—" remember well the great
trust you have undertaken." The King's Favourite was
to be the King's sentinel and truth-teller, as it were the
guardian angel of the King's reputation. The King saw
him, if not as a guardian, at least as angelic. " Steenie,"
James called him, for he was as beautiful as St. Stephen
when " all that sat in the council, looking on him, saw
his face as if it had been the face of an angel." The original
Stephen had been so transformed when he looked up to
heaven ; George Villiers was looking up to the less trans-
lucent heaven of a Favourite's vision. During these weeks
of anxiety, and of growing intimacy between the Creature
and his Creator, there was determined the later mastery of
the Creature. James, standing firm against the wrath of
Somerset, unconsciously began to betray his strength into
the sympathy of Somerset's successor, his " slave and
dog." After all his battle against it, he was, in a few years,
to be led, very firmly and very far, by his nose.

CHAPTER TWELVE

The Body of the House of Commons

SOMERSET was in the Tower, a prison which was not the least of the treasures offered by England to her King. He had had formerly nothing but Edinburgh Castle to compare with it, and from Edinburgh captives escaped. From the Tower few escaped. It stood by James, an ever untreacherous friend, till he had no more use for it. It never abandoned him ; he, rather, abandoned it.

In 1616 two bodies lay under its stones, that of Overbury and that of Arabella Stuart. The Lady Arabella had been the King's cousin, and had been forced to be his rival. He had been very definitely aware of her before his succession, but once that was achieved he bore no grudge, nor (less surprisingly) did she. He increased her income ; she assured him of her loyalty. She desired for herself only a quiet life, and James desired for her the same thing. They existed in friendship for six years, until, at the age of thirty-four, she revealed the secret of her love.

James had told her she might marry any of his subjects ; he would not allow her to marry any foreigner, Spanish or other. That, in his eyes, would be a matter " tickle to this crown." There was, however, a great English house— the Seymours—who themselves had through the Greys some claim to the Throne. James had forgotten them ; he remembered only too late when he heard of secret meetings between Arabella and the Lord William Seymour. He interfered at once. He forbade them to marry, and extracted from Seymour a promise to abandon the lady. Within four months the lovers were secretly married.

R

Nothing was more natural or more foolish. The King saw in this deliberate disobedience to the Throne an intention aimed at the Throne; to him its secrecy made its intention more flagrant. Seymour was sent to the Tower; Arabella to custody at Lambeth. She had, the King said, " eaten of the forbidden tree." The fruit, in her mouth sweet as honey, was to her belly very bitter. They corresponded. The King heard of it, and sent Arabella farther away, to Durham. But at Barnet she fell ill, and ill she remained until, disguised as a man, she escaped to take ship for France. Her husband was to escape and join the ship. He escaped; he missed the ship, and took another to Ostend. There, waiting for his mistress, he heard at last she had been retaken by a ship dispatched in pursuit. The King's vibrating nerve of kingship maddened him. He sent her to the Tower, to closer guard. There, her mind gave way as her heart broke. Imbecile, but watched, she lived four years, and died. In Scotland, John Wemyss and Margaret Twinstan had been more fortunate, but they had not touched that neuralgic thread in the physical nature of James Stuart.

There had been other prisoners, some names of Scottish fame. Andrew Melville—of all people !—had found himself compelled to be a neighbour in captivity of the lords and princes of the earthly kingdom he despised. He and other ministers had been brought to London, by royal command, to argue the everlasting question of the freedom of the General Assembly. There they were compelled to attend Anglican services and preached at by Anglican divines. So far, one cannot pity them; it is as pleasant as unusual to see thoroughly good people getting their deserts. But Melville dropped into Latin verse — a pasquinade on Popish ceremonies. He was brought before the Council. His old bad habits got the better of him; he caught and shook the sleeve of the Bishop of London,

crying out that this was the mark of the Beast. The
Beast, its crown being still unwounded, incited James to
send Melville to the Tower for four years, after which—in
1611—he was allowed to go overseas.

There also was Patrick Ruthven, held for no crime but
belonging to the hated House of Gowrie; there was the
Earl of Northumberland, held for carelessly allowing
Thomas Percy, of the Powder Plot, to belong to the King's
gentlemen pensioners without oath taken. There was
Raleigh. Over all these hung the suspended anger of the
King; all these in prison let sound, more freely and more
gaily, the hunting-horns of Royston. There now dwelled
Somerset, and there, by another operation of Divine
Justice, was to lie for a little the swollen wrath of Sir
Edward Coke.

Of Raleigh it may be simpler to speak later. For all
this imprisonment, and all the safe custody of so many
various potential or actual traitors, did not catch the real
sedition. The King had at last cell after cell for his
enemies. It would once have been all that he needed.
But now not one of those cells, nor all, could hold the body
of enmity that was forming against him. The history of
James's reign is the tale, domestically, of the precipitation,
out of the liquid mass of the gentlemen of England, of the
explosive salt of the House of Commons. James himself
was one of the first to realize it ; in 1621, when a deputation
waited on him, he cried out in a sardonic jest : " Bring
chairs for the ambassadors." He attributed to them,
justly, in his anger what his dogmas denied them, the
assumption of the mystical corporality of Kings.

At first, in those happy days of mutual relaxation,
innocent and ignorant, nothing seemed less likely. Both
sides were intent on a natural enjoyment. Even so, the
enjoyments of the gentlemen were more austere than the
pleasures of the King. Many of them were disposed to a

Puritanic conformity ; most of them to a conscientious harrowing of their Catholic fellows. The King's remarkable tenderness troubled them. His efforts towards religious peace shocked them. But his need of and demands for money shocked them also, both in body and soul—at the moment when, at Westminster, the House of Commons was already adolescent. Under Elizabeth it had been a baby ; under James it was a solemn, rich, selfish, pedantic, and verbose young man. It also had a kind of spiritual homosexuality ; it was married to itself. It had nearly all James's vices, and an entirely different set of virtues. Its pedantry was at a disadvantage, because so many of the laws to which it had to appeal were technically on James's side. Its selfishness was at an advantage, because it had money and James had not. In verbosity the two were about equal. Neither, when it came to the point, could ever talk the other down. Each of them claimed a mysterious source of " liberty and power," which the King called Prerogative and the Commons Privilege. The defeat of Prerogative has enabled us to believe in Privilege, unless indeed we look up the prescient scripture of James Stuart and remark that " it is ofttimes a very deceivable argument to judge of the cause by the event." Prerogative might so easily have won, and then we should all have platitudinously talked of royalty as we do now of democracy. It did not. At first—before they met—all was thought to be well between the King and his Commons. But with the meeting came the change. James in his first speech enlarged, with his curious literal conceit, on the thankfulness which he felt to the English for so comfortably receiving him, and, at much greater length, on " the blessings which God in my Person hath bestowed upon you all." He, in his Person, his material impregnated flesh, had brought them peace—peace with foreign nations, peace between the two parts of the one island. " I am

the Husband, and all the whole Isle is my lawful Wife ; I
am the Head, and it is my Body ; I am the Shepherd, and
it is my Flock : I hope, therefore, no man will be so
unreasonable as to think that I, as a Christian King under
the Gospel, should be a Polygamist and husband to two
wives ; that I being the Head, should have a divided and
monstrous Body ; or that being the Shepherd to so fair a
Flock . . . should have my Flock parted in two." The
intimate metaphors were unfortunate. Hardly had the
masculine voice of the Husband, Head, and Shepherd
ceased than the voice of the Wife, Body, and Flock was
heard replying. There was some dispute over one of the
elections. The Husband declared that he, in his Chancery,
was the only judge of election returns. The Wife insisted
that she was herself the judge ; it was part of her wifely
privileges. The Head declared that such privileges apper-
tained to the Body only by his permission ; the Body
asserted that they were part of its own inalienable nature.
The Shepherd, in this case, proposed a compromise ; the
Flock bleated an agreement, but they kept together and
their " baas " were all in a musical harmony. As the years
swept by, two of the great concerns of man—money and
theology—divided those two instincts still more. The
other two—Art and Science—did not much appear. The
great question of the Union with Scotland was very dear
to the King's heart. He did not want to return there, but
he wanted to have his ancient kingdom one with his new.
As he liked to use the good Scots language, as he liked to
pleasure his Scottish friends, so he wanted to feel in himself
the comfortable sensation of unity. He desired to experience the perfected royalty ; his person was hurt by the
division. The Commons had no such sense of division.
They were asked to permit the operation of an intruding
nature ; to absorb into their own body the uncouth and
greedy Siamese twin of the Northern Kingdom. They

showed themselves very reluctant. They demurred, wrangled, and procrastinated. James found it impossible to understand what they were about. Within a few years after his coming into his kingdom, he found himself confronted with a mass of vague hindrance not much more tolerable than the more obvious rocks of offence of his youth. The royal nature found itself lost in. a Boyg, through which it could never discover its way to anything that it really wanted, and in which, among the verbose reverberations of loyalty, its ear might at any moment be offended by the sudden raucous bark of " Privilege ! Privilege ! "

His desire for a perfect union between the two kingdoms was thwarted. He had expected it to be so simple and swift, and it proved so complicated and slow. The Commons, instead of hurrying on with the Union to please the King, were spending time over such domestic delights as the possible abolition of Purveyance and Wardship to please themselves. The King and the Commons, in that first session of 1604, both in the same place and at the same time, expected gratification. As a result the House spent a fortnight drawing up an immense Apology for its proceedings, and James adjourned them with what was in effect a flourishing Apology for his own, in which he pathetically complained, with some exaggeration, that in Scotland he had been thought not only King but Councillor, whereas in England he was despised as Councillor and depreciated as King.

His first Parliament lasted with prorogations from 1604 to 1611. Sometimes such an incident as the Gunpowder Plot would bring the two parties together. Too many other incidents drove them apart.

There were all the Scottish followers, some in place and power, some only seeking it, but all offensive to the insular profit of the English. There were vulgar shows and revels, offensive to the gentlemanly public thrift of the English. There was the King's softness towards Papistry; it was discovered—the Cardinal Bellarmine let it out in the course of the great controversy—that James had once written to the Pope addressing him as " Most Holy Father." Explanations put the responsibility on the Scottish Secretary Balmerino, who had tricked the King into signing, but no one believed the explanations, unless possibly Bellarmine, who, having scored his point, was uninterested. At a later period there was division, if not dispute, on the observance of Sunday. The King in 1617 had issued a *Declaration of Sports*, in which he encouraged his people, after Divine service, in dancing, archery, leaping, vaulting, Maypoles and May-games, Whitsun-ales, and morris dances, but not bear- and bull-baiting, nor interludes, nor bowling. The Commons in 1621 introduced a Bill for the better observance of Sunday, politely arranging that there should be no clauses which actually conflicted with the *Declaration*. One member in opposition pointed out that King David danced, and asked in effect what right had they to fly in the teeth of King David and King James ? The Commons declared that so profane a person could not be tolerated, and that his seat was forfeited. But before then there had been incidents on the other side.

Certain gentlemen of Leicestershire and thereabouts had been busy extending their enclosures, to such an extent that there was local rioting. The King appointed a Commission to investigate, and warned the members to see that the Justice of the King took no hurt through the impoverishment of the poor by the encroachments of the rich. Such an incident had nothing to do with the privileges of the House. But the unwritten privileges of many country gentlemen who shifted their neighbours' landmarks were offended by the prerogatives of Majesty; and the prerogatives of Majesty to spend its money as it liked were offended by the reluctance of the Commons to supply money to be spent. A merchant named Bates had had a case of currants removed from the docks without paying the customs duty. Thrown into the Marshalsea, he declared that he believed the duty to be illegal, since it had been imposed by the King without Parliament. The King appealed to the Judges of the Court of Exchequer. The merchants appealed to the House of Commons. The Judges declared in favour of the King. The Commons embodied such impositions in a list of grievances. This new word began now to sound in voices even harsher and fiercer than those which cried " Privilege ! " It became militant.

Science, we used to be told (before it altered all that one night without satisfactorily explaining how or why), insisted that every effect had its cause. In history we can often observe effects looking for plausible causes. The Grievances of the Commons are an instance. They searched the centuries for precedent justification ; sometimes they found it, sometimes they did not. Their real cause was contemporaneous, emotional, adolescent, and therefore inadmissible. They set out to make it historic, intellectual, and mature. They did not succeed. But in the years that went by as they developed their thesis, and enlarged their privileges, and sharpened their grievances, opportunity was given for the true cause itself to become historic. In the matter of Mr. Bates's currants the Commons invoked the statutes of Edward I. and Edward III. for arguments and assurances. They had a grand debate in which they all but unanimously concluded that the intention of the knights and clerics of the Middle Ages had been to restrain the King from taxing merchants unless the merchants agreed to be taxed.

In the Parliaments of 1614 and 1621 the search for the historic cause which was none, and the force of the contemporaneous cause which was all, grew stronger. The King was compelled to yield before the massed Grievances because he was in desperate need of the subsidies which were convoyed by the Grievances. Many other methods of raising money were tried. Benevolences, free gifts from his subjects to the King, were tried, but they were always difficult and never sufficient. The sale of honours—knighthoods and peerages—was tried, and the compulsory bestowal of honours. But much of the money that should have come to the Crown remained in the Court, and James was the last person in the world to extract his own dues from any one with whom he was on friendly terms. In the end the King was always driven back on Parliament, and the Parliament was the Boyg. It was a fog in which the Blatant Beast prowled, barking out " Privilege ! " and " Grievance ! " It barked at his domestic ecclesiastical policy and at his foreign policy. It barked on behalf of Puritan ministers and against Roman recusants. Even Cecil could not manage it. Cecil indeed was becoming an obvious failure. He had appeared to be the coincidence of two points—of the King and the Families—and now he found himself to be rather the loop which joined them, an elastic loop drawn to a greater and greater strain. In 1610 he had made efforts to arrange a contract between them by which the King should make certain concessions and the Commons should grant a permanent income. It failed, and the strain on his own mind, which, in fact, had very little elasticity in it, became greater. He " animated the Negative," said his cousin, Francis Bacon, in an admirable phrase. " His friends fall from him apace," wrote Chamberlain ; " I never knew so great a man so soon and so generally censured." At last, in 1612, " the little great man," as he came to be called, died. On the day of the funeral the common people made an attempt to throw down the fences of his " new impaled ground " in Hertfordshire.

They were prevented, and the modern hiker can pace, for miles and miles, by the railings which still impale the estates of the successors of Cecil.

The King after the Minister's death attempted to be his own Minister. A spasm of energy held him to it for some time, with the help of Somerset and Overbury, and then deserted him. But as he had said after Thirlstane's death that he would have no one in office whom he could not hang, so now he was determined to use only "meaner men." Bacon was at hand, but he would not use Bacon. It was a significant limitation of James's nature that he never did. He made him Lord Keeper, but that Bacon's mere indefatigable legal and loyalist industry compelled. James Stuart had not the greatness which is implicit in the recognition of greatness ; the single exception is Donne. His learning was profound but sterile, and the neighbour-hood of the great creative imaginations was not for him. He was, said Clarendon, " very quick-sighted in discerning difficulties and raising objections, and very slow in master-ing them, and untying the knots he had made ; in a word, he knew not how to wrestle with desperate contingencies, and so abhorred the being entangled in such." Clarendon was writing of politics, but his sentence has a wider scope. To the younger Scottish James it is something less than fair ; the King had had to wrestle often enough with desperate contingencies. But it had been against his will, and he had thought, relaxing in England, that he was free of them, nor indeed did the propinquity of the Commons seem to him so desperate as all that. It was too vague, too verbose, too multitudinous, too obviously temporary, though obviously tiresome, a contingency. But in matters of the spirit Clarendon was right. He was not made to wrestle with desperate contingencies there, and he abhorred the being entangled in such. It is but to say he was not a great man. For great men, whether they abhor them or not, wrestle with, and are nourished and live by, such contingencies. The very play which exhaled a delicate tribute to James from the cauldron of the witches is itself an example of such a one which was thrust on Shakespeare in *Macbeth*. Whether Shakespeare or Bacon or, in a less but true kind, Donne or even Andrewes, all of them there knew more than the King. He abhorred and avoided the desperate contingencies of the soul.

The reward—the inevitable result, rather—of that wrestling is a certain natural domination. " They are Powers," says Wordsworth, speaking of such minds, and their power is felt, each after his kind and after his kind of wrestling—Dante or Napoleon or Beethoven. But what then of James's doctrine of Kings ? It is certain that all kings have not wrestled with such desperate contingencies, but James (could he and would he have indulged in this argument) might have answered that his idea of monarchy postulated the bestowal of such power by God on certain chosen souls, so that, being spared the wrestling, they yet have the power. Their authority is not from themselves ; it is attributed to them, in act by God, in belief by their subjects. Something of the sort is held, by the whole Roman Church, concerning the person of the Pope ; it is why he need not be a saint. It must be admitted that James would more easily have believed it about the Pope than the Pope about James. But it does seem to be in some such attributed power we must find the basis of government—certainly of monarchical government. Perhaps so we are less likely to fall—but we are not anyhow very likely to fall—into the error of (say) the deplorable Thackeray, who took such trouble to remind us that Louis XIV. was an ordinary man and might have ordinary pains. Every one knew it. Every one anywhere near James the First knew that he had gout and was weak, and had a Scottish accent and fiddled with his clothing. Every one

then as now can compare him with his favoured few.
Masculine beauty moves always near him, deferential and
grimacing. The exquisiteness of one lovely figure after
another satisfies the King, so far as the continual presence
of something that he is not and cannot be can satisfy him.
The majesty of the mortal god (we know, but he knew and
they knew) is helpless there ; he cannot add one cubit to
his stature, nor can all the sorceries or the sciences of his
day strengthen those weak legs or reduce that huge tongue.
The bitter absurdity of his figure draws these others about
it ; a circle of lordliness and grace moves widdershins round
him, as if he too called up spirits, and had remembered all
the spells to invoke them and forgotten the single necessary
spell which could make him as one of them. So instead of
that spiritual spell we have the aping of it, the physical
familiarities—the leering eyes, the pawing hands, the stammering royal endearments, and beauty responding in turn
with flatteries that seem more bestial and less credible
even than those with which Elizabeth toyed. But then
we are, certainly, under one disadvantage ; we do not see
the King. To do that, it is necessary to look with other
eyes—as with those of Francis Bacon, who, daily accustomed to him and to his smiling and haughty intimates,
beheld continually emerging from that fantastic circle the
lofty and immaculate figure of the elect of God, the sovereign
and serene prince of wisdom and justice. And the mere
fact is that he did.

James neglected Bacon ; he appointed " mean men " ;
he went on trying to dominate the Commons, who were
by now subconsciously attributing a similar power to
themselves. The Addled Parliament of 1614 produced
nothing but addle. The more serious Parliament of 1621
resulted in gestures. Before it had met there had come
about in 1617 the fall of the great house which had stood by
Cecil to invite James—the Howards. Henry Howard died

in 1614. Thomas Howard, Earl of Suffolk, had been shaken by the Somerset collapse, but he had not fallen. He was Treasurer. His cousin, the Lord Charles Howard, Earl of Nottingham, was High Admiral; his son-in-law, Lord Knollys, was Master of the Wards. The "mean man" who had been appointed Secretary of State, Sir Thomas Lake, was a client of the Family. In 1618, alarmed and angry at the rise of Villiers, they produced a new neophyte, young Monson, nephew of Sir Thomas of the Overbury trial. He was made to wash his face every day with posset curd; he was tricked and pranked up; he was sent to receive the Communion from the Archbishop.[1] It was a fiasco; the King had him warned off, though some hoped he "would come forward, not perhaps soon, but pede-tantim." Villiers struck in return. Suffolk was accused of bribery and malpractice, and compelled to resign. In the next year Nottingham also—not before it was time— was compelled to resign. Villiers, after some hesitation on his part, was made High Admiral by the King, as the King's mother had made Bothwell Admiral of Scotland. James composed a Latin poem expounding the suitability, since Neptune controlled both liquid waves and swift horses, of the Favourite being at once Admiral and Master of the Horse.

He had, about this time, an opportunity of a little detective work. There had been a great quarrel between Sir Thomas Lake's daughter, Lady Roos, and Lady Roos's husband's grandfather's young wife, Lady Exeter. Lady Roos accused Lady Exeter of actual incest with her husband

[1] It is easy to feel that, for so austere a mind, the Archbishop got himself rather curiously mixed up with the King's masculine Favourites. But it is necessary to remember that the post of Favourite was almost part of the constitution, that it meant the holder of the King's particular and personal favour, and therefore was a necessary part of the great offices of State. Abbot, a Puritan, had seen nothing improper in his efforts to get Villiers chosen.

and attempted murder against herself. Lord Roos, to escape his wife and her mother, Lady Lake, had fled as far as Rome, and even farther, for he died there. In heaven— he died a Catholic—there is no marrying. The ladies were brought forth before the Star Chamber and the King. Lady Roos swore that Lady Exeter had acknowledged her guilt in a private interview, overheard by Lady Roos's maid, Sarah Swindon. Sarah swore to it. There were also (as there always are) letters. The letters turned out either forgeries or unprocurable ; one witness said he had used an incestuous letter from Lady Exeter to Lord Roos in order to light his pipe. The King suspected Sarah very grievously. He remembered the occasions on which he had detected imposture among the professed victims of witchcraft. He caused her to be carried down to the house at Wimbledon where the alleged interview had taken place ; he went down himself. He turned the large rolling eyes of Majesty on Sarah and told her to go wherever she had stood, hidden by the tapestry, to overhear. She did, and the King, in triumphant glee, beheld her from the knees downward clearly visible below the too-short hangings. He confronted the wretched Sarah with the fact, and sent her back, a convicted perjurer, to London. In the general collapse of the accusation she was sentenced to branding, whipping, and life-imprisonment, unless she confessed ; which she did, and was, after a few months, set free. Lady Roos also confessed and was released from prison, though when, later on, Gondomar the Spanish ambassador interceded for her complete pardon, the King said that he could not do it, "unless the Church of Rome believes in the seven deadly sins, for on my life she is guilty of them all."

The fall of the Howards and the friends of the Howards did but leave the mysterious claims of Prerogative and Privilege more securely entrenched, and when battle opened more highly incensed. In 1621 monopolies were attacked, and the Lord Chancellor Bacon fell. By now the King had gone far in his personal and political schemes of regaining a Protestant crown for his daughter and a Catholic bride for his son. The Commons viewed the Catholic bride, the more that she was also Spanish, with feelings ranging from regret to horror. They viewed the prospect of contributing subsidies for the European war with feelings ranging from agreement to regret. John Pym explained the duty of persecution of Catholics—" not to punish them for believing or thinking, but that they might be disabled to do that which they think and believe they ought to do." The House presented more ornate Grievances—one of which was the proposed marriage of the King's son. The King, informed by Gondomar, wrote a stern letter warning them off any discussion of the prerogative royal, mysteries of State, and the Prince's match ; he added that he thought himself " very free and able to punish any man's misdemeanours in Parliament, as well during their sitting as after," and he should not fail to do it. He probably did not know it, but with those words he changed the Boyg. It hardened before him into an iron door that stood between him and his kingdom. His son would see the iron door turn to iron men, and be destroyed by them within his kingdom. The Commons, in a sentence of incredible length, declared their inalienable privilege of free speech—" our undoubted right and inheritance." It was on the presentation of that declaration that the King cried out for stools for the ambassadors. He sent an answer, in which he compared them to robbers who took a man's purse and then said they did not mean to rob him. Let them beware how they entrenched on his prerogative so as to enforce him to retrench on their privileges. There were further passages, but they only made the division clearer. On December 18, 1621, the Commons protested the inviolable and sovereign nature of their body, and of the members of that body. The candles had been lit in their chamber. They had the Protestation read, passed it, and resolved that it should be entered upon the Journals of the House. It ran :

" The Commons now assembled in Parliament, being justly occasioned thereunto, concerning sundry liberties, franchises, and privileges of Parliament, amongst others not herein mentioned, do make this protestation following :

" That the liberties, franchises, privileges, and jurisdictions of Parliament are the ancient and undoubted birthright and inheritance of the subjects of England ; and that the arduous and urgent affairs concerning the King, State, and defence of the realm and of the Church of England, and the making and maintenance of laws, and redress of grievances, which daily happen within this realm, are proper subjects and matter of counsel and debate in Parliament ; and that in the handling and proceeding of those businesses every member of the House hath, and of right ought to have, freedom of speech, to propound, treat, reason, and bring to conclusion the same :

" That the Commons in Parliament have like liberty and freedom to treat of those matters, in such order as in their judgments shall seem fittest, and that every such member of the said House hath like freedom from all impeachment, imprisonment, and molestation other than by the censure of the House itself, for or concerning any bill, speaking, reasoning or declaring of any matter or matters touching the Parliament or Parliament business ; and that, if any of the said members be complained of and questioned for anything said or done in Parliament the same is to be shewed to the King by the advice and assent of all the Commons assembled in Parliament before the King give credence to any private information."

On the next day they were adjourned. Christmas went by. On December 30, the King in Whitehall, strong in his own inviolable nature, sent for the Journals, and, his Council standing about him, tore out the page containing the Protestation of that alien growth.

The Spanish ambassador was the one person who was thoroughly pleased. The King would never call another Parliament ; he would not be able to interfere in the wars then raging in Europe. The people—he did not, in fact, mean the people but the gentlemen—were desperately offended, but they were disunited, without leaders or strong places. " They are rich, and live comfortably in their houses ; so that it is not likely there will be any disturbance." He was wrong. It was because they were rich and lived comfortably in their houses that they were able to maintain the mystical triune chastity of wealth, gentility, and godliness, and within thirty years another January was to close with the death of another King.

CHAPTER THIRTEEN

AUTHORITY FORGETS

IT is necessary, in order to feel the force of the concern which dominated the King during the last years of his life, and inflicted on him a spiritual defeat he had not till then experienced, to go back a little from the moment of the Protestation of the Commons : say, to 1616 when he was fifty. He was then still active in body and mind, though he suffered increasingly from fits of the gout in one and from fits of gloom in the other—" a kind of morosity," wrote the gossips, a year or two later, and added that the sight of my lord of Buckingham set all quiet again. He was becoming dependent on the Favourite. The Authorized Version had been put forward by his authority five years earlier, that book in which more than in any other, outside Shakespeare, the desperate contingencies of men are treated, and one more desperate contingency than any man ever endured. In 1616 the King's own collected works were published by his authority under the editing of Bishop Montague, who translated some into Latin, including the *Counterblaste against Tobacco*. The King regarded this as one of his more humorous efforts ; the Bishop, translating, called it a *ludus*, a light *jeu d'esprit*. Few have so thought of it since, but perhaps few have read it. Even more than Shakespeare, who died in this year, James Stuart is known by the titles of his books rather than by their contents.

The *Counterblaste* had originally been published in 1604. " If my grounds," wrote the King, " be found true, it is all I looke for ; but if they cary the force of persuasion

with them, it is all I wish, and more than I can expect."
He went on to deal with smoking as a barbarous habit
brought in " by a father so generally hated "—meaning
Raleigh—used upon deceitful grounds of health, and giving
rise to sins towards God and foolish vanities before the
world. He disparaged its medical success, which according
to the old doctrine of humours, was thought to be due
to the dry and hot fumes rising into the cold and moist
nature of the brains. James denied the major—that
unlike things were good for unlike. He denied the minor
—that tobacco was simply hot and dry, saying that it had
also " a certain venomous quality," witness the hateful
smell. He denied that it purged the system of " rheums
and distillations," arguing that " this stinking smoake
being sucked up by the Nose, and imprisoned in the colde
and moyst braines, is by their colde and wett facultie,
turned and cast foorth againe in waterie distillations, and
so are you made free and purged of nothing, but that
wherewith you wilfully burdened your selves."

Some argued that its general use proved it good, to
which the King scornfully replied : " Such is the force of
that naturall Self-love in every one of us, and such is the
corruption of envie bred in the brest of every one, as we
cannot be content unlesse we imitate every thing that our
fellowes doe, and so proove our selves capable of every
thing whereof they are capable, like Apes, counterfeiting
the maners of others, to our owne destruction." He
mocked at the number of troubles it was supposed to cure.
" It cures the Gowt in the feet, and (which is miraculous)
in that very instant when the smoke thereof, as light, flies
up into the head, the vertue thereof, as heavie, runs downe
to the little toe. It helpes all sorts of Agues. It makes
a man sober that was drunke. It refreshes a weary man,
and yet makes a man hungry. Being taken when they
goe to bed, it makes one sleepe soundly, and yet being

taken when a man is sleepie and drowsie, it will, as they
say, awake his braine, and quicken his understanding. . . .
O omnipotent power of Tobacco ! "

Tobacco-drinking was no better than a lust, a branch
of the sin of drunkenness ; it was an extravagance and a
disgraceful indulgence. Some of the gentry bestowed
three or four hundred pounds a year upon this " precious
stink," merely to turn their insides into kitchens. Friends
could not meet but what they must be in hand with
tobacco, and he that did not smoke was accounted peevish
and no good company. Mistresses could not entertain
their lovers better than by giving them pipes of tobacco.
The sweetness of man's breath was becoming wholly lost,
and not only of man's, for, " which is a great iniquitie,
and against all humanitie, the husband shall not bee
ashamed, to reduce thereby his delicate, wholesome, and
cleane complexioned wife, to that extremitie, that
either shee must also corrupt her sweete breath there-
with, or else resolve to live in a perpetuall sinking
torment."

Therefore, the King concluded, " Have you not reason
then to bee ashamed, and to forbeare this filthie noveltie,
so basely grounded, so foolishly received and so grossely
mistaken in the right use thereof ? In your abuse thereof
sinning against God, harming your selves both in persons
and goods, and raking also thereby the markes and notes
of vanitie upon you : by the custome thereof making
yourselves to be wondered at by all forraine civil Nations,
and by all strangers that come among you, to be scorned
and contemned. A custome lothsome to the eye, hatefull
to the Nose, harmefull to the braine, dangerous to the
Lungs, and in the blacke stinking fume thereof, neerest
resembling the horrible Stigian smoke of the pit that is
bottomlesse."

He was active also in other small affairs of the mind,

still practising detection. One of his judges and a serjeant-at-law fell into disfavour in October because they had caused certain reputed witches to be hanged at Leicester. James, coming that way later, made inquiries into the case, examined and tested the boy who was supposed to be bewitched, discovered trickery, and showed a countenance of disapproval to the lawyers concerned. He demanded scepticism as well as credulity in cases of witchcraft, but he was more able to combine both than most of his servants.

Francis Bacon, his Attorney-General, was made a member of the Privy Council this year, and was to be Lord Keeper the next. Sir Peter Young, the tutor of long ago, received his last promotion; he became master of St. Cross Hospital. In the previous year the self-austere mind of John Donne had allowed himself to take orders at last; the King, who admired his theological learning and divine knowledge, made him a royal chaplain this year and gave him other preferment. There was something in common between the two men—their delight in curious learning and their devout piety. On March 24, 1617, Donne, preaching for the first time at Paul's Cross, before a great assembly—Bacon, Abbot, Winwood, and many other notables—sent out, in the reverberation of his sombre sentences, his own testimony to the King's chief desire : " It is the Lord that hath done it, and it is wonderful in our eyes. . . . that a King, born and bred in a warlike nation, and so accustomed to the sword, as that it had been directed upon his own person, in the strength of his age, and in his Infancy, in his Cradle, in his mother's belly, should yet have the blessed spirit of peace so abundantly in him, as that by his Councils and his authority he should sheathe all the swords of Christendom again."

Of the King's more immediate circle Somerset had

vanished and Villiers had arrived. In 1616 he was knighted and pensioned ; he received the Garter ; before the end of the year he was made a Viscount. In 1617 he became Earl of Buckingham and in 1618 Marquis. He appears to us almost as the archetypal Favourite of dreams ; certainly he was at last the ideal Favourite of the dreams of King James. He was everything that a Favourite ought to be—splendid, generous, devoted, proud, intelligent, honourable, and capable. He was quick-tempered, but he bore no grudges. He bore no great gratitude either, not even in the end to the King. Without the mature masculinity of Arran or the more vulgar violence of Somerset, his imperious nature achieved something that neither of them—that no one since the early D'Aubigny—had been able to do ; he conquered James Stuart. Even more astonishingly he conquered James Stuart's son. He did it with no help but that of his own spiritual nature. He diverted the royal integrity of James and made a friend of the royal integrity of Charles. There were at first sharp passages between Charles and Steenie, but James had reconciled them. At a great banquet, given by Buckingham, and called " the Prince's feast," the King said publicly that he hoped his posterity " will so far regard their father's commandments and instructions as to advance that house (of Villiers) above all others whatsoever." Fate, overhearing the wish, inspired Charles to carry it out to an extent that left even the royal house of England, in his father's person, something under-advanced ; so careful should men be of every idle word, lest they are stripped of excuse in the day of fulfilment. As if in an easy grasp of magnificence the Favourite's aspiring spirit embraces and holds both father and son—and, for one brief moment, even the Parliament as well. He meets the Commons in the Great Hall where the King once met them, the Prince standing by his side to support him, and imposes himself and his intentions on them, in a golden glory of rage and honour and battle. The line of splendid masculine beauty could hardly have had a more magnificently spectacular conclusion. Even when, three years later, it was indeed concluded by Buckingham's assassination, it ended with a spectacle. King James meanwhile, between those two spectacles, had, oddly and unnoticeably, died—still talking Latin.

The Prince Charles, however, was not very noticeable, except to his father, till the end of 1616. In November he was created Prince of Wales ; there was then no other child of the King's in England. All three—Henry, Elizabeth, Charles—had followed James southward, along with or after Anne of Denmark, who pursued in the new kingdom the same bird of happiness which she had sought in vain in Scotland. Masques, progresses, schemes of building, occupied her. Every now and then she made some small effort to influence her husband ; every now and then, as at the rise of Villiers, he caused her to influence him. On occasions of the second kind she was always successful ; of the first, rarely. She gave birth to two other children, girls, Mary and Sophia, who died in infancy. She pursued joy for sixteen years, and either abandoned or found it at last in 1619 when she died. She was heavily in debt, and in the general straits of the Crown her funeral was a difficulty. The Lord Treasurer Cranfield refused to buy cloaks for it on credit, and there was no money to pay for them. Eventually the difficulty was got over even with superfluity. The funeral took place on May 13 (she had died on March 2) : " a drawling tedious sight— 280 poor women, an army of mean fellows, the number of lords and ladies very great, but a poor show, which perhaps was because they were apparelled all alike, or that they came laggering all along, even tired with the length of the way and the weight of their cloaks, every lady having twelve yards of broad cloth about her, and the countesses sixteen." [1]

In that "drawling tedious sight" Anne of Denmark disappears. She had, even so, outlived her eldest son by six years. Henry had died of typhoid fever in 1612, calling out for his sister Elizabeth. The girl was very dear to both her brothers, more perhaps than they were to each other. Henry was growing up into the chivalric, slightly rambustious, prince of romantic tradition. In spite of the *Basilikon Doron* there had come a rift between him and his father, no more though more showy than between most children and their parents. Henry was the kind of prince who looks ideal from a distance, as James looks despicable ; the closer one comes, the more doubtful one becomes. He was good-humouredly superior to his lame and ailing brother Charles ; he promised, when he was King, to make him Archbishop of Canterbury, so that he might hide his lame leg under his robes. He made a hero of Raleigh in the Tower, and cried out against James for keeping such a bird in captivity. It did not increase the King's willingness to release the bird, especially as from its cage it wrote letters on policy to the Prince. Henry fell in love with Frances Howard, until he heard of amorous relations between her and the Favourite Carr ; then, at a Court function, when some one showed him the lady's glove, he exclaimed scornfully before them all that it had been stretched by another hand. It was the lady's great-uncle, the Lord Henry Howard, who remarked that the Prince,

---

[1] It is sad how death involves death. At the funeral a young gentleman named Appleyard of Lynne, and (some said) of Oxford, was killed by the falling of a stone from Northumberland House, " one of the S's that formed the battlements," under pressure from those who stood on the leads. " He was removed," wrote a contemporary clerical gossip, " to St. Martin's churchyard, where divers flocking to see him, amongst the rest a scrivener's wife, beheld the sad spectacle, and was so affected by it, that, returning home to her house, she immediately died."

if ever he came to reign, would prove a tyrant. Promise
of magnificence can be allowed him ; but magnanimity is
a more subtle song. The fever intervened, and James
was credited with having poisoned his royal and filial rival.

He had, for some time before Henry's death, been
concerned with prospects and plans for the marriage of
his two elder children. The dream of universal peace
coming in his own person, had changed its details. It
no longer envisaged a General Council of unity, but rather
the union of dynasties. With a marriageable son and a
marriageable daughter—and another son in reserve—the
King had visions of wedding one to Catholicism and one
to Protestantism, so that contending principles of the
Christian verity might become his children by blessed
nuptials, and he himself, growing old in his high seat of
the west, a peacemaker without guile, might overlook
throughout Europe the peaceful generations of his spiritual
descendants. He still believed it to be possible for men
not absolutely to have to kill one another for details of
their creed. It was certainly part of the ill-luck that
pursued him that he should be the last English King to
sign a warrant for the burning of heretics. They were
two Arians, and it made a good deal of difference in James's
eyes that they denied the Deity of Christ altogether. The
King condescended to argue in person with one of them,
but he would not be convinced, and the outraged royal
rationalist had him carried to the fire.

The great concluding episode, therefore, in James
Stuart's life is the marriage union of his children and of
religions in his children. It is accompanied by all the old
elements of laughter and slaughter ; it is clouded by the
vapours of egotism which wreathe themselves into the all
but megalomaniac figure of the grotesque King patri-
archally lording it over nations, and are dispersed only to
show an equally grotesque figure weakly scolding his

imperious supplanters, Buckingham and Charles. The episode begins with the single stream of the blood of Raleigh ; it opens on to the multitudinous streams of the blood of the Thirty Years War abroad and the Civil War at home. His daughter loses a crown ; his son loses a bride. The universe about him hoots with laughter at what is happening and what is yet to happen : " very tragical mirth." In the midst of the agitations and alarms, the King, distracted and driven, ill and ageing, has to go against his own intelligence and to forfeit his own desires. And as his own mother and father had hurried from the stage in order to leave it free for him, so he himself seems to be pushed and hustled away so as to leave it clear for his son. It is—just for a moment—almost impossible to make out exactly whether he is dead or alive ; we discover only by glancing aside at the short and dignified person of Charles—the Prince ? no ; Charles the First. So we know that King James is indeed dead.

Elizabeth, after some talk of Gustavus Adolphus and some of the King of Spain, had been, just before Henry died, contracted to Frederick, the Elector Palatine. He was a Protestant prince of Middle Europe, one of the subordinate princes of the Empire, owning direct allegiance to the Emperor. The marriage was celebrated in February 1613, with great pomp, and among other plays performances of *Othello* and the *Tempest*.[1] *Henry VI*. would have been more prophetic. The royal pair left England in April, and James was free to turn with renewed concern to the future of his single remaining son.

He had thought, for Henry, of a French, a Spanish, a Savoyard princess. Raleigh, writing to the Prince, had

---

[1] *Othello* at a marriage ! But Shakespeare's contemporaries seem to have taken his tragedies less seriously than we do. In 1606, as an entertainment for Boxing Night, the Court witnessed *King Lear*. Have we been wrong all these years ? Is *Lear* really a joke ?

disparaged a Spanish marriage ; he thought, justly, that the Spanish power was already failing. The Prince himself had privately made difficulties about the difference of creed. He said he could not allow of " two religions in one bed." The King was inclined to think it was the best place for two religions. Ordinary facts of life had a wonderfully reconciling effect on all but fanatics, and he did not conceive that his children—by nature or grace—would be fanatics. Henry, however, died, and Charles was less difficult.

As between France and Spain, the King's own choice was made. The Spanish monarchy seemed to him still—what the French was so soon to become—the greatest in Europe ; it was certainly the most ostentatiously Papalist. Also, it had been the monarchy which had loomed most terrifically over him in his early days of kingship, when strange vessels hid in the mouth of the Clyde, and blank letters went south from the lords of the Scottish north. James was too sure of himself to feel he needed help from external things ; no Spanish alliance could have made him more of a King than he knew he was. Yet he would have found a measure of satisfaction if and when the marriage of the Infanta of Spain to the Prince of Wales should have exhibited him in the full glory of his estate, when the slandered child of barbaric Stirling should have become the beloved father of Europe's oldest kings. There was also another balance in which the match swayed equal with a blacker weight. That weight was the Commons. It seems doubtful if James was ever quite sure whether he wished to threaten the Commons with Spain, or Spain with the Commons—in order to gain from either his own desire. He probably (it would have been very natural) wanted to do both ; to make the Commons vote money lest he should be led into the arms of King Philip, and King Philip hasten the marriage and the dowry lest he should

be compelled to lead the Puritan passions of the Commons.
The dowry was an important element. James was not
primarily concerned with it, but he never forgot it.

At that time the Spanish ambassador, Diego de Sarmiento, Count Gondomar, was a man after the King's own
heart. He made of him as much a Favourite as he could of
a foreign ambassador. They talked Latin together, Gondomar deliberately speaking false. The King corrected him.
The ambassador, with an exquisite compliment, answered :
" Sir, I speak Latin like a gentleman, but you like a
pedant." It was a tribute that could only be paid to a
King—who is above gentlemen, and hardly to any King
but James—who was equal to pedants. Gondomar established his intimate influence ; he was a very able man.
He as well as Buckingham renewed, at this other end of the
King's life, something of the political vision which Esmè
D'Aubigny had awakened in youth, but of a more austere
and haughty kind. He inflected the mind of the King with
the tenses of the verb *to rule* as it was spoken in Spain.
Occasionally he made a slip ; he forgot that James treasured
an actual royalty. And he hardly ever understood that
both James and Charles treasured their religion as Catholic.
It was comprehensible. Gondomar was an ardent Spanish
Catholic, and he saw the conversion of England—always
just round the corner.[1]

In this same year 1616, negotiations being already
privately under weigh, the King surprised and alarmed
the ambassador by releasing Raleigh from the Tower.

The whole story lies among the more sinister shadows of
James Stuart's career. It is the second affair in which,
though the King could be proved right in every detail of
his intentions and acts, he would still be left in the wrong

---

[1] He was, however, amusing. When the old Countess of Buckingham
was the centre of suits : " the land," he wrote, " was never nearer conversion, since now they pray to the Mother rather than to the Son."

at the end, and the first is the execution of his mother. Raleigh's death was not so intimate a thing, and the easy popular censure of James is largely based, partly on an assumption of a national feeling which, if indeed it existed at all then as it now does, he certainly did not share, and partly on a failure to understand the things for which he did care. He did not particularly want to execute Raleigh. But he wanted still less to have his European, dynastic, religious, and personal schemes spoiled by Raleigh. That they would have been, the influence of Gondomar persuaded him. It is, perhaps, the first sign of a certain loss of power in him that he was so persuaded.

Raleigh had been in the Tower for thirteen years, living part of the time in a little house he had built for himself within the precincts. In 1616 he was sixty-four. He was yearning for freedom, and for one more chance of gold and glory. There was a mine, he knew, in Guiana, on the Orinoco : if the King would let him go ! He got into touch with the anti-Spanish party at Court ; he persuaded—it is said he bribed ; at last he succeeded. James let him out. But to be let out was not enough for him, nor was it all the King expected. He was to justify his release by finding the gold, by bringing it back in quantities, and by doing so without causing any inconvenience, let alone harm, to the Spanish settlements. The Spanish ambassador heard of the project and protested. The King assured him that it would be all right. The ambassador refused to believe it. He pointed out the danger of a war with Spain. But the possibility of receiving a mass of gold independently both of the English Commons and the Spanish Court weighed with the King. He had never much cared for Raleigh even before the mysterious plots ; it is likely that to James the magnificent Elizabethan seemed to have more than a touch of Francis Hepburn, Earl of Bothwell, about him, and if Raleigh failed or did ill he was willing

that he should suffer for it.   If necessary, the King said,
he should be sent to be hanged in the plaza at Madrid.   But
he insisted on letting him go.   He consulted the Council,
a number of whom were strong supporters of Raleigh.
The Council advised that the expedition should proceed.
Raleigh was compelled to write a letter in which he promised
not to commit outrage on Spanish subjects.   Gondomar
was exactly informed of the intentions of the expedition,
and of the ships composing it.   But Raleigh was always
inclined to " talk big."   He mentioned to Bacon the
possibility of seizing the Mexico gold fleet.   Bacon said
that would be piracy.   " Oh no ! " Raleigh answered.   " Did
you ever hear of men who are pirates for millions ?   They
who aim at small things are pirates."   It is likely that what
he said to Bacon he said to others.   The Spanish Court,
alarmed, sent warnings out to the West.   James, having,
he thought, made everything clear, and having the support
of the Council, let Raleigh go.

He sailed.   The tragic result is familiar.   He returned,
with the blood of Spaniards and the ash of a Spanish town
upon the hands of his followers, if not on his own.   His
son had been killed in the assault ; his friend who had
ordered the assault had committed suicide.   He had lost
many men by sickness and battle.   He had no gold.
The Spanish Government, through the passionate voice of
its lofty ambassador, was demanding his immediate
execution or his delivery to them for execution in Spain.

The influence of Gondomar and the King's vision of a
reconciled Spain, his own dislike of Raleigh, and his equal
dislike of Raleigh's sort of buccaneering adventure, moved
him heavily.   It was assumed everywhere that Raleigh
was to blame.   The King spoke of his crimes.   But though
James supposed him guilty he still insisted that he must
be shown to be guilty.   Gondomar, protesting that Raleigh
was in England and had not been hanged, and implying

the inferiority of the international honour of the King of England to that of the King of Spain, touched the inflamed nerve too rashly. James flung his hat on the ground and went into a storm of anger. He cried out that such might be justice in Spain, it was not in England—no one there was condemned without trial, no, not if he had murdered the Prince of Wales. The ambassador dilated again on the town burnt and the men slain, and recovered the ground he had lost. The King promised that Raleigh should be sent to Spain unless that King preferred to have him hanged in England . . . which King Philip did.

When at last the examinations took place it became clear, not certainly that Raleigh had ordered any attack on Spain, but that he thought it always a noble and glorious deed to attack Spain—always and in all places. The old man of sixty-six maintained the tradition of his youth. The more the Commissioners examined, the more it seemed to them that Raleigh had never much minded whether Spain were attacked, or whether indeed there were ever a mine for him to find. It remained true that he himself had not lifted sword against Spain ; all the fighting had been done by the detachment of his men whom he had sent up the Orinoco, while he himself, at their wish, remained at the mouth to guard them against possible attacks by the Spanish fleet. But it remained also true that to acquit or pardon him would be equivalent to throwing an insult in the face of Spain, and to declaring that the King of England was, like his great predecessor, indifferent to international rights in the New World.

Half-right and half-wrong, the King determined to carry out his promises to Gondomar, and the Favourite supported him. But, legally, Raleigh was already attainted and in effect dead. The Commissioners proposed that there should be another semi-public examination, which should be a trial in everything but name. But James

was, quite undoubtedly, afraid of Raleigh's public appear-
ances and public speeches.　At Winchester in 1603 Raleigh
had, " by his wit, turned the hatred of men into com-
passion."　As if he were back again in some old state of
being where a ruffian adventurer might dominate the
King's courts and even lay hands on the King, James
hushed the final acts up and hurried them on.　His policy,
his domestic and foreign futures, were in danger ; he made
haste to aid them.　Raleigh was formally asked what he
could say why the sentence of 1603 should not be executed.
He said he had held since then the King's commission, and
that discharged the old judgment.　They told him nothing
but an absolute pardon could discharge it.　He said he
could do nothing then but throw himself on the King's
mercy.　He was put to death the next morning in Palace
Yard, saying of the axe that slew him, " This is a sharp
medicine, but it is a sound cure for all diseases."

It had been the last passage between the Elizabethan
and Jacobean age, and the Jacobean was left alive.　The
age that appears to hide its processes in its exhibition of
natural passion was destroyed by an age that hides its
passion in its exhibition of logical process.　The rational
age of cause and effect survived ;　we can hardly forgive
it.　Nor, as if ashamed of its own inevitable success, did
it easily forgive its King, and it used its own nature against
its King.　International rights and international promises
meant little to Raleigh—" no peace with Spain beyond
the line "—and much to James.　But there was a personal
honesty in Raleigh's anarchy and something of a personal
dishonesty in James's legal destruction of Raleigh.　As if
the universe determined to avenge the one and punish
the other, the House of Commons by similar means destroyed the dynasty.　It so ordered its past as to explain
its present.　It produced national rights which slew the
King as the King had produced international rights to

slay Raleigh, and as in both cases they were rights which the victim neither understood nor admitted, so in both cases there shows in the conquerer a certain dishonesty, or at least duplicity, of spirit. Of the other great Elizabethans then left alive, the Lord Keeper Bacon was searching out the everlastingly rational plan of the universe; the Dean of St. Paul's, John Donne, was searching for the irrational path of the Maker of the universe. There was one other—the lawyer, Edward Coke, and he had become the champion of the new political rationalism. He discovered precedents and declared principles; in his own person he betrayed the Elizabethan age to its logical successor. He was a very rich man, and though we must not say he used his legalism to defend his riches, it is certain that his legalism had that effect. He helped to destroy Raleigh; he helped to destroy Bacon; he helped —very greatly he helped—to destroy the King. After the discovery by the Commons of their mystical inviolacy in 1621 James threw him into the Tower for presumptuous speeches. The Prince Charles interceded for " Sir Edward Coke." James said perversely that he knew no such person. Charles tried again with " Master Coke." James swore he knew no Master Coke neither, but there was one Captain Coke, leader of the Faction in Parliament. Captain Coke was in the Tower, and there for some months he remained. Like Columbus or Galileo, but with less excuse, he had discovered a new world—the world of the legal rights of the House of Commons—and he suffered for it. But James, about that time, began to cease his persecutions. He let out Coke; he had already let out Northumberland and Ruthven (to whom he gave a pension of £500 and sent him to live at Oxford). The Tower was emptied of its prisoners; the lions, whose snarling and fighting the King liked sometimes to watch, roared there alone.

In less than a year after the smell of Raleigh's blood

T

had soothed the Spanish horse of the King's policy, the German horse plunged and reared at the sudden glow of a crown. Frederick the Elector Palatine, the husband of the young Elizabeth, was offered, by the revolting Bohemian Protestants, the Crown of Bohemia. They had formally deposed their previous King, the Catholic Ferdinand, but as Ferdinand had just been elected Holy Roman Emperor the reception of the Crown by Frederick ordained for the new king every kind of trouble. He had sent a special embassy to England to ask the advice of his father-in-law, James. James said to him gloomily : " Do not expect to leave here quickly." Unfortunately the Elector Palatine felt himself compelled to act quickly. James, meditating on the dangerous position in which his son-in-law was likely to be found, desired strongly to know whether the Bohemians were justified by the constitution of their kingdom in their offer of the Crown. He disapproved of horses changing riders in the middle of a stream of religious strife, and indeed at any time. But if the fundamental laws of Bohemia allowed it, he would not stand in Frederick's way. Before he could find out, news arrived that Frederick had accepted the crown. James, preparing patriarchal counsel, was annoyed at being made to look a fool, as he thought, in the eyes of Europe. He was angered at the certain folly and possible criminality of his son-in-law, and he did not propose to spend the bones of a single Englishman in support of the new King. With Bohemia he refused to interfere ; " for conscience, because it was unlawful to dethrone a king on religious grounds ; for honour, because the Elector had sought but not followed his advice ; for example, because he liked not that subjects should dethrone their king." He hoped that he and the King of Spain might mediate between Frederick and Ferdinand, but he would send a small army to defend Frederick's hereditary dominions. Meanwhile the Imperial general, at the head

of an army largely Spanish, defeated Frederick outside
Prague. " I expected this," James said. God allowed
such things to happen to usurping monarchs. But when
Frederick was swept out of the Palatinate also, and was
compelled to fly to the Netherlands, James assumed that
things had gone farther than God meant. He determined
to restore his son-in-law. But he determined to do it
peaceably.

So difficult a union of ideals—legality and peace—
appealed to no one else in Europe. So difficult a union of
mediators—James and Philip—appeared unlikely to every
one else. But it could be discussed, and while it was
being discussed James was unlikely to act. He summoned
the 1621 Parliament, to procure subsidies if war should
become necessary. The House of Commons was enthusiastic over war and less enthusiastic over subsidies. They
attacked monopolies, and overthrew Bacon, and desired
the strict observance of Sunday, and presented Grievances.
They were dissolved. " A King of England has no reason
but to decline a war," James commented. " The sword
is in his hand; the purse in his subjects'. If he begins war
he will be allowed to continue it only on conditions that
break the heart of Majesty."

He had reason so to judge. His good intentions had
built for him a chamber in which he was more and more
compelled to sit in the company of ruin and something like
death. He had, since he came to England, by a farther
indulgence of his comfort, discouraged any knowledge of
the propinquity of actual death. Its violence and darkness belonged to a world of experience he desired to forget.
Mourning for the Queen his predecessor was dropped ; so,
later, with even more speed, was mourning for Anne of
Denmark. By a chance of illness, but not entirely without
his assenting choice, he had been present at the death-beds
neither of his wife nor his son. Now in his leisure hours

he avoided the metaphorical death of his hopes in coarser
delights, taking refuge in rough horseplay and crude jests.
He was full of sorrow ; the Palatinate was lost and his
daughter a fugitive, the Parliament was hostile and seditious, his estate was squandered about him. He had
desired " to win all men's hearts," and this was everywhere
the disheartening result. He had already, in 1619–20,
published a book of *Meditations* on St. Matthew xxvii.
27–29,[1] in which he compared the crown of a King to the
Crown of Thorns. But he could not sit with his melancholy;
he had no calling to the solitary way of the mystic. Now,
after supper, instead of masques or revels or curious arguments, he had certain of his gentlemen-in-waiting called,
and there was playing of fiddles and singing of bawdy songs
and making of bawdy jokes, and mounting and tilting,
one on another's back, and invention of practical jokes ;
so that the King would laugh and forget his woes. He
bound George Villiers more closely to him by assisting the
Favourite's marriage to Katharine, daughter of the Earl
of Rutland, an old Catholic peer, though he insisted that
the lady should be converted to the Church of England
first, which, most happily, she was. The Marquis and the
Marchioness wrote to him joint letters of devotion, and
invited their benefactor to stay with them. He went ; he
wrote verses congratulating them and invoking children,
and when, as the years went by, the children came, he had
them in his palaces, vicariously paternal. " Little children
did run up and down the King's lodgings like little rabbit-
starters about their burrows."

[1] From his own Authorized Version :

" Then the soldiers of the governor took Jesus into the common hall,
and gathered unto him the whole band of soldiers.

" And they stripped him, and put on him a scarlet robe.

" And when they had platted a crown of thorns, they put it upon
his head, and a reed in his right hand : and they bowed the knee before
him, and mocked him, saying, Hail, King of the Jews ! "

It was not Buckingham's marriage but his friendship that was to press most heavily upon the King. James had exhorted his children to advance the house of Villiers ; the last of his children, whose amity with Villiers James himself had established, advanced him very far in his own heart. There grew up between the Prince of Wales and Buckingham a close love. They were both, in different ways, the King's workmanship, and the workmanship, though still deferential, began to hem in the worker. One day at the Council he found them both united in opposition.

It was in 1623 that their union and opposition became marked and victorious. The slow negotiations with Spain had dragged on, seriously hampered by the Spanish refusal to oppose the Emperor over the Palatinate. Gondomar was a strong supporter of the match, for he thought it would be the most likely method of restoring England to Catholic unity. But James, longing to give his daughter her rights and Europe his peace, was talking as if Spanish aid in the recovering of the Palatinate would be a necessary part of the marriage treaty. Gondomar conceived a better method of discussion than with an ageing, legalistic, and Protestant King in London ; he hoped for an easier settlement with a young romantic Prince in Madrid. He revived an old idea which had been dropped—let Charles come himself to Spain. The proposal permeated successfully the minds of the Favourite and the Prince. They determined to go.

The Christmas of 1622 came and passed before they spoke of it to their lord ; a festival broken by a curiously reminiscent incident. For on Twelfth Night the young gentlemen of Gray's Inn, willing to make a startling end of the revels, borrowed from the Tower as much artillery as they could, and in the dead of night fired it off. James, in his bed, heard the warlike thunder. The perils of his past youth repossessed him. He scrambled to his feet, crying,

" Treason ! treason ! " The whole Court was roused, and sprang on guard. The Earl of Arundel, who was in attendance, came hurrying to the Bedchamber with his sword drawn, as if in a rescue of the King's person. The palace for those few minutes became like Holyrood or Stirling, and the step of Bothwell was heard on the stairs, the shouting of Mar and Morton in the hall. Quiet was restored ; the royal person discovered itself to be safe. But the youthful frolics of Gray's Inn had unwittingly prophesied the spiritual approach, if not of Bothwell, at least of Charles and Buckingham. In less than a month after that outbreak, in the February, they came together to the King. They had audience. They explained to him their desire— or rather their intention—to go themselves directly to Spain. Taken by surprise, and over-persuaded, he agreed. He was then left by the young men to think of it, and the more he thought the more alarmed he became. When in the morning they returned they found he had wholly changed his mind, and that the change was accompanied by a storm of anger and fear. He told them they were all wrong ; that for them to put Charles into the hands of the Spanish Court would mean new and exorbitant demands, that the journey would alarm and anger the English, that it would be derogatory to his own dignity, a hazard to the safety of the Prince, and utter ruin to Buckingham. He begged them, with such tears of passion as he had hardly shed since the days of the Ruthven lords, not to press on him a thing against his reason and understanding and interest. He said that it would break his heart if they did.

Charles said coldly that they had his Majesty's promise, he hoped he would not violate it. Buckingham was more imperious, if not more haughty. He said that if his Majesty broke his promise no man would trust him more ; he had been talking to some pitiful rascal ; it would be

unforgivable now to refuse. Between them they drove
the King into another reluctant agreement. He let himself
be cheered ; he spoke of companions. Sir Francis Cottington, who had already gone to and from Spain, was proposed
as one, and James ordered him to be brought. Buckingham
whispered to Charles that he would be against the journey.
Charles said briefly : " He durst not." He came ; the
King said : " Cottington, here are Baby Charles and
Steenie, who have a great mind to go by post into Spain,
to fetch home the Infanta, and will have but two more in
their company, and have chosen you for one. What
think you of the journey ? " Cottington was startled and
shocked, and alarmed at having to speak. He answered,
in considerable nervous anxiety, that he could not think
it wise, for the Spaniards would certainly make new
demands, and all that had been done towards the match
would prove fruitless, once the Prince was in their hands.
The worst fears of the King returned. All the dangers of
darkness and the unknown leapt upon him. He cried out
in a frenzy of tears, " I told you this before. I am undone.
I shall lose Baby Charles." He threw himself on his bed,
and lay there for some moments sobbing, until he heard
Buckingham denouncing and threatening Cottington for his
insolence in offering an opinion instead of merely explaining
the best road. James pulled himself together and inter-
posed. " Nay, by God, Steenie, you are very much to
blame to use him so. He answered me directly to the
question I asked him, and very honestly and wisely." He
defended his servant successfully, but he could not successfully maintain his opinion. Against his judgment, his will,
and his desire, in the face of his real terror of losing the
Prince for ever, the allied determination of the two young
men broke him. He gave way, and in a few days the
adventure was begun. The King mastered his affections
and his fears, and, like greater poets, received from his

emotions an artistic impulse towards verse (Jack and Tom
Smith were the names adopted by the travellers).

> What sudden change hath darked of late
> The glory of the Arcadian state ?
> The fleecy flocks refuse to feed,
> The lambs to play, the ewes to breed ;
> The altars smoke, the offerings burn,
> Till Jack and Tom do safe return.

> . . . . . .

> What may it be that moves this woe ?
> Whose want affects Arcadia so ?
> The hope of Greece, the prop of arts,
> Was princely Jack, the joy of hearts !
> And Tom was to our royal Pan
> The chiefest swain, and truest man.

> . . . . . .

> Love is a world of many Spains,
> Where coldest hills and hottest plains,
> With barren rocks and fertile fields
> By turns despair and comfort yields ;
> But who can doubt of prosperous luck,
> Where love and fortune doth conduct ?

> Thy grandsire, godsire, father, too,
> Were thine examples so to do ;
> Their brave attempts in heat of love,
> France, Scotland, Denmark, did approve.
> So Jack and Tom do nothing new,
> When love and fortune they pursue.

> Kind shepherds that have loved them long,
> Be not too rash in censuring wrong ;
> Correct your fears, leave off to mourn,
> The heavens shall favour their return !
> Commit the care to royal Pan,
> Of Jack his son, and Tom his man.

" The words of Mercury are harsh after the songs of
Apollo," and after this prophecy the King found the words
of the English Mercuries as disturbing as ever he had
expected. The reception which they had in Spain was as
satisfactory as they could wish. But it was warm with

the expectation of the august visitor's conversion. It was hoped that from so devoted a lover almost anything might be gained. The Mercuries, not entirely understanding this, wrote hopefully to the paternal Apollo. But James at bottom was still unhappy. His hopes of the marriage warred with his fears for Charles's safety. He wrote frequently ; he sent jewels and necessaries. He sent to his slave and dog Steenie the patent of his advancement to a Duchy, while he himself looked after the Duchess at home. He also sent warnings.

" MY SWEET BOYS,—God bless you both, and reward you for the comfortable news I received from you yesterday (which was my coronation day), in place of tilting ; and God bless thee, my sweet gossip, for thy little letter, all full of comfort. I have written a letter to the Condé d'Olivares, as both of you desired me, as full of thanks and kindness as can be devised, and indeed he well deserves ; but in the end of your letter ye put in a cooling card, anent the nuncio's averseness to this business, and that thereby ye collect that the Pope will likewise be averse ; but first ye must remember that in Spain they never put doubt of the granting of the dispensation—that themselves did set down the spiritual conditions. These things may justly be laid before them ; but I know not what ye mean by my acknowledging the Pope's spiritual supremacy. I am sure ye would not have me renounce my religion for all the world ; but all that I can guess at your meaning is, that it may (be) ye have an allusion to a passage in my book against Bellarmine, where I offer, if the Pope would quit his godhead, and usurping over kings, to acknowledge him for the chief bishop, to which all appeals of churchmen ought to lie *en dernier resort*, the very words I send you here inclosed, and that is the farthest my conscience will permit me to go upon this point ; for I am not a monsieur

T *

that can shift his religion as easily as he can shift his shirt, when he cometh from tennis.

" I have no more to say in this ; but God bless you, my sweet Baby, and send him good fortune in his wooing, to the comfort of his old father, who cannot be happy but in him. My ship is ready to make sail, and only stays a fair wind. God send it her ; but I have, for the honour of England, curtailed the train that goes by sea of a number of rascals. And, my sweet Steenie gossip, I must tell thee that Kate was a little sick within these four or five days of a headache, and the next morning, after a little casting, was well again. I hope it is a good sign that I shall shortly be a gossip over again, for I must be thy perpetual gossip ; but the poor fool Kate hath, by importunity, gotten leave of me to send thee both her rich chains ; and this is now the eighth letter I have written for my two boys, and six to Kate. God send me still more and comfortable news of you both, till I may have a joyful, comfortable, and happy meeting with you ; and that my Baby may bring home a fair lady with him, as this is written upon our Lady-day.

" *25th of March*, 1623.   JAMES R."

" MY SWEET BOYS,—The Spanish ambassador let a word fall to Grislie, as if there would be some question made, that my Baby's chaplains should not do their service in the king's palace there ; but he concluded that that business would be soon accommodated. Always, in case any such difficulty should be stucken at, ye may remember them that it is an ill preparation for giving the infanta free exercise of her religion here, to refuse it to my son there, since their religion is as odious to a number here, as ours is there ; and if they will not yield, then, my sweet Baby, show yourself not to be ashamed of your profession, but go sometimes to my ambassador's house and have your service there, that God and man may see ye are not ashamed of your religion.

" But I hope in God this shall not need. And so, God bless you, my sweet Boys ; and after a happy success, return and light in the arms of your dear dad.

" *From Whitehall, the 7th of April.*   JAMES R."

By June, Cottington returned with the message that the Infanta would not be allowed to come for a year, though Charles might marry her before then if he would remain with her in Madrid. The King, on June 14, 1623, sent a lamentable cry back.

" GREENWICH, *June* 14, 1623.

" MY SWEET BOYS,—Your letter, by Cottington, hath stricken me dead ; I fear it shall very much shorten my days, and I am the more perplexed that I know not how to satisfy the people's expectation here, neither know I what to say to the Council, for the fleet that staid upon a wind this fortnight, Rutland and all aboard, must now be staid, and I know not what reason I shall pretend for the doing of it ; but as for my advice and directions that ye crave, in case they will not alter their decree, it is, in a word, to come speedily away, and if ye can get leave, give over all treaty. And this I speak without respect of any security they can offer you, except ye never look to see your old dad again, whom I fear ye shall never see, if you see him not before winter. Alas, I now repent me sore that ever I suffered you to go away. I care for match, nor nothing, so I may once have you in my arms again. God grant it, God grant it, God grant it ; amen, amen, amen ! I protest ye shall be as heartily welcome as if ye had done all things ye went for, so that I may once have you in my arms again ; and God bless you both, my only sweet son, and my only best, sweet servant, and let me hear from you quickly, with all speed, as ye love my life ; and so God send you a happy and joyful meeting in the arms of your dear dad. JAMES R."

He maintained, as far as possible, a clear countenance before his Court, but grief and loneliness were gaining power over him, and he could not conceal them. His tears came more easily. He asked those round him : " Do you think I shall ever see the Prince again ? " " The King is in a stupor," wrote a Venetian to the Doge. He was willing to do anything to recover his son and his Favourite. In July he swore to observe the Spanish conditions for the marriage, both public and private, concerning the freedom of the Infanta in the exercise of her religion, the opening of her church to the general public, the education of the children under her care, the freeing of Catholics from the penal laws, and so on. There was nothing in the articles which strikes us as unusual. But the chaplains of the King of England had been refused entrance into the rooms Charles occupied in the Palace at Madrid, and it was certain that the Commons of England would prove as far from toleration as the Court of Spain. James, with laborious sincerity, warned the ambassador that all his oaths could not mean more than that he would endeavour to persuade the Commons to compliance in those things that concerned them.

There had been considerable agitation in the country over the Prince's journey. The romantic view of the young lover speeding to bring home his bride was entirely lost in the equally romantic but more horrific view of the bride's nationality and religion. Prayers for the Prince put up in some churches included petitions for his safe delivery from the house of Rimmon, and orders had to be issued that such intercessions were to ask only " that God should return our noble Prince home again, and no more." One neat-minded cleric, in fact, used those very words—" God return our noble Prince home again—and no more." It is still a question whether he was such a fool as he sounded. In another church the preacher became so daring that the parson caused a psalm to be sung over his intercessions. It was rumoured that Plymouth or some other port was to be put into the Spaniard's hands ; the actual proposal had been less startling, being only that the English Catholics should be given control of some fortified city as a guarantee. Rumours that the King was at heart a Papist again spread : at the very time that James was making ineffectual efforts to persuade the Spanish Government to take steps to restore the fugitive Frederick to his Palatine Electorate. " I do not like," he said later, " to marry my son with a portion of my daughter's tears." The University of Oxford " made verses in praise and commendation of this happy match," and presented them to the King by the hands of the Vice-Chancellor. But the University was an exception ; it was carrying its devotion to lost loyalties even to the invention of new.

To the agitated King and the disturbed country presently came news that, in spite of all, the marriage covenant would not stand. The English gentlemen in attendance behaved roughly to a priest sent to attend one of their number. Buckingham was generally unpopular. Charles was unhappy about the Palatinate. Both of them thought the Spaniards were playing with them. At last the Prince determined to return. On August 28 he took the oath to the marriage contract, and on September 2, leaving his proxy with the ambassador Bristol, he set out. A Cardinal asked him if he wished his travelling carriage to be open ; he answered with a sneer that he would not dare decide without consulting the Junta of Spanish Theologians.

Perhaps never since their delivery from the Powder Plot had the King and his people been so at one as in their delight at the return of the wanderers. But James was merely overjoyed to recover his son and his "slave and dog." The rest of England was overjoyed that the Prince had been brought safely out of Rimmon, without one of Rimmon's daughters to wife ; that is, with the destruction of the King's policy. Of his policy at that moment James did not think. Between blazing bonfires and shouting crowds, the clashing of church bells, and tables spread in the streets, the Prince and the Duke came to London and passed through it on their way to Royston. In St. Paul's, at a solemn service, the Psalm *In exitu Israel* was sung as an anthem of thanksgiving. By a happy chance the Prince met near Tyburn a number of felons going to execution ; he caused them to be set free. Debtors in prison had their debts discharged by unknown benefactors. London was illuminated all night. At Royston the King waited, weeping and laughing for joy. On October 6 they came ; he hurried down to meet them. They fell on their knees ; he flung out his arms and embraced them. Baby Charles and Steenie had come home ; on the staircase, united once more, they all wept together.

But they had not come home, as James—and perhaps the Spanish Government—supposed, to allow negotiations still to drag on. Both the Prince and the Duke felt themselves to have been insulted, and were prepared to avenge the insults. Charles had failed to persuade Spain to promise to restore the beloved Elizabeth ; and he was determined that she should be restored. Both of them painted in dark colours to James the dishonourable procrastination of Spain. The King had wanted them back ; he now had them back. Before he had well finished the indulgence of his simple passion, he was being hurried down a new path between them. In their first interview the Prince turned on his father, saying : " I am ready to conquer Spain if you will allow me to do it." *Beatus pacificus*, but there are other Beatitudes concerning those whom men revile and curse, and what if the pacificator is one of them ? Buckingham shook a burning torch of war in the air ; the old King shrank from it. " What ! " he exclaimed to Charles in December, " would you engage me in a war in my old days, and make me quarrel with Spain ? " He was still sending long letters and proposals to the exiled Frederick and to the Spanish King ; he still hoped vaguely and vainly for the pacification of Europe. They both refused him. Bristol in Madrid was compelled to attempt to postpone the betrothal ceremony, the Spanish King felt himself to be insulted, and the whole effort failed. No grandchild of James Stuart would ever carry in his veins the mingled Scottish and Spanish blood.

It was not enough that the supplanters of the King should threaten Spain ; they must also, for what seemed to him a monstrous conflict, arrange for him a more monstrous alliance. They invoked that multitudinous body of profane rule which was the House of Commons. They determined on a Parliament, for they had determined on war. It was to have met on February 16, 1624, but James postponed it for three days—the Duke of Lennox had died. The son of D'Aubigny had passed to warn his father among the shades of the near coming of his father's lover.

James Stuart came to open his Parliament. He had, on the conclusion of the last, torn from their Journals the resolution of the House of Commons in which they presumed to advise him on policy. Now he invited their advice " for the glory of God, the peace of my Kingdom, and the weal of my children." In matters of religion he begged them to " judge me charitably as you would have me judge you." He assured them he had never intended to endanger it. " I never did think with my heart or speak it with my mouth." For the Spanish marriage, his

Secretaries, assisted by Buckingham and the Prince, would
give them an account.

The account was given—by Buckingham. On that
day the Houses, not in their own place but in the hall of the
palace where the King was used to call them to confer,
heard the Favourite's tale with approval and applause.
In their own chambers afterwards they followed his pointing. War! said Eliot. War! said Coke. War with
Spain that would cost little, for it would be paid for by
seizure of Spanish ships and treasure! War, inexpensive,
religious, patriotic war! They plunged into their old
habit of improving the recusancy laws; they denounced
the royal alliance with Spain, and prepared a petition to
this effect to the King. James sent to Buckingham saying
that he had a bad cold and could not then receive it. The
Favourite wrote in reply: " In obedience to your commands I will tell the House of Parliament that you, having
been upon the fields this afternoon, have taken such a fierce
rheum and cough as, not knowing how you will be this
night, you are not yet able to appoint them a day of
hearing; but I will forbear to tell them that, notwithstanding your cold, you were able to speak with the King
of Spain's instruments, though not with your own subjects."

By now George Villiers was rather the Favourite of the
Commons than of the King—" never any man," said Sir
Edward Coke enthusiastically, " deserved better of his
King and Country." A grotesque alteration of fidelity
had taken place; at last the will of the King was, in
effect, a captive. He was sent to make another speech
to the Houses. " My delay hitherto was upon hope to have
gotten it without a war. I held it by a hair, hoping to have
gotten it by a Treaty, but since I see no certainty that way,
I hope that God, who hath put it into your hearts so to
advise me, and into my heart to follow your advice, will
so bless it, that I shall clear my reputation from obloquie,

and in despite of the Devil and all his instruments show that I never had but an honest heart."

Through the year 1624 one way and another his spiritual captivity was enhanced, and now, though perhaps he did not know it, he had no more time to wait. When he was young he had yielded often, *pour mieux sauter*, but now he was too old to spring. He had indulged his emotions ; he was now compelled to indulge the emotions of others. He could hardly see the Spanish ambassadors alone ; the Duke was always there. He could hardly tell the Parliament what he wanted ; the Prince explained for him. He was their prisoner, but only because he was at last the weak captive of his affections. He needed, and knew he needed, both of those intimates, and he clung to them though he knew that they were moving on an unwise path. He allowed the Prince to promise the Parliament, and he himself promised, never again to interfere at the request of a foreign prince with the domestic laws against the Catholics. He allowed Bristol, his ambassador in Madrid, to be recalled and kept in seclusion and under threat of impeachment, lest he should tell a story of the Madrid visit which did not wholly chime with Buckingham's. He allowed his Treasurer Cranfield, Earl of Middlesex, who had done more than any other man for the finances of England, but who was wholly against war, to be impeached at Buckingham's instigation. But he fought feebly against it, warned by that still vivid sense of things which had so often helped him. He warned them, with a good deal of feeling, that the prosecution of Middlesex was " such a wound to the Crown as would not be easily healed." They remained high and unmoved. He flung at the Duke : " By God, Steenie, you are a fool, and will shortly repent this folly ; you will find, in this fit of popularity, you are making a rod with which you will be scourged yourself." He turned angrily on Charles, saying : " You will live to have your bellyful of parliaments," and went on to warn the incredulous Prince that when he himself was dead "you will have too much cause to remember how much you have contributed to the weakening of the Crown by this precedent you are now so fond of." But he could not stay them ; Middlesex was tried and condemned. When the new treaty of marriage and friendship with France was brought forward he allowed himself to sign a promise in favour of the Catholics, irreconcilable with the promise lately given to the Parliament ; sitting in a room in Cambridge, and using a rubber stamp for his signature, his hands, like his legs, being badly crippled with gout.

Meanwhile he was sometimes carried out in his litter, being too weak to hunt any longer, but having, for the love of his old great days, the game driven in front of him, or he was borne down to see the flights of a new set of hawks at the brook—as at that Christmas of 1624 which he spent in his chamber, going neither to the chapel nor to any of the plays, but only in fair weather to renew those fairer memories of delight. He had written before the Feast to Charles :

" MY ONLY SWEET AND DEAR CHILD,—Notwithstanding of your desiring me [not] to write yesterday, yet had I written in the evening, if at my coming in out of the park such a drowsiness had not come upon me, as I was forced to sit and sleep in my chair half an hour. And yet I cannot content myself without sending you this billet, praying God that I may have a joyful and comfortable meeting with you, and that we may make at this Christenmas a new marriage, ever to be kept hereafter ; for, God so love me, as I desire only to live in this world for your sake, and that I had rather live banished in any part of the earth with you, than live a sorrowful widow-life without you. And so God bless you, my sweet child and wife, and grant

that ye may ever be a comfort to your dear dad and
husband,   JAMES R."

The Prince was his father's wife, as the Duke was
his dog. The King's mind took refuge in fancies more
intimate than even he had used before. The material
kingship of his body by such metaphors drew those other
two closer and closer to him, or so persuaded itself that it
did. In the verbal images of that closing corner of his
own cerebral kingdom he took refuge from the terrible
domination which went abroad over the kingdom without.
" Sweet heart," he called Buckingham ; it was a phrase
of the affections of the day, but the two words seem to
possess a grotesque life of their own when they are met
also in one of Charles's letters to the Duke—" Now, sweet
heart, let me know what I can do in this or anything else
to serve thee." A twisted rivalry tingles in them ; except
that the King has no power, and the Prince no need, to
be a rival, nor would the Duke permit it, for he had chosen
his love.

Once in those months, accentuating their relations, the
world broke in. The Spanish ambassadors, working against
the French alliance, sought to gain the King's private ear
and failed. At last, by a sleight of hand, while one Spanish
gentleman spoke to the Prince and the Duke, another
slipped a paper into the King's hand, begging him to read
it secretly. He did so ; it begged him to admit a special
emissary to a private audience. He agreed ; he heard hints
of strange seditious purposes on the part of the Duke.
He cried out that indeed Buckingham had " ten thousand
devils in him," but he could not believe there was evil
intended. Before the intrigue could go farther, the Duke
descended and put a stop to it. Unfortunately the emissary
had a mistress, who (still more unfortunately) was in the
pay of Dr. John Williams, Bishop of Lincoln and Lord

Keeper (there had been no Chancellor since Bacon fell).
The news of the attack had been told to her by her lover,
to the Bishop's messengers by her, to the Prince by the
Bishop, and so to the Duke.   But later the Spaniards made
one more effort.   They touched once more the nerve of
royalty ;   they solemnly assured James that the Duke
intended to dethrone him if he refused to make war on
Spain.   For one moment the love of his heart seemed about
to rob the old man of the treasure of his soul.   He drove
straight to the Duke and the Prince at St. James's, and
there, shaken and weeping, told them of the Spanish
accusation.   He refused to believe it.   But he insisted—
once more—that law must be kept, that Buckingham must
deal with the accusation, if it were properly formulated.
This, however, when it came to so sharp a point, could not
be done.   The ambassadors made a general statement
which was laid before the Privy Council.   Buckingham
was declared innocent of all treasonable intentions.   The
King was content.

At least, though Buckingham had taken away his hope
of international peace, he gave him in the end some peace
of intimate love.   The armies of the Thirty Years' War
were marching and countermarching.   There were raised
in England and sent to join them a rabble of soldiers and
vagabonds, under the command of the German adventurer
Mansfield.   This riotous and looting army was got out of
England and taken over to Europe—where it was forbidden
to disembark, first by the French, afterwards by the Dutch
authorities.   Pestilence and famine struck the vessels ;
" scarce a third landed," and the whole design failed.
Meanwhile Buckingham was planning naval movements.
There was to be a fleet sent against Spain in the name of
the King of England ; another " in the name of the King
of Bohemia."   Shakespeare in poetry had provided
Bohemia with a sea-coast, but George Villiers in fact pro-

mised her a fleet. Amid these sordid, horrible, and magnificent preparations and catastrophes, the King on March 5, 1625, fell ill. He caught " a tertian ague "; he heard of the death of the Marquis of Hamilton, one of his old Scottish friends, and he felt his own. He exclaimed : " I shall never see London again." A week later they brought him to Hampton Court ; the Prince and the Duke attended. Buckingham and his mother, the old Countess, provided him with medicines and plaisters, much to the anger of the royal physicians. The grotesque buffoonery of Fate which followed James was faithful to him to the end. The King grew worse ; the old woman still peremptorily administered remedies. When, in the very next year, the magnificent Favourite was impeached, the thirteenth article of accusation based itself on his high misdemeanour in so presumptuously thrusting his remedies on the Person of the King. The very last of all the royal captivities took place. A third old woman, neither his mother nor his godmother, but the greedy and fussy mother of the latest and longest beloved of that tragi-comic life, secluded and nursed and dominated him. He still grew worse. On March 22, the Lord Keeper, the Bishop of Lincoln, came to him. The King had liked and advanced him ; they had talked of much curious knowledge and antique ecclesiastical lore. They had, between them, converted the lady whom the Favourite had married from the Roman to the English Church. The Bishop, nevertheless, had sometimes ventured to oppose Buckingham ; once at such a time the King had said to him : " You are a stout man ; you durst do more than I myself." He came, that Tuesday, to James, and found him already past the wit and laughter he had for so long so greatly enjoyed. In the morning, after speaking to the doctors, he went to the Prince, and asked for permission to warn the King. He received permission ; he went in and kneeled down. There, with that formal but real

U

approach which James had loved, he begged the King's Majesty to receive from him the message that Isaiah brought to Hezekiah : *Set thy house in order*, for his days could be but few in this world, but the best remained for the next. The King answered that he was satisfied : he asked for assistance at his going to Christ. On that day, except while he slept, he made preparation, speaking sometimes in the Latin which had been his comfort and his conceit, and using that correct accent which Buchanan had taught him in Stirling. On the Thursday he made confession and received absolution. He professed before all present that he died in the Faith of the Church of England, " whose doctrine he had defended with his pen, being persuaded that it was according to the Mind of Christ." They communicated to him the Sacred Body and Blood. He spoke of it joyfully, and seemed in a way of recovery. But by the Friday he grew less conscious, and the world in which he had played his fantastic part began to fade as fantasies do. The Lord Keeper remained in constant attendance. The outer chambers were thronged, but the King's chamber was quiet. He lingered through the day ; he moved, he said, still in Latin, " *Veni, Domine Jesu !* " and died.

CHAPTER FOURTEEN

THE ORATION OF JOHN DONNE

THEY embalmed him. It was said that, when the physicians opened his body, they found " his heart of an extraordinary bigness, all his vitals sound, as also his head, which was very full of brains ; but his blood was wonderfully tainted with melancholy ; and the corruption thereof supposed the cause of his death." They brought him up to Denmark House, Charles I., all in black, very pale, attending. There, some days before the interment in Westminster, John Donne preached over him. The preacher was a man of fifty-two ; he himself had but six more years to live. By his own testimony he owed to James the occasion of his own soul's second birth ; he owed to him his priesthood, and all that his priesthood had meant to him of wrestling with angels in the night. " When I sit still and reckon all my old Master's royal favours to me, I return evermore to that—that he first inclined me to be a minister." " I received mercy as I received the ministry." Somerset had once asked the King to make John Donne a clerk of the Council, but the King had refused, saying he knew Donne was a learned man, and would be a learned divine and a powerful preacher, " and my desire is to prefer him that way." By that obstinacy Donne was driven into secret searchings of his spirit, and in those searchings he found the way of the last spiritual search. It might have happened in many ways ; it did happen in that way. It is to James Stuart that the deep and sublime rhetoric of the sermons is, by occasion, due, and to him that the discovery of God which shadows and

illuminates that rhetoric is also due.   They were diverse in
their powers, those two poets : the one remained the
apprentice he called himself, the other became a master.
They were diverse in their habits : James Stuart turned
from death-beds, while the other ran forward in thought to
his own.   The one evaded desperate contingencies ; the
other was a conqueror of many kinds of despair.   The
learning of James is a grotesque parody of Donne's ;   the
piety of James is but a pale wraith of Donne's ;   the
one has but the half-shameful body, where the other burns
as the living soul.   But though the one compared to the
other seems always little more than the corpse which on
that day of approaching sepulchre it indeed was, lying deaf
and blind under the passion that flowed above it, yet it
was the corpse of greatness, it was greatness turned, as if
by witchcraft, into a poor waxen image of itself.   James
Stuart was never a great man, yet in his absurdity he is
more like a twisted shape of greatness than many more
ordinary men.   He had tolerance and laughter and knowledge and intelligence ;   he liked men and women, he
desired great things.   The gossips and controversialists
laughed and sneered, and our generations follow them.
Yet once at least, in the midst of so much pleasant mirth,
it is permissible to remember that Francis Bacon praised
James Stuart living and John Donne lamented him dead,
and that it is not safe too easily to despise a man they
honoured, though he were the King, nor wise too easily to
suppose that they honoured him with a servile insincerity,
because he was the King.   They knew him in all his
absurdity—clumsy, weak, conceited, continually sipping his
wines, continually arguing his theories.   They saw and felt
him ;   they touched his hand with their lips and were not
ashamed—the hand which, it is said, he rarely washed
because he wished to keep it soft, and so would only
moisten the ends of the fingers with a damp cloth ;   the

hand with which, against his will and only at the petition of his English subjects, he touched for the King's evil; the hand which pulled the ears and stroked the cheeks and smoothed the clothes of the members of his circle of beautiful forms—Lennox, Arran, Gray, Somerset, Buckingham, and other circles of lesser splendour beyond them; the hand which fiddled with his own clothing and his own body, and smoothed and soothed the material flesh of Majesty; the hand that scribbled those maundering sentimentalities and those explicit doctrines, and guided the reins of his horse on his happy hunting days, and in an extremity could reach for a sword.

On that day when the deepest of the Metaphysical poets, the equal of all but the very few greatest among both our poets and our devotees, spoke of the most metaphysical of all our kings, it was that dead hand that he had seen and known, upon which he declaimed. " I kiss your dirty hands," George Villiers had written to his " dear dad and gossip." Raising even those last words as it were to higher terms, speaking of the august father of his priestly vocation and the pious gossip of his holy search, the voice of Donne that day rose up the spirals of his imagination of the hand, dropping through the declivities of sound, and again climbing and crying, in lamentation and resignation, crying of the hand, the royal hand, of James Stuart, King of Scotland and England :

" When you shall find that hand that had signed to one of you a *Patent* for *Title*, to another for *Pension*, to another for *Pardon*, to another for *Dispensation*, Dead: That hand that settled Possessions by his *Seale*, in the *Keeper*, and rectified *Honours* by the *sword*, in his *Marshall* and distributed relief to the *Poore*, in his *Almoner*, and *Health* to the *Diseased*, by his *immediate Touch*, Dead : That Hand that ballanced his *own three Kingdomes* so equally, as that none of them complained of one another, nor of him, and carried the *Keyes* of all the Christian world, and locked up, and let out *Armies* in their due season, Dead ; how poore, how faint, how pale, how momentary, how transitory, how empty, how frivolous, how Dead things must you necessarily thinke *Titles*, and *Possessions*, and *Favours*, and all, when you see that Hand, which was the *hand of Destinie*, of *Christian Destinie*, of the *Almighty God*, lie dead ?   It was not so *hard* a hand when we touched it last nor so *cold* a hand when we kissed it last. . . ."

CHRONOLOGY

1566 Charles James Stuart born (June 19).
1567 Abdication of Mary. Coronation of James (July 29). Murray Regent.
1569–79 Education at Stirling.
1579 Morton seizes the King (April). Arrival of D'Aubigny (September).
1580 Fall of Morton.
1582 Raid of Ruthven.
1583 Escape of the King.
1584 Arran in power. Rise of the Master of Gray.
1585 Publication of *Essayes of a Prentise*. Flight of Arran.
1586 League with England.
1587 Execution of Mary. Feast of Peace to the lords.
1588 The Armada.
1589 Defeat of Huntly and Bothwell. Marriage to Anne of Denmark (November).
1590 Examination of the witches.
1591 Bothwell Raid. Murder of Murray.
1592 Bothwell Raid. The Spanish blanks.
1593 Bothwell seizes the King, and is defeated.
1594 Bothwell Raid. Birth of Prince Henry.
1595 Flight of the Catholic Earls.
1596 The Octavians. Defeat of the Kirk. Submission of Edinburgh.
1597 Triumph of the King. *Demonology*.
1598 The *Trew Law*.
1599 *Basilikon Doron*.
1600 Gowrie Conspiracy.
1603 Accession to England.
1604 Hampton Court Conference. Project of the Union. *Counterblaste against Tobacco*.
1605 Gunpowder Plot. *Apologie for the Oath of Allegiance*.
1607 Coming of Robert Carr.
1610 Failure of the Great Contract.

1612 Death of Cecil and of Prince Henry.

1613 Marriage of Elizabeth. Essex nullity.

1614 Coming of Villiers. Addled Parliament.

1616 Rise of Villiers. Somerset Trial. Raleigh freed. *Collected Works*.

1618 Execution of Raleigh. Fall of the Howards.

1619 Death of Anne.

1620 Defeat of the Elector Palatine.

1621 The Protestation of the Commons.

1623 The Spanish visit.

1624 Meeting of the Commons. Triumph of Buckingham. Impeachment of Middlesex.

1625 War. Recusancy laws. Defeat and death of the King.

SHORT BIBLIOGRAPHY

JAMES I. . . . *Court and Times* (Birch, 1848); *Life of Prince Henry* (Birch, 1760); *Court of* (Goodman, 1839); *Life* (Harris, 1772); *Life* (Henderson, 1904); *Progresses* (Nichols, 1828); *Memoirs* (Osborne, 1658); *Court and Character* (Weldon, 1650); *Historie of James the Sext* (1804).

Works : Collected (1616); Political Works (McIlwain, 1918); *Essayes of a Prentise* (Arber, 1895); *New Poems* (Westcott, 1911); *Lusius Regius* (Rait, 1901).

LETTERS . . *Elizabeth and James* (Bruce, 1849); *Correspondence of Cecil* (Bruce, 1861 ; 1766); *Kings of England* (Halliwell-Phillipps, 1846); *Original Letters* (Ellis, 1825–46; 1843); *Patrick, Master of Gray* (1835); *Wotton* (Pearsall Smith, 1907); *Bowes* (Stevenson, 1842).

MEMOIRS . *Robert Carey* (1808 ; Powell, 1905); *Lord Herries* (Pitcairn, 1836); *Sir James Melville* (Thomson, 1827); *Rev. James Melville* (Pitcairn, 1842); *David Moysie* (1830).

HISTORIES . *Historical Collections* (Rushforth, 1659–1701); *Memorials from Sir Ralph Winwood* (Sawyer, 1725).

Scotland (Tytler, 1828–43 ; Hill Burton, 1867–70 ; Hume Brown, 1899–1909 ; Lang, 1900–7); *Criminal Trials in Scotland* (Pitcairn, 1833); *Kirk of Scotland* (Calderwood, 1842–9); *Church of Scotland* (Spottiswoode, 1847–51); *King James's Secret* (Rait, 1927).

England (Clarendon ; Lingard, 1854–5 ; Froude, 1856–70 ; Gardiner, 1863–9 ; Trevelyan, 1926 ; Belloc, 1925–31 ; *Political*, 1907); *Church History* (Fuller, 1655 ; Dodd and Tierney, 1839–43); *State Papers ; State Trials.*

Lives, etc. . *D.N.B.* ; *Elizabeth* (Milton Waldman, 1933 ; Neale, 1934) ; *Walsingham* (Conyers Read, 1925) ; *Raleigh* (W. Stebbing, 1899 ; Milton Waldman, 1928) ; *Bacon* (Spedding, 1861–74) ; *Scrinia Reserata* (*John Williams*—Hacket, 1693) ; *Villiers* (Wotton, 1651) ; *Donne's Sermons* (Alford, 1839 ; Pearsall Smith, 1920) ; *Works of Ben Jonson* (Herford and Simpson, 1925) ; *Nugae Antiquae* (Harington, 1779).

INDEX

305

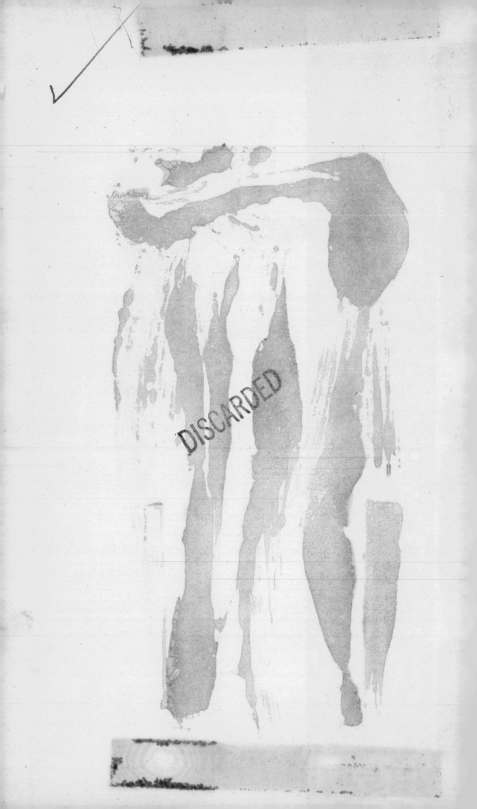